Developing Enterprise Java Applications
with J2EE™ and UML

Developing Enterprise Java Applications with J2EE™ and UML

Khawar Zaman Ahmed

Cary E. Umrysh

♦♦ Addison-Wesley

Boston • San Francisco • New York • Toronto • Montreal
London • Munich • Paris • Madrid
Capetown • Sydney • Tokyo • Singapore • Mexico City

The publisher offers discounts on this book when ordered in quantity for special sales. For more information, please contact:

Pearson Education Corporate Sales Division
201 W. 103rd Street
Indianapolis, IN 46290
(800) 428-5331
corpsales@pearsoned.com

Visit AW on the Web: www.awl.com/cseng/

Library of Congress Cataloging-in-Publication Data

Ahmed, Khawar Zaman.
    Developing Enterprise Java applications with J2EE™ and UML / Khawar Zaman Ahmed,
    Cary E. Umrysh.
        p.   cm.
    Includes bibliographical references and index.
    ISBN 0-201-73829-5
    1. Java (Computer program language)   2. Business—Data processing.   I. Umrysh,
    Cary E.   II. Title.
    QA76.73.J38 A35 2001
    005.13'3—dc21   2001046452

ISBN 0-201-73829-5
Text printed on recycled paper
1 2 3 4 5 6 7 8 9 10—CRS—0504030201
First printing, October 2001

To my late father and my mother,
and to Heike and Yasmeen.
—Khawar

To my wife Socorro for her support
during this lengthy project,
and to my sons Jordan and Joshua.
—Cary

Contents

Foreword

The history of software engineering is, in effect, the history of abstraction. As complexity rises, we respond by raising the level of abstraction in our programming languages and in our methods. Thus, we have seen the move from C to Java, from structured methods to object-oriented design, and from classes to design patterns to architectural frameworks.

J2EE, the Java 2 Platform, Enterprise Edition, is such a framework. J2EE is a comprehensive platform for deploying complex systems. It raises the level of abstraction for the development team by offering a set of mechanisms (JSP, Enterprise JavaBeans, servlets) and services (JDBC, JNDI, JMS, and RMI to name a few), enabling the team to focus on its core business value instead of building infrastructure.

As good as J2EE is, however, there is a large semantic gap between what J2EE provides and what must be crafted for the business. Bridging that gap can only be achieved given a strong, foundational understanding of J2EE together with a sound architecture for the domain-specific system. The Unified Modeling Language (UML) comes into play here, for the UML is essentially the language of blueprints for software. Visualizing, specifying, constructing, and documenting the key elements of a system are essential as complexity rises, and this is the very reason for the UML's existence.

Khawar and Cary bring all of these elements together in this book to help you bridge that semantic gap. Not only do they cover all of the essential pieces of J2EE thus helping you build a foundational understanding, they also explain how best to use J2EE's mechanisms and services. This book will also guide you in applying the UML to model your systems built upon J2EE, thus enabling you to better reason about and communicate the analysis and design decisions your team must make in building quality software.

The authors have a deep understanding of J2EE and the UML and a strong sense of the best practices that can lead you to the effective use of both. Their experience in building production systems comes through in their writing, and especially in their comprehensive case study.

There is an essential complexity in building enterprise systems; this book will help you master much of that complexity.

—Grady Booch
Chief Scientist
Rational Software Corporation

Preface

Developing complex software requires more than just churning out lines of code. As a software architect or developer involved in an industrial project, you must understand and be able to leverage critical software subdisciplines such as architecture, analysis and design techniques, development processes, visual modeling, and the underlying technology to be successful.

This book brings all these diverse elements together from the Java 2 Platform, Enterprise Edition (J2EE) development perspective to provide a holistic approach for the reader. Specifically, this book tries to answer the following key questions:

- What is the Unified Modeling Language (UML), and how is it relevant to J2EE development?
- How do Java and UML relate to each other?
- What are the key concepts in software architecture?
- How does a software development process fit into the J2EE software development equation?
- How can analysis and design help you to arrive at a better J2EE application design?
- What are the key J2EE technologies, and how do they fit together?
- How can you leverage the UML for J2EE development?

Rather than reinvent the wheel, the approach taken in this book is that of bringing together known works, such as Jim Conallen's Web Modeling Profile and the Sun Java Specification Request-26 for UML/EJB Mapping Specification.

To provide a practical illustration of the topics discussed, this book guides you through a sample J2EE application development project using the Rational Unified Process (RUP) and the UML. A working implementation is provided. Suggestions for further enhancements are also listed to assist you in continuing your exploration of the UML and J2EE technologies.

Intended Audience

This book is suitable for anyone interested in learning about the UML and how it can be applied to J2EE development. Current J2EE application developers will learn how to apply the UML to J2EE application development. UML practitioners will benefit from learning about the J2EE in the context of the UML. And software professionals interested in learning both the UML and J2EE will be able to get to a productive state faster facilitated by the intertwined contextual discussion.

After reading the book, you will

- Be able to effectively utilize the UML for developing J2EE applications
- Learn about the key J2EE technologies (EJB, JSP, and servlets) at a technical level
- Know when to use Model 1 versus Model 2 architecture, and identify situations where patterns such as value object and session bean chaining may be appropriate
- Understand software architecture concepts such as decomposition, layering, components, frameworks, patterns, and tiers
- Be able to apply techniques such as use case analysis, analysis object discovery, and analysis to design transformation to your J2EE project
- Understand the notion of software development processes and the fundamentals of some of the currently popular processes
- Learn how to start using the RUP for your J2EE project

This book only covers the Java language to the extent of providing a mapping of key Java concepts to the UML. Consequently, some familiarity with Java is assumed (knowing C++ or a similar language should be sufficient to get the basics from the examples). Prior knowledge of, or experience with, the UML, J2EE, or enterprise application development is not a prerequisite, but is certainly helpful.

How to Use This Book

If you are new to the UML and J2EE, you will get the most out of this book by reading it completely in a sequential manner.

Those who are comfortable with the UML and are primarily interested in learning about J2EE (or how to apply the UML to J2EE) can jump directly to Chapters 9–16.

On the other hand, if you know J2EE and mostly want to learn about UML, you should concentrate on Chapters 1–8, and then skim through the remaining portions of the book.

You will get the best results if you get your hands on a good modeling tool and try to apply visual modeling to a problem of your own!

Chapter Summaries

Chapter 1: *Introduction to Enterprise Software* provides a high-level overview of enterprise software development and related technologies.

Chapter 2: *Introduction to the J2EE* covers the basics of the Java 2 Platform, Enterprise Edition. It provides an overview of the basic technologies and the APIs, which form the J2EE.

Chapter 3: *Introduction to the UML* provides an overview of the UML and a quick introduction to the UML basics.

Chapter 4: *UML and Java* provides an overview of the Java language's mapping to the UML and covers some of the basic UML constructs.

Chapter 5: *Overview of Activities* introduces the notion of software development processes and outlines the approach taken in the book.

Chapter 6: *Architecture,* which is an important aspect of good software, introduces the notion of software architecture and provides an overview of some of the concepts in software architecture.

Chapter 7: *Analyzing Customer Needs* shows you how to apply UML use cases to better understand customer requirements. No matter how cool the software, if it does not meet the customer's requirements, it is a failure!

Chapter 8: *Creating the Design* focuses on analyzing the requirements further and creating the initial design for the case study. This chapter discusses how to translate the requirements you have gathered into software.

Chapter 9: *Overview of J2EE Technologies* lays the groundwork for the J2EE technologies we discuss in the remaining chapters.

Chapter 10: *Servlets* provides an overview of the Java servlet technology, discusses how they are modeled in the UML, and then shows a representative application of UML and servlets to the case study. Java servlets are ideal for the request-response oriented Web paradigm.

Chapter 11: *JavaServer Pages* teaches you about JSPs, when to use them, and how to use them in the sample project. JavaServer Pages (JSP) combine the power of servlets with the flexibility of HTML pages.

Chapter 12: *Session Beans* discusses how session beans are used in the middle tier and how to best model and utilize them. Session beans are one of the three types of enterprise beans provided in the J2EE. The chapter concludes with the usage of session beans in the context of the case study.

Chapter 13: *Entity Beans* focuses on the entity bean concept, its advantages and issues, and how to effectively model it in the UML. Entity beans provide a convenient way to objectify the stored data.

Chapter 14: *Message-Driven Beans* covers the technology and how to model them in the UML. Message-driven beans are a new addition to the J2EE Enterprise JavaBean specification.

Chapter 15: *Assembly and Deployment* discusses how UML can help assembly and deployment of a distributed application.

Chapter 16: *Case Study* discusses the details of the example used in this book including general requirements, restrictions, and such.

References for further reading include books, articles, and online sources.

A **Glossary** containing specialized terms and their meanings is provided for quick reference. An **Index** is provided for quick lookup and reference.

Conventions

We use several notational conventions throughout this book. A short list is provided for your reference:

- Italicized words are used to highlight key concepts or terminology.
- References to terms such as **javax.servlet.http.HttpServletResponse** are used to identify the exact J2SE or J2EE classes for further details. For example, in the preceding term the user is being referred to the HttpServletResponse class, which is found in the http package located in the servlet package of the javax package.

- Boldface text is used to identify keywords and reserved words in the context of Java/J2EE, for example, **ejbCreate**.

- Code samples are shown in a slightly different format to distinguish them from plain text, for example, `public void acceptOrder() {`

Acknowledgments

We would like to acknowledge the contributions of all those who helped make this book possible.

Our sincere thanks to Kirk Knoernschid, Todd Dunnavant, Dave Tropeano, Atma Sutjianto, Kevin Kelly, Terry Quatrani, Carolyn Hakansson-Johnston, Ingrid Subbotin, Jim Conallen, Loïc Julien, Dave Hauck, James Abbott, Simon Johnston, Tommy Fannon, Hassan Issa, and all others who provided direct or indirect input, clarifications, ideas, feedback, guidance, and reviews at various stages, from before inception through to completion. Their help was instrumental in defining and redefining the work, in eliminating inaccuracies, in creating additional material, and in the end, the result is a better product overall.

A special thank you to Todd Dunnavant. He not only reviewed multiple drafts cover to cover, he also generously provided in-depth written explanations, suggestions, and comments on various topics that we were only too happy to incorporate in the book.

Kirk Knoernschid's succinct review was most helpful in getting us to focus and remedy some of the key deficiencies in an earlier, draft version. Thank you for that.

Khawar would like to acknowledge and thank Kevin Kelly for his guidance and mentoring. Kevin's insights and ideas were immensely useful throughout this project.

Dave Tropeano's review of a very early draft directly led to a revectoring of our overall approach and the addition of at least two full chapters. The final version is better because of it, and we have Dave to thank.

Our thanks to Rational Software and its management for fostering a work environment in which such endeavors can be undertaken. We would especially like to thank Steve Rabuchin for his willingness to go the extra mile to help others pursue their ideas and achieve their goals. We would also like to thank Jim McGee, Roger Oberg, Magnus Christerson, John Scumniotales, Matt Halls, and Eric Naiburg. Had it not been for the encouragement and support of these individuals, this book would neither have been conceived nor written.

We are very grateful to the staff at Addison-Wesley for their support throughout this project. We especially thank Paul W. Becker and his assistant Jessica Cirone who assisted, reminded, guided, and prodded us through the publishing process. Many thanks to Anne Marie Walker who, through her thoughtful editing, transformed our semi-coherent passages into readable paragraphs. Thanks also to Kathy Glidden of Stratford Publishing Services, Inc. for her skilled project management in the critical production stage.

We benefited immensely from others who have worked on or written about the UML, J2EE, and related topics. To that end, we would like to thank the various authors whose books, articles, and Web sites are listed in the References section. Their works helped expand our understanding of the subjects.

Last but most importantly, we would like to thank our families for their patience and support throughout these last several months. Khawar would like to thank his wife Heike and his daughter Yasmeen for their cheerful and understanding attitude and for their support during this long commitment. Heike's diligent proofreading and corrections to the draft at various stages were invaluable and resulted in the elimination of numerous late-night typos and incoherent sentences. Cary would like to thank his wife Socorro for all her support and helpfulness during this lengthy project.

—K.Z.A.
—C.E.U.

Chapter 1

Introduction to Enterprise Software

■

What Is Enterprise Software?

■

Evolution of Enterprise Software

■

Enterprise Software and Component-Based Software

■

Summary

If you have heard of terms such as Business-to-Business (B2B) and Business-to-Consumer (B2C), you are already familiar with enterprise software at some level. B2B and B2C are just some of the more popular manifestations of enterprise software.

This introductory chapter offers a more in-depth exploration of enterprise software and the challenges and opportunities that accompany it.

What Is Enterprise Software?

The term *enterprise* refers to an organization of individuals or entities, presumably working together to achieve some common goals. Organizations come in all shapes and sizes, large and small, for-profit and nonprofit, governmental and nongovernmental.

Chances are, however, that when someone uses the term enterprise, they mean a large, for-profit organization, such as Intel, General Motors, Wal-Mart, Bank of America, or eBay.

Enterprises generally have some common needs, such as information sharing and processing, asset management and tracking, resource planning, customer or client management, protection of business knowledge, and so on. The term enterprise software is used to collectively refer to all software involved in supporting these common elements of an enterprise.

Figure 1-1 depicts enterprise and enterprise software graphically.

The figure shows an enterprise software setup that is essentially a collection of diverse systems. Software is organized along the various functions within the organization, for example, sales, human resources, and so on. A firewall is provided to safeguard enterprise data from unauthorized access. Some software systems such as those for sales and inventory management interact; however, most are fairly isolated islands of software.

Enterprise software may consist of a multitude of distinct pieces today, but enterprises have gradually come to realize that there is a strong need for their diverse systems to integrate well and leverage each other wherever appropriate for maximum enterprise benefit. B2B and B2C are good examples of such integration and leveraging.

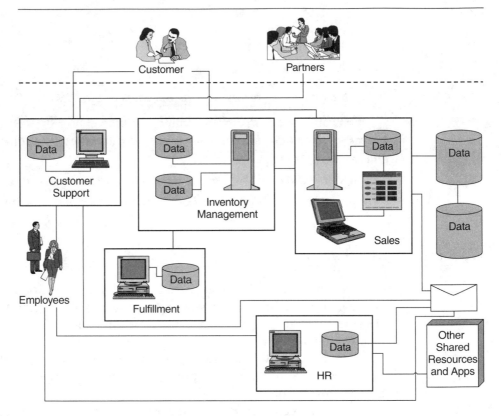

Figure 1-1 Enterprise and enterprise software

Some of the potential ways an enterprise hopes to leverage integrated enterprise software follows:

- By integrating its customer support and in-house product knowledge, an enterprise could provide new and better services to its customers via the Web.

- By linking its marketing machine with the online world, an enterprise could reach a much larger audience online.

- By linking its sales management and inventory, an enterprise may be able to devise specific, lower cost Web sales channels to reach an untapped market segment.

- By providing a front end to one of the services used by its employees, such as the internal office supply ordering system, and tying it into the accounting system, the enterprise could lower the overall cost and improve employee efficiency.

- Making the enterprise HR system available online could be used as a way to give employees more control over their health and 401(k) choices and reduce the overall administrative costs to the enterprise.

- By automating one of its human resource intensive operations and making it available on an anytime, anywhere basis, an enterprise could provide better service to its customers while reducing the overall operational costs.

Challenges in Developing Enterprise Software

Successful enterprises tend to grow in size, hire more people, have more customers and more Web site hits, have bigger sales and revenues, add more locations, and so on. In order to support this growth, enterprise software must be scalable in terms of accommodating a larger enterprise and its operations.

Enterprises encounter constraints as they grow. One common constraint is the computer hardware's inability to scale as the enterprise's processing needs increase. Another constraint is the enterprise's ability to put more people in the same physical or even geographical location. Thus, the challenge of distribution comes into the picture. Multiple physical machines solve the processing needs but introduce the challenge of distributed software. New building or geographical locations address the immediate need, but they introduce the challenge of bringing the same level of services to a diversely located enterprise.

Connecting previously separate systems in order to gain enterprise-scale efficiencies can be a major challenge. Legacy systems were typically designed with specific purposes in mind and were not specifically conceived with integration with other systems in mind. For example, human resource management perhaps was treated as a distinct need without much interaction with financial management, and sales management had little, if anything, to do with customer support. This disjointed approach to software development often resulted in excellent point products being purchased to address specific needs, but it commonly resulted in software architectures that were difficult to integrate.

A related challenge is the need to deal with a multivendor environment. Partly out of evolution, and partly out of necessity, enterprise software has often ended up with similar products from multiple vendors used for the same purpose. For instance, although the HR application might be built on an Oracle 8i database, the customer support application might rely on Microsoft SQL Server.

Enterprise software also typically requires some common capabilities, such as security services to safeguard the enterprise knowledge, transaction services to guarantee integrity of data, and so on. Each of these requires specific skills and knowledge. For instance, proper transaction handling requires strategies for recovering from failures, handling multiuser situations, ensuring consistency across transactions, and so on. Similarly, implementing security might demand a grasp of various security protocols and security management approaches.

These are just some of the common challenges that must be addressed when dealing with enterprise software development.

Evolution of Enterprise Software

Not too long ago, mainframes ruled the world, and all software was tied to this central entity. The advantages of such a centralized approach included the simplicity of dealing with a single system for all processing needs, colocation of all resources, and the like. On the disadvantage front, it meant having to deal with physical limitations of scalability, single points of failure, limited accessibility from remote locations, and so on.

Such centralized applications are commonly referred to as *single tier* applications. The Random House dictionary defines a *tier* as "one of a series of rows, rising one behind or above another." In software, a tier is primarily an abstraction and its main purpose is to help us understand the architecture associated with a specific application by breaking down the software into distinct, logical tiers. See Chapter 6 for a more detailed discussion of tiers.

From an application perspective, the single most problematic aspect of a single tier application was the intermingling of presentation, business logic, and the data itself. For instance, assume that a change was required to some aspect of the system. In a single tier application, all aspects were pretty much fused; that is, the presentation side of the software was tied to the business logic, and the business logic portion had intimate knowledge of the data structures. So any changes to one potentially had a ripple effect and meant revalidation of all aspects. Another drawback of such intermingling was the limitations it imposed on the reuse of business logic or data access capabilities.

The client-server approach alleviated some of these major issues by moving the presentation aspects and some of the business logic to a separate tier. However, from an application perspective, the business logic and presentation remained very much intermingled. As well, this *two-tier* approach introduced some new issues of its own, for instance, the challenge of updating application software on a large number of clients with minimal cost and disruption.

The *n-tier* approach attempts to achieve a better balance overall by separating the presentation logic from business logic and the business logic from the underlying data. The term *n-tier* (as opposed to *three-tier*) is representative of the fact that software is not limited to three tiers only, and can be and indeed is, organized into deeper layers to meet specific needs.

It should be noted that each tier in an n-tier does not imply a separate piece of hardware, although that is certainly possible. A tier is, above all, a separation of concerns within the software itself. The different tiers are logically distinct within the software but may physically exist on the same machine or be distributed across multiple machines.

Some examples of the types of advantages and benefits offered by n-tier computing are

- *Faster and potentially lower cost development:* New applications can be developed faster by reusing existing, pretested business and data access components.

- *Impact of changes is isolated:* As long as interfaces remain unchanged, changes on one tier do not affect components on another tier.

- *Changes are more manageable:* For example, it is easier to replace one version of a business component with a new one if it is residing on a business tier (on one or a few dedicated servers) rather than having to replace hundreds or thousands of client applications around town, or around the globe.

Figure 1-2 illustrates enterprise software organized along these single, two, and n-tiers.

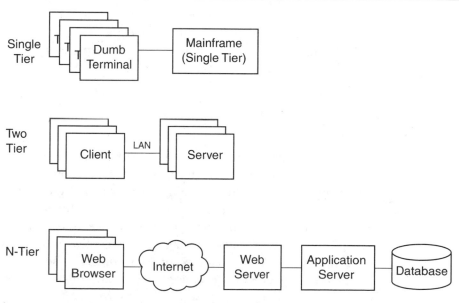

Figure 1-2   Architectural evolution of enterprise software

Enterprise Software and Component-Based Software

When the object-oriented software approach burst onto the software development scene, it was widely expected that adoption of object-oriented software development techniques would lead to reuse, but this hope was only partially realized. One of the reasons for this partial success was the fine granularity of the objects and the underlying difficulty of achieving large-scale reuse at that level due to the more strongly coupled nature of fine-grained objects.

Software components are designed to address this precise issue. Unlike an object, a software component is designed at a much higher level of abstraction and provides a complete function or a service. Software components are more loosely coupled. Using interfaces the components have deliberately exposed, they can be combined together rapidly to build larger applications quickly and are more cost-effective.

Component-based software, of course, requires that components from different sources be compatible. That is, an underlying common understanding, a contract if you will, is required on which the components are to be developed.

Various *component models* have been developed over the years to provide the common understanding. Microsoft's ActiveX, later COM, and Sun Microsystem's applets and JavaBeans are examples of such component models.

Distributed component models have also been developed to address component-based software in the context of distributed enterprise software and associated challenges discussed earlier. Such component models essentially provide an "operating system" for distributed and component-based software development. Examples of these include DCOM, Microsoft DNA (now Microsoft.NET), and Sun Microsystem's Enterprise JavaBeans (EJB), which is part of the Java 2 Platform, Enterprise Edition (J2EE).

Summary

Enterprise software has undergone a gradual evolution in pursuit of providing ever-greater value to the enterprise. Enterprise software faces some distinct challenges. These include, among others, scalability, distribution, security, and the need to work with a diverse set of vendor technology. Various evolutionary architectural approaches have been tried over the years to meet such challenges. An increasingly popular solution revolves around using a distributed component model to develop superior enterprise software. Such distributed component models hold promise, but they are still in their infancy.

Chapter 2
Introduction to the J2EE

Sun Microsystems has organized the Java 2 Platform along three specific focused areas, or editions: Micro Edition (J2ME), Standard Edition (J2SE), and Enterprise Edition (J2EE).

Of those products, J2EE is the most relevant to developing enterprise Java applications.

What Is the Java 2 Platform, Enterprise Edition?

The J2EE defines an architecture for developing complex, distributed enterprise Java applications.

J2EE was originally announced by Sun Microsystems in mid-1999 and was officially released in late 1999. The J2EE, being relatively new, is still undergoing significant changes from release to release, especially in the area of Enterprise JavaBeans (EJB).

The J2EE consists of the following:

- Design guidelines for developing enterprise applications using the J2EE
- A reference implementation to provide an operational view of the J2EE
- A compatibility test suite for use by third parties to verify their products' compliance to the J2EE
- Several Application Programming Interfaces (APIs) to enable generic access to enterprise resources and infrastructure
- Technologies to simplify enterprise Java development

Figure 2-1 illustrates the relationship between the J2EE platform elements graphically.

The platform builds on the Java mantra of "Write Once, Run Anywhere" via a group of technologies and a set of APIs. These are, in turn, supported and bound by three key elements, namely the reference implementation, the design guidelines, and the compatibility suite.

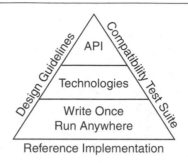

Figure 2-1 The J2EE platform elements

A Brief History of J2EE

How J2EE came about is quite interesting. Java, originally named Oak, was conceived as a software language for developing applications for household appliances and other such devices. With the Internet revolution, Java gradually evolved into a language for client-side development with capabilities such as applets and JavaBeans. Along the way, several Java APIs, such as Java Database Connectivity (JDBC), were developed to address market needs for generic access and usage of resources typically required by enterprise software applications.

It was clear soon after Java's introduction that the use of Java on the client side in a browser-based systems environment faced some serious challenges, such as the latency involved in the loading of Java libraries over the Internet before a client-side Java application could start up. However, Java's relative simplicity, platform-independent architecture, and rich set of APIs as well as its Web enabled nature were strong positives for its use in enterprise software development.

This ease of use and Web enabled nature of Java led to a relatively wide adoption of Java for Web-centric development. Developers used Java technologies, such as applets, for visuals and dynamic output that could easily be added into standard HTML pages on Web sites.

Although Java applications could be run on servers, Java initially did not offer any specific capabilities for server-side use. Sun realized the potential for using Java as a language for Web-based applications and sought to adapt it for the server side via the Java Servlet specification. Once the adaptation occurred, the Web client could call into a Java program running on a remote server, and the server program could process the request and pass back meaningful results. The concept of the *servlet* was born and has been utilized fairly heavily for enterprise application development. Servlets, however, were never really designed to handle complex issues related to customer transactions, session concurrency, synchronization of data, and so on.

EJB, originally released as an independent specification by Sun Micro-systems, was intended to simplify server-side development by providing a very large set of out-of-the-box services to handle the key enterprise application development issues.

The concept of n-tier architecture has been around a long time and has been successfully used for building enterprise-scale applications. Sun's embracement of the n-tier development model for Java, and introduction of specific functionality to permit easier server-side development of scalable Web-based enterprise applications, gave Java the critical missing ingredient it needed in this arena.

The J2EE is the result of Sun's effort to align the disparate Java technologies and APIs together into cohesive Java development platforms for developing specific types of applications. Three Java platforms currently exist. Each successive one listed can conceptually (but not necessarily technologically) be considered a superset of the previous one:

- *Java 2 Platform, Micro Edition (J2ME):* Platform for the development of software for embedded devices such as phones, palm tops, and so on.

- *Java 2 Platform, Standard Edition (J2SE):* Most familiar of the Java 2 platforms. It is also known as the Java Development Kit (JDK) and includes capabilities such as applets, JavaBeans, and so on.

- *Java 2 Platform, Enterprise Edition (J2EE):* Platform for developing enterprise-scale applications. It is designed to be used in conjunction with the J2SE.

Figure 2-2 provides an overview of the three existing Java 2 platforms.

Why J2EE?

You are probably asking: So, why use the J2EE? Isn't it too new and unproven? What does it really offer? Is it just another fad?

Let's start with the newness aspect. Although the J2EE packaging is new, specific pieces that make up the J2EE have been around for a while. For instance, the JDBC API is well established. Servlet technology has also been used for some time as a lightweight and maintainable alternative to the Common Gateway Interface (CGI)[1] scripts.

---

1. An older approach used for processing user input provided via the Web and for providing dynamic content based on the input.

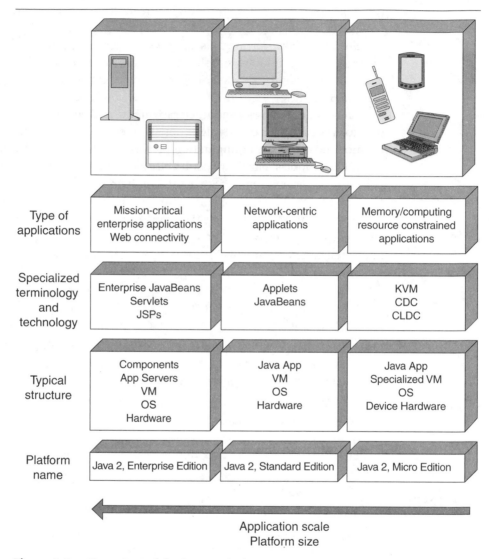

The following is the content of the figure:

Type of applications	Mission-critical enterprise applications Web connectivity	Network-centric applications	Memory/computing resource constrained applications
Specialized terminology and technology	Enterprise JavaBeans Servlets JSPs	Applets JavaBeans	KVM CDC CLDC
Typical structure	Components App Servers VM OS Hardware	Java App VM OS Hardware	Java App Specialized VM OS Device Hardware
Platform name	Java 2, Enterprise Edition	Java 2, Standard Edition	Java 2, Micro Edition

Application scale
Platform size

Figure 2-2 Overview of the Java 2 platforms

J2EE also offers some promising benefits. As described in the following paragraphs, these include features that enable developers to focus on developing business logic, on implementing the system without prior detailed knowledge of the execution environment, and on creating systems that can be ported more easily between hardware platforms and operating systems (OSs).

Enterprise software development is a complex task and can require extensive knowledge of many different areas. For instance, a typical enterprise application development effort might require that you be familiar with interprocess communication issues, security issues, database specific access queries, and so on. J2EE includes built-in and largely transparent support for these and similar services. As a result, developers are able to focus on implementing business logic code rather than code that supports basic application infrastructure.

The J2EE enterprise development model also encourages a cleaner partition between system development, deployment, and execution. Because of this, developers can defer deployment details, such as the actual database name and location, host specific configuration properties, and so on, to the deployer.

J2EE supports hardware and OS independence by enabling system services to be accessed via Java and J2EE rather than underlying system APIs. For this reason, enterprise systems that conform to the J2EE architectural specification can be ported fairly easily between different hardware systems and different OSs.

Perhaps one of the greatest J2EE benefits is its support for componentization. Component-based software has numerous advantages over traditional, custom software development:

- *Higher productivity:* Fewer developers can achieve more by putting together an application from prebuilt, pretested components rather than implementing a custom solution from scratch.
- *Rapid development:* Existing components can be put together rapidly to create new applications.
- *Higher quality:* Rather than testing entire applications, component-based application developers can concentrate on testing the integration and the overall application functionality achieved via the prebuilt components.
- *Easier maintenance:* Because components are stand-alone to begin with, maintenance such as upgrades to individual components is much easier and more cost-effective.

Although some level of software componentization does exist, it is a far cry from the type of componentization prevalent in other industries, such as electronics or automobiles. Imagine the diminished electronics industry if each and every chip required needed to be handcrafted in order to put together a new electronic gadget.

J2EE facilitates componentization in many ways. A few examples follow:

- The "Write Once, Run Anywhere" nature of Java makes it appealing for developing components for a diverse set of hardware systems and operating systems.

- J2EE offers a well thought-out approach for separating the development aspects of a component from its assembly specifics and its assembly aspects from its deployment details. Thus, components developed independently can be readily integrated into new environments and applications.

- J2EE offers a wide range of APIs that can be used for accessing and integrating products provided by third-party vendors in a uniform way, for example, databases, mail systems, messaging platforms, and so on.

- J2EE offers specialized components that are optimized for specific types of roles in an enterprise application. For example, enterprise components can be developed in different "flavors," depending on what they are expected to accomplish.

Component marketplaces have already started to emerge. A recent Gartner Group study forecasted that by 2003, 70 percent of all new applications would be built from components. J2EE, with its support for component-based development (CBD), rapid adoption, and broad industry support, should play a prominent role in this switch to CBD.

A Brief Overview of J2EE

The J2EE technologies and APIs cover a broad spectrum of enterprise Java development. It is unlikely you will use each and every aspect of the J2EE in your enterprise Java development effort. But it is always helpful to have the big picture in mind, so the intent in this section is to make you aware of what is in the J2EE.

In the rest of the book, we cover the technologies in the context of modeling them with the Unified Modeling Language (UML). We also cover some, but not all, of the APIs. If you are interested in a specific API, see the References section at the end of this book for a list of resources for further reading.

Technologies

To understand the J2EE technologies, you must first understand the role of the container in the J2EE architecture. All current technologies in the J2EE rely on this simple yet powerful concept.

Figure 2-3 illustrates the role of the container within the J2EE.

A container is a software entity that runs within the server and is responsible for managing specific types of components. It provides the execution environment for the J2EE components you develop. It is through such containers that the J2EE architecture is able to provide independence between

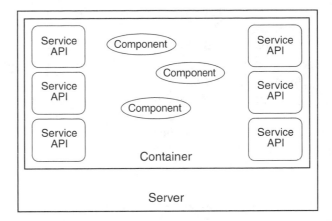

Figure 2-3   The container concept

development and deployment and provide portability between diverse middle tier servers.

A container also is responsible for managing the life cycle of components deployed within it and for things such as resource pooling and enforcing security. For instance, you can restrict the ability to access a specific method to a small group of callers. The container would then enforce this restriction by intercepting requests for that method and ensuring that the entity requesting access is in the privileged list.

Depending on the container type, it may also provide access to some or all of the J2EE APIs.

All J2EE components are deployed and executed within some kind of a container. For instance, EJBs run within the EJB container, and servlets run in the Web container. In all, the J2EE has four different kinds of containers:

- *Application container:* Hosts stand-alone Java applications
- *Applet container:* Provides an execution environment for applets
- *Web container:* Hosts the Web components, such as servlets and JavaServer Pages (JSP)
- *Enterprise container:* Hosts EJB components

Servlets

Servlets are Web components capable of generating dynamic content. They are one of the most frequently used J2EE components found on the World Wide Web today. They provide an effective mechanism for interaction between the server-based business logic and the Web-based client, and they provide a lightweight and more manageable alternative to the popular CGI scripting approach.

Because servlets are simpler and require fewer resources in general, some developers prefer to use these components along with JSPs almost exclusively in their implementations rather than making use of the more complex EJB components. This practice might make sense for very simple enterprise applications, but quickly becomes a less than optimal choice whenever transaction support is needed in the application.

Servlets are best used to handle simpler tasks, like gathering and checking for valid inputs from the entry fields of a Web page. When the preliminary checks are done, the data should then be passed to a more suitable component to perform the actual task at hand.

Servlets run inside the servlet container (also referred to as the servlet engine) hosted on a Web server. The servlet container manages the life cycle of a servlet and translates the Web client's requests, made via protocols such as the Hypertext Transfer Protocol (HTTP), into object-based requests. Likewise, the container translates the response from a servlet and maps the response object to the appropriate Web protocol.

JSP

JSPs are another type of J2EE Web component and have evolved from servlet technology. In fact, portions of JSPs are compiled into servlets that are then executed within the servlet container environment.

JSPs came into being to make it easier for members of a Web team to maintain the portions of the system that support Web page presentation without requiring them to be traditional programmers. Nonprogrammers typically maintain the presentation code in the HyperText Markup Language (HTML). This is harder to do when that HTML is generated by Java statements contained within servlets.

JSPs permit Java code to be embedded within a structured document such as HTML or eXtensible Markup Language (XML). This allows the presentation code to be easily maintained as regular HTML code and shields nontechnical contributors from code editors, and so on.

Because JSPs allow for very complex Java code to be embedded within these HTML or XML documents, some developers chose to use this method during the early days of JSP technology. However, it is generally good practice to keep the Java code within a JSP relatively simple.

Some other Java technologies that have been around for a while, like JavaBeans, also tie into the use of JSPs. They help to make it less complicated to display larger amounts of data for things like tables in Web pages.

EJB

The EJB specification is at the very core of the J2EE platform. It defines a comprehensive component model for building scalable, distributed server-based enterprise Java application components.

There are three types of EJBs:

- *Session beans* are best used for transient activities. They are nonpersistent and often encapsulate the majority of business logic within an enterprise Java application. Session beans can be stateful, meaning they retain connections between successive interactions with a client. The other type of session bean is stateless. In the case of a stateless session bean, each successive invocation of the session bean by the same client is treated as a new, unrelated activity.

- *Entity beans* encapsulate persistent data in a *data store,* which is typically a complete or partial row of information found in a database table. They provide automated services to ensure that the object-oriented view of this persistent data stays synchronized at all times with the actual data residing in the underlying database. Entity beans also are often used to format this data, either to assist in the business logic of the task at hand or to prepare the data for display in a Web page. As an example, in a database table of employees, each record could map to an instance of an entity bean.

- *Message-driven beans* are designed to be convenient, asynchronous consumers of Java Messaging Service (JMS) messages. Unlike session and entity beans, message-driven beans do not have published interfaces. Rather, message-driven beans operate anonymously behind the scenes. Message-driven beans are stateless and are a new type of EJB component introduced in J2EE 1.3.

The Model-View-Controller (MVC) architecture, originally used in the Smalltalk programming language, is useful in understanding how these different J2EE technologies fit and work together. For those unfamiliar with MVC architecture, the basic idea is to minimize the coupling among objects in a system by aligning them with a specific set of responsibilities in the area of the persistent data and associated rules (Model), presentation (View), and the application logic (Controller). This is illustrated in Figure 2-4.

The Model is responsible for maintaining the application state and data. It can receive and respond to queries from the View and can provide notifications to the View when things have changed.

The Controller updates the Model based on execution of application logic in response to user gestures (e.g., dialog buttons, form submit requests, etc.).

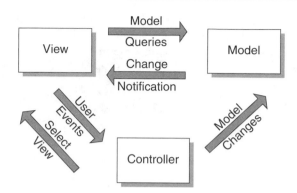

Figure 2-4 Model-View-Controller architecture

It is also responsible for telling the View what to display in response to user gestures.

The View is responsible for the actual rendering of the data provided by the Controller.

To illustrate, consider a simple clock application developed using the MVC approach. The Model in this case is essentially responsible for keeping track of time. Time is automatically updated at predefined intervals (a microsecond, millisecond, or some other unit) through some built-in mechanisms in the Model. It also provides operations so other entities can query the Model and obtain the current time, but it does not care or know how the time is to be displayed.

The responsibility for displaying the time falls on the View; however, the View can take different forms. For example, it may take the form of an analog display whereby two (or three) hands are used to display the time. It can easily be a digital display consisting of several digits as well. As time changes, the Model notifies the View, and the View updates to reflect the new time.

Keep in mind that clocks require some mechanism for updating the time, for example, when daylight savings time goes into effect. On a clock rendered in a Web browser, the user may have the capability to indicate a change in time by using some Graphical User Interface (GUI) controls or by typing in a new time. The Controller receives the user gestures for such changes and updates the Model by calling the appropriate operations defined on the Model to reflect the new time.

A Model may have several simultaneous Views. For instance, a clock application running on the Web may have several users utilizing it at the same time, using different representations, such as analog, digital, and so on.

APIs

There are several APIs within the J2EE. Some of the more popular ones are discussed in the following sections.

JDBC

Interaction with databases is an integral part of an enterprise Java application. The JDBC API is squarely focused on making this aspect easier for the enterprise Java developer.

The JDBC API, which is similar in spirit to Microsoft's Open Database Connectivity (ODBC) API, simplifies access to relational databases. It consists of a generic, vendor independent interface to databases. Using the JDBC makes your applications portable and your database skills applicable across a wider range of vendor platforms.

The majority of the JDBC API already exists as part of the J2SE. It is not limited to use only with the J2EE. There are however a few extensions that the J2EE version adds, mostly to support some advanced functions for the J2EE containers to use, like connection pooling as well as some additional support for JavaBeans.

The JDBC API provides a common interface in order to shield the user from vendor specific differences as much as possible. JDBC implementations are supplied by the database vendor, so different databases can act differently under the covers.

In enterprise applications, you do not necessarily need to use JDBC directly. For example, you can use entity beans to make the necessary database calls for you. The practice of using JDBC directly is expected to become less common as application servers provide more sophisticated and well-tuned support for entity beans.

Java Naming and Directory Interface (JNDI)

In the context of JNDI, "naming" actually refers to a naming service. Naming services allow you to look up, or refer to, an object. A file system is an example of a naming service.

A directory service is similar to a naming service and provides enhanced searching capabilities. In fact, a directory service always has a naming service (but not vice versa).

There are various naming and directory services available, so the challenges on this front are quite similar to those in the area of databases. JNDI is designed to address those challenges by providing a generic and uniform way to access the services.

The complete JNDI API already exists as part of J2SE, although it is listed as an enterprise feature. Most distributed enterprise applications make use of this service at some point. For example, any use of EJBs in an enterprise application necessitates that JNDI be used to find the associated EJB Home interfaces.

JMS

A messaging service allows communication among distributed applications using self-contained entities called messages. Such communication is typically asynchronous.

Various vendors provide messaging oriented middleware. The JMS provides a uniform and generic interface to such middleware.

JMS can be used directly in an enterprise application or via a type of EJB known as a message-driven bean. Message-driven beans are new in J2EE 1.3.

Remote Method Invocation (RMI)

RMI enables access to components in a distributed environment by allowing Java objects to invoke methods on remote Java objects. The method is actually invoked on a proxy object, which then arranges to pass the method and parameters onto the remote object and provides the response from the remote object back to the object that initiated the remote method invocation.

RMI is not exclusive to J2EE. However, RMI is at the heart of some J2EE technologies, such as EJB.

Other J2EE Technologies and APIs

In this section, we list some other J2EE technologies and APIs that are either in existence now or are expected to become part of J2EE in the future.

J2EE Connectors

J2EE Connectors provide a common architecture to use when dealing with Enterprise Information Systems (EIS) as the data store. These large systems tend to be prevalent in huge enterprises, and they can be very complex to deal with.

Java Transaction API (JTA)

A transaction refers to a grouping of multiple operations into a single "atomic" operation. Thus, if part of a transaction fails, the other, previously executed operations are "rolled back," that is, undone, to ensure sanity of the system.

The JTA provides a generic, high-level API for transaction management. It is primarily used for large, distributed, often complex transaction processing, usually involving a number of large, remotely connected systems.

Java IDL

The Java Interface Definition Language (IDL) provides interoperability support for the Common Object Request Broker Architecture (CORBA) and the industry standard Internet Inter-Orb Protocol (IIOP). It includes an IDL-to-Java compiler and a lightweight Object Request Broker (ORB).

RMI-IIOP

RMI-IIOP refers to RMI using the IIOP as the communication protocol under the covers. IIOP is an Object Management Group (OMG) standard. Because CORBA uses IIOP as the underlying protocol, the use of RMI-IIOP makes interoperability between RMI and CORBA objects simpler. RMI-IIOP is typically also more efficient than RMI over the Java Remote Method Protocol (JRMP).

Java Transaction Service (JTS)

JTS is a transaction manager service that supports JTA and makes use of IIOP to communicate between remote instances of the service. Like JTA, it is used in large distributed system situations.

JavaMail

JavaMail provides an API to facilitate interaction with e-mail messaging systems in a vendor independent fashion. This API consists primarily of a set of abstract classes that model a Java-based e-mail system. It is intended for building sophisticated e-mail-based applications. Note, however, that it is possible to provide e-mail support in an application without using the JavaMail API.

Summary

J2EE offers a well thought-out architecture for developing complex enterprise Java applications.

J2EE's combination of technologies—namely EJB, servlets, and JSPs—and its generic API (JDBC, JavaMail, JMS, etc.) give its users various advantages. Thus, developing a J2EE application simplifies the overall task of developing large-scale distributed applications.

Some of the key challenges that are simplified by J2EE include distribution of applications across multiple processes and processors, security, transactions, persistence management, and deployment.

Chapter 3

Introduction to the UML

The Unified Modeling Language (UML) is a graphical language for the modeling and development of software systems. It provides modeling and visualization support for all phases of software development, from requirements analysis to specification, to construction and deployment.

The UML has its roots in several preceding object-oriented notations.[1] The most prominent among them being the notations popularized by Booch, Rumbaugh, et al. and Jacobson, et al. So, even though the UML has been formalized for just a few years, its predecessors have been used to design and specify software-intensive systems since the early 1990s.

The unification of the competing notations came about in the mid to late 1990s. In early 1997, several consortia submitted responses to an Object Management Group (OMG) Request for Proposal for a common metamodel to describe software-intensive systems. A consortium headed by Rational Software submitted the UML 1.0 specification. This incorporated the leading features of several modeling notations including those of Booch, Rumbaugh, and Jacobson. At the request of the OMG, most of the competing consortia cooperated with the group led by Rational to refine UML 1.0 into UML 1.1, which was accepted by the OMG in late 1997.

UML continues to evolve under the direction of the OMG. For example, recently proposed extensions provide common notations for data modeling, Web application modeling, and mapping J2EE constructs to UML.

The UML has broad industry support. By virtue of being the specification supported by the 850+ member OMG, it is the de jure software industry standard for visual modeling and development. The fact that all leading tools for modeling software-intensive systems now support UML makes it the de facto standard as well.

---

1. The distinction between notation and methodology is a common source of confusion. The UML is a notation that can be applied using many different approaches. These approaches are the methodologies.

UML Overview

The central idea behind using the UML is to capture the significant details about a system such that the problem is clearly understood, solution architecture is developed, and a chosen implementation is clearly identified and constructed.

A rich notation for visually modeling software systems facilitates this exercise. The UML not only provides the notation for the basic building blocks, but it also provides for ways to express complex relationships among the basic building blocks.

Relationships can be *static* or *dynamic* in nature. Static relationships primarily revolve around the structural aspects of a system. Inheritance relationship between a pair of classes, interfaces implemented by a class, and dependency on another class are all examples of static relationships.

Dynamic relationships, on the other hand, are concerned with the behavior of a system and hence exist at execution time. The messages exchanged within a group of classes to fulfill some responsibility and flow of control within a system, for example, are each captured in the context of the dynamic relationships that exist within a system.

Both static and dynamic aspects of a system are captured in the form of UML diagrams. There are several types of UML diagrams. They are organized along specific focal areas of visual modeling called *views*.

The following types of diagrams are provided by the UML:

- *Use case diagram:* A use case diagram shows use cases, actors, and their relationships. Use case diagrams capture the precise requirements for the system from a user's perspective. See Chapter 7 for a detailed discussion of use cases in the context of enterprise Java application development.

- *Class diagram:* A class diagram shows the static relationships that exist among a group of classes and interfaces in the system. Some common relationship types are inheritance, aggregation, and dependency. See Chapter 8 for more details on classes, interfaces, and class diagrams.

- *Object diagram:* An object diagram provides a snapshot view of the relationships that exist between class instances at a given point in time. An object diagram is useful for capturing and illustrating, in a static fashion, complex and dynamic relationships within the system. See Chapters 12 and 13 for additional coverage of how object diagrams are used in the context of enterprise application design and development.

- *Statechart diagram:* State machines are excellent for capturing the dynamic behavior of the system. They are particularly applicable to event driven, reactive systems or objects where event order is important. Statecharts are also useful for modeling the behavior of interfaces. For more information on using statecharts in the context of J2EE, see Chapter 12.

■ *Activity diagram:* An activity diagram is an extension of a statechart diagram and is similar in concept to a flowchart. An activity diagram allows you to model the system's behavior in terms of interaction or flow of control among distinct activities or objects. Activity diagrams are best used for modeling workflows and flow within operations. See Chapter 7 for further discussion of activity diagrams.

■ *Interaction diagram:* Interaction diagrams are used for modeling the dynamic behavior of a system. There are two kinds of interaction diagrams in the UML:

   ■ *Sequence diagram:* Used for modeling the message exchange between objects in a system. Sequence diagrams also capture the relative time ordering of messages exchanged.

   ■ *Collaboration diagram:* The message exchange is captured in the context of the overall structural relationships among objects.

   The two diagrams are equivalent, and it is possible to convert from one to the other easily. Interaction diagrams are commonly used to model the flow of control in a use case and to describe how objects interact during the execution of an operation, such as the realization of an interface operation. Interaction diagrams are discussed in Chapter 8.

■ *Component diagram:* A component represents the physical manifestation of a part of the system, such as a file, an executable, and so on. A component diagram illustrates the dependencies and relationships among components that make up a system. A component typically maps to one or more classes, subsystems, and so on. Components and component diagrams are discussed in Chapter 15.

■ *Deployment diagram:* A deployment diagram shows the architecture of a system from the perspective of nodes, processors, and relationships among them. One or more components typically map to a deployment node. In the context of J2EE, deployment diagrams are useful for modeling and developing the distributed system architecture. Deployment diagrams are discussed in Chapter 15.

The UML is a comprehensive subject worthy of a book itself (and in fact, several good ones have already been written!). Only the most relevant aspects are covered in this book. Refer to the References section at the end of this book for a list of some excellent books on the UML that provide a more in-depth discussion of specific areas of the UML.

Why Use the J2EE and the UML Together?

Any reasonably proficient programmer can develop a piece of software that will do the job—for a while. But building an enterprise system that is maintainable, scalable, and evolvable is a different matter altogether. And these days, when a system must evolve at a breakneck pace or face obsolescence, it is all the more important to take the long term view because you *will* need to maintain, scale, and evolve the system you are building!

It is possible to survive and thrive for a while by coding, compiling, fixing, and deploying your application. Sooner rather than later, you will most likely find that your system is not able to scale to the new growth demands. This is because your system probably was not architected and designed so that it could evolve easily in the face of new requirements.

The UML provides the tools necessary for architecting and building complex systems, such as those required for an enterprise. It supports, among other disciplines, requirements engineering, architecture-level design, and detailed design. In addition, UML modeling tools are evolving to where they can be used to impose consistent design patterns upon a J2EE-based system model and to generate a significant portion of the system's executable source code.

UML's support for requirements engineering is mainly manifested in its support for use cases, which are used to understand and communicate functional requirements. Using UML for requirements modeling, in conjunction with a use case driven development process, facilitates traceability from requirements to design. Traceability, in this context, implies the ability to determine the elements in a design that exist as a result of a specific requirement. In a use case driven development process, specific design elements are created for the purpose of satisfying a use case. Thus, traceability is often achieved implicitly.

Such traceability has various benefits. For example, the ability to identify the impact of changes in requirements on the design can not only simplify the task of modifying a system to meet new requirements, but also help focus testing of the system after the changes are complete. Similarly, the ability to determine the requirements that led to the existence of specific design elements can assist in eliminating unnecessary design elements.

Let's walk through a simple scenario to illustrate this. Imagine that your project has a requirement *R1*. In the use case model, you create a use case named *deliver* in response to *R1*. In the analysis model, two classes *compute* and *route* are created to fulfill the use case. The use case is realized by a *deliver use case realization* and classes **compute.java** and **route.java** are created to fulfill the *deliver use case realization*. If there is a change to *R1,* can you easily determine which classes will likely need to be tested? Conversely, can you justify the existence of **compute.java** in the implementation model?

As the functional requirements change or new ones are added, the system model can be examined to determine which portions of the system's architecture and detailed design are impacted by the changes.

UML includes modeling constructs that can help developers understand how large-scale portions of the system interact at runtime and depend upon each other at compile time. Additionally, UML modeling tools can include checks to ensure that design details do not violate architecture-level constraints. Such tools thereby can help ensure that the quality of the system's architecture is maintained through multiple releases.

UML diagrams, such as interaction diagrams, activity diagrams, and class diagrams, can be used to understand and document complex interactions within the system. These help in the analysis of the problem and also provide a detailed record of the as-designed behavior and structure of the system. So when it is time to incorporate new functionality in the system, you know what the design intent was and what the inherent system limitations are.

In addition to supporting the ability to create generic UML models, UML modeling tools are evolving rapidly to a point where they will help impose consistent, accepted patterns of object interaction into a system design. For example, consider the challenge of determining when to make use of session beans versus entity beans, when to use stateful versus stateless session beans, and when to use JavaServer Pages (JSP) versus servlets. In the future, these types of design decisions may be codified within a tool and applied upon demand.

Finally, using UML enables developers to move to a true visual development paradigm. In addition to enabling developers to impose consistent modeling patterns into their designs, modern UML modeling tools generate an increasing amount of highly functional J2EE source code. As a result, developers can concentrate on higher value design activities and leave much of the labor-intensive coding to the modeling tools. A visual representation is also excellent for communicating the design among the team. In addition, it can be used effectively to ramp-up new team members rapidly.

Challenges in Modeling J2EE in the UML

One of the authors recalls trying to replace a leaky rear differential seal on his car. The repair manual called for a specialized tool to remove the seal, but he took one look at it and decided the job could be done with his wrench set and pliers. He eventually managed to replace the seal, but it took him weeks, and somehow the oil never stopped leaking!

The challenge in using unadulterated UML for J2EE modeling is somewhat similar. You may get the job done, but your efficiency and likelihood of success will be diminished.

More specifically, the specifications that make up the J2EE offer some distinct modeling challenges, for instance:

- An Enterprise JavaBean (EJB) class implements the business methods in the Remote interface, but not the interface itself. This is contrary to the standard UML concept of interface realization.
- An EJB, by definition, is related to a Home and Remote interface. It is necessary that a UML modeler consistently honor this architectural pattern.
- Servlets and EJBs have deployment descriptors associated with them.
- Unlike most other Java classes, EJBs, servlets, and JSPs are packaged in a specific type of archive file along with their deployment descriptors.
- Entity bean attributes map to elements in a database.
- EJBs have the notion of transactions and security.
- Session EJBs can potentially have significant dynamic behavior.
- Different persistence schemes can be employed by entity beans.
- JSPs are logically a hybrid in that they have both client and server aspects to them.

Given the drive to deliver better software in less time, another objective in modeling J2EE is to be precise enough to permit UML-based modeling tools to be able to process your model and provide value-added capabilities related to J2EE.

Extension Mechanisms in the UML

We are quite sure the creators of UML did not have J2EE on their minds when they created the UML. Fortunately for us, they had enough foresight to recognize that in order for the UML to last any length of time, it would have to be capable of evolution and adaption to new languages and constructs.

The UML provides three mechanisms for extending the UML: stereotype, tagged value, and constraint.

Stereotype

A stereotype allows you to create a new, incrementally different model element by changing the semantics of an existing UML model element. In essence, this leads to the addition of new vocabulary to the UML.

```
<<interface>>
  Control
```

Figure 3-1   A class with stereotype

In the UML, a stereotyped model element is represented by the base model element identified with a string enclosed within a pair of guillemets («»). A pair of angle brackets (<< or >>) can also represent a guillemet.

The use of stereotypes is fairly common in everyday UML usage, and it is quite acceptable to create stereotypes to model concepts/constructs if the stereotype adds clarity. As an example, the UML itself describes the *extend* and *include* relationships via the <<extend>> and <<include>> stereotypes.

A stereotype can be defined for use with any model element. For instance, stereotypes can be used with associations, classes, operations, and so on. An example of a stereotype is shown in Figure 3-1. A stereotype may optionally be shown via an icon. An example is shown in Figure 3-2. Note that Figure 3-1 and Figure 3-2 are equivalent. We make extensive use of the iconic representation in this book.

Tagged Value

UML model elements typically have properties associated with them. For example, a class has a name. A tagged value can be used to define and associate a new property for a model element in order to associate additional information to the model element.

A tagged value is defined as a *tag, value* pair in the following format: {tag=value}. For instance, the UML construct class has a name, but normally there is no way to identify the author of the class. A tagged value of {author=Khawar} could be used to associate the author's name to the class model element.

An example of a tagged value is shown in Figure 3-3.

Control

Figure 3-2   Representing an interface using an icon

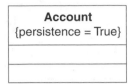

Figure 3-3   Tagged value example

Constraint

As its name implies, a constraint in the UML allows you to specify restrictions and relationships that cannot be expressed otherwise. Constraints are great for specifying rules of how the model can or cannot be constructed.

A constraint is expressed as a string placed between curly braces such as {constraint} .

For example, if the order of the associations within a group of interconnected classes was important, you could use a constraint on each association to clearly identify its order in the relationship. An example of a constraint is shown in Figure 3-4.

It's one thing to have the facilities to do something, and quite another to actually do it. The whole point of having the UML is to provide a common vocabulary, so extending the language at anyone's whim is counter to the purpose as well as the spirit of the UML.

Generally, when a need arises to adapt the UML for a specific purpose, the suggested process is to create a new UML profile, and at an appropriate point, submit it to the OMG, which is the body responsible for the UML and for standardization. This allows other interested parties to contribute to the profile and ensure its adequacy for the specialized needs from all points of view.

A UML profile does not actually extend the UML. Instead, it uses the UML extension mechanisms to establish a uniform way of using the existing UML constructs in the context of a new domain. Thus, a UML profile is essentially a

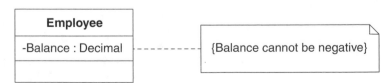

Figure 3-4   An example of a constraint

collection of stereotypes, constraints, tagged values, and icons along with the conventions for using them within the new domain.

Some examples of UML profiles that already exist or are in the works include

- UML profile for Software Development Processes
- UML profile for Business Modeling
- Data Modeling
- Real-Time Software Modeling
- XML DTD Modeling
- XML Schema Modeling
- UML EJB Modeling
- Web Modeling

The first two profiles in the list are documented in the OMG UML specification document. The remaining profiles are either published or submitted, or are being used in the industry, or are under consideration for development.

The Approach to J2EE UML Modeling

The approach we've taken in this book is to reuse existing and proven approaches for modeling specific concepts in the UML and reduce the extensions to the absolute minimum necessary.

Significant work has already been done in the form of a proposed UML profile for EJBs, developed via the Java Community Process (JSR 26). The UML notation for J2EE reuses that work to a large degree. Effort has also been put forth on the Web Modeling profile.[2]

So, rather than focus on the mechanics and intricacies of J2EE UML mapping, we attempt to highlight how specific facilities within the UML can be effectively used to model J2EE applications and derive the most benefits in the process.

Consequently, our modeling focus is on activities such as:

- Understanding and identifying the overall role a specific J2EE technology may play in an enterprise application
- Identifying strategies for dealing with intertechnology relationships

---

2. As documented in *Building Web Applications with UML* by Jim Conallen, Addison-Wesley, 1999.

- Understanding dynamic behavior of components
- Developing a suitable architecture for the enterprise application
- Identifying and maintaining the dependencies

Summary

The UML provides a rich set of constructs for modeling complex systems and is ideally suited for modeling enterprise Java applications.

UML modeling is more than the visual presentation of a specific J2EE technology. The true value of UML becomes apparent as it is applied to solving challenges that are hard to solve without the aid of modeling. Such challenges include, among others, behavioral modeling, identification of dependencies, significant relationships, and development of a resilient architecture for the enterprise application.

Chapter 4
UML and Java

- Representing Structure

- Representing Relationships

- Summary

UML and Java may be languages for software development, but they exist in different planes of reality. UML occupies the visual world, whereas Java is textual in nature.

UML is also richer than Java in the sense that it offers more abstract and powerful ways of expressing a particular concept or relationship. However, there is generally only one way to represent that concept or relationship in the Java language.

For example, a Java variable declaration can be expressed in multiple ways in UML.

This chapter provides an overview of some key UML concepts related to classes and how they relate to the implementation world. The primary purpose is to review the basic mapping for the benefit of those who may be new to the UML world. A secondary purpose is to identify ways in which the use of UML notation can effectively enhance the significance of a specific piece of Java code without actually altering the equivalent Java code.

Representing Structure

Structural concepts, such as class and interface, are fundamental to both Java and the UML. This section identifies how these concepts map to Java and the UML.

Class

In the UML, a Java class is represented via a compartmentalized rectangle. Three horizontal compartments are used:

- *Name compartment:* Shows the Java class name
- *Attribute compartment:* Lists variables defined on the class, if any
- *Operations compartment:* Shows methods defined on the class, if any

Figure 4-1 shows a simple Java class without any variables and methods.

Java	UML

`public class Account{`
 	
`...`
 	
`}`
	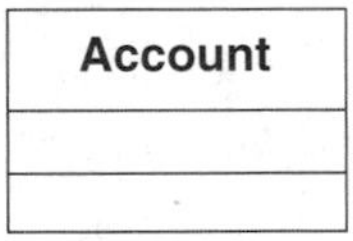 **Account**

Figure 4-1 A class in Java and the UML

An abstract class is identified by italicizing the class name.

A stereotype may be used alongside a class name to unambiguously identify it as a specific type of Java class, such as an applet (we discussed the concept of stereotypes in Chapter 2). You can also use stereotypes to identify specific types of classes (such as <<Business Entity>>) in your particular domain vocabulary to make the classes more meaningful wherever they appear.

A word of caution: if you are using a UML tool for Java code generation, note that the tool may use the stereotyping mechanism to affect code generation.

Figure 4-2 shows a stereotyped class.

Variable

Java variables may manifest themselves in various ways in the UML. This is one instance where modeling adds a dimension not apparent in the source code.

Java	UML

`public class Clock extends Applet{`
 	
`...`
 	
`}`
	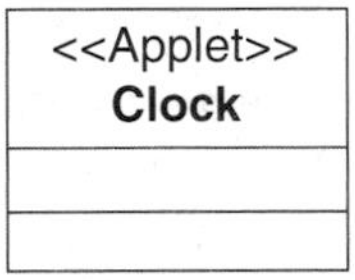 <<Applet>>
	Clock

Figure 4-2 A stereotyped class

Java	UML
| ```
public class Employee

{

    private float yearsOfService;

    public String lastName;

    public String firstName;

    public String socSecNum;

    public String employeeID;

    ...

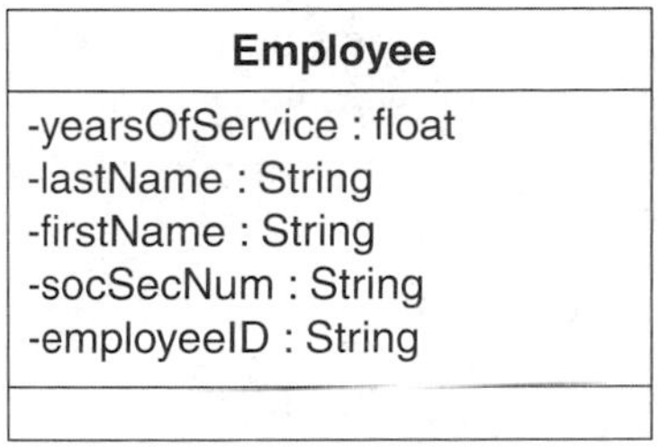

}
``` | **Employee**<br><br>-yearsOfService : float<br>-lastName : String<br>-firstName : String<br>-socSecNum : String<br>-employeeID : String |

Figure 4-3   A class with attributes

The simplest form of variable declaration is to list it within a class's attribute compartment. Underlining the attribute indicates the *static* nature of the variable. The visibility of an attribute is indicated by preceding the attribute with + for public, # for protected, and - for private. Figure 4-3 shows a class with attributes.

This form of declaration may come about for basic data that is needed for the class. Such variables do not generally have any specific significance from a broader modeling perspective. Examples include variables you require for storing basic pieces of information that make an object what it is, variables required for internal logic, and so on. Such variables are based on objects that usually cannot be decomposed further.

Variables may also manifest themselves due to an object's relationships with other objects (for example, a collection of some sort). We discuss such relationships and their usage in the "Representing Relationships" section later in this chapter.

Method

Methods are the equivalent of operations on a class in the UML. They are shown in the third compartment for a class. Visibility scope of UML operations is
```

defined using the same convention used for class attributes, as described in the "Variables" section.

Underlining the operation's name is used to differentiate a static method. Listing the operation in italics in the operation compartment shows that the method is abstract. You can, of course, hide or show details depending on the significance of the detail. For instance, in Figure 4-4, the full operation signatures are not shown by choice.

Object

Although both Java and UML have the concept of an object, there is no direct mapping between a UML object and Java code. This is so because objects are dynamic entities, which are based on class definitions. Java applications are

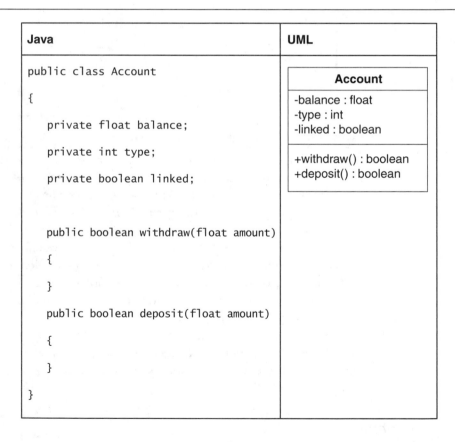

Figure 4-4   A class with attributes and operations

Java	UML
No Java code equivalent	<table><tr><td>checking : Account</td></tr><tr><td>balance : float type : int linked : boolean</td></tr></table>

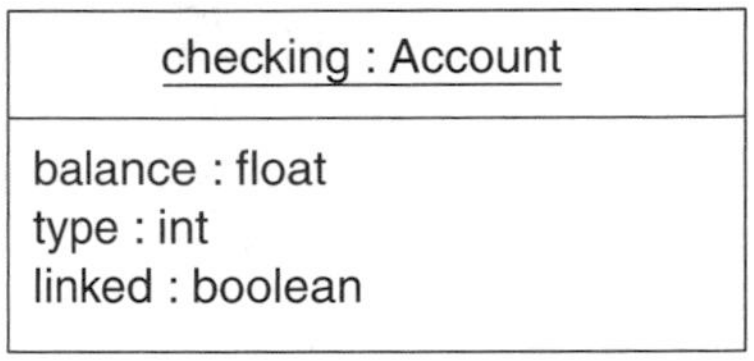

Figure 4-5   An object

written in terms of Java classes that result in the creation of Java objects when the application is actually executed.

In the UML, objects are used to model dynamic aspects of the system via interaction diagrams. A rectangle with an object name, and/or a class name, is used as the notation for an object. Sometimes it is desirable to show the attribute values for the object in a given situation. This can be done using a rectangle with two partitions showing the attributes of the class. See Figure 4-5.

Interface

In the UML, a Java interface is depicted as a class stereotyped with <<interface>>. Stereotyped classes may optionally have icons associated with them. In the case of an interface, the UML iconic representation is a small circle. This iconic representation is commonly used for representing Java interfaces when modeling in the UML.

Figure 4-6 shows the standard interface representation.

Java	UML
| ```
public interface Control{

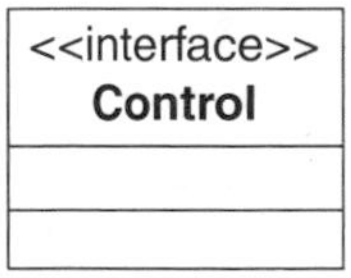

...

}
``` | <table><tr><td>&lt;&lt;interface&gt;&gt;<br>**Control**</td></tr><tr><td></td></tr><tr><td></td></tr></table> |

Figure 4-6   An interface
```

Java	UML

`public interface Control{`
 	
    `...`
 	
    `}`
	Control  ○———

Figure 4-7   Alternate representation of an interface in the UML

Figure 4-7 shows an alternate and more compact form of representation.

Either approach is acceptable from a modeling perspective and really comes down to your individual preference. This book makes extensive use of the icon representation for diagrams presented.

Package

A Java package maps to a UML package. Packages may be logical, meaning you may only use them as a grouping mechanism. Packages can also be physical, meaning they result in a physical directory in the file system.

The UML package is represented as a folder, as shown in Figure 4-8. Packages may be stereotyped to distinguish the type of package, for example, using <<subsystem>> to identify the package as a subsystem. (A subsystem refers to a group of UML elements and represents a behavioral unit in a model. It can have interfaces as well as operations. Subsystems are typically significant from an analysis and design perspective. There is no direct mapping between a subsystem and a Java language construct.)

Java	UML
`Package Widgets;`	 **Widgets** (folder)

Figure 4-8   A package

Representing Relationships

Relationships play a key role in capturing and modeling the important structural aspects of a Java application.

Some of these relationships, such as inheritance, can be explicitly identified in the Java language via predefined keywords. Others are not as easily identifiable in Java code but can nonetheless be represented.

Inheritance

The UML concept of generalization is analogous to inheritance in Java. Generalization maps directly to the **extends** keyword and is shown visually via a line with a triangle at the end nearest the super class. See Figure 4-9.

Realization

In Java, a class may implement one or more interfaces. The Java keyword **implements** maps to the concept of realization in UML.

In the UML, realization can be shown in two different ways. If the stereotyped class approach is used for representing an interface, realization is shown via a dashed line with a triangle at the end touching the interface. If the circle notation is used for an interface, a plain, solid line connecting the interface and the implementing class is used.

These approaches are shown in Figure 4-10 and Figure 4-11. Note that the approach shown in Figure 4-11 is shorthand for the approach shown in

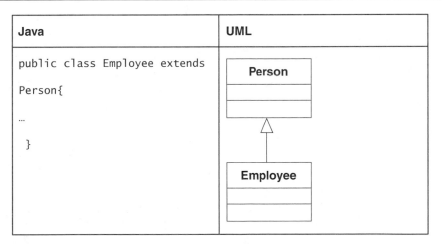

Figure 4-9   Representing the inheritance relationship

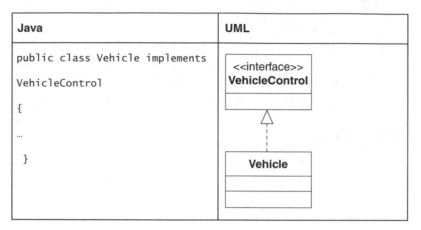

Figure 4-10 UML realization

Figure 4-10. It is inappropriate to mix the two. For example, showing an interface via a circle and using the dashed line with a triangle would be inappropriate.

Dependency

Anytime a class uses another class in some fashion, a dependency exists between the two. The relationship is that of the user depending on the class

Java	UML

public class
 	
Vehicle
 	
implements
 	
VehicleControl
 	
{
 	
...
 	
}
	VehicleControl ⊸ **Vehicle**

Figure 4-11 Alternate representation of interface realization

that it is using. In the UML, a dependency is shown via a dotted line with an arrow touching the class that is causing the dependency.

A dependency exists if a class:

- Has a local variable based on another class
- Has a reference to an object directly
- Has a reference to an object indirectly, for example, via some operation parameters
- Uses a class's static operation

Dependency relationships also exist between packages containing classes that are related. Dependencies between packages are shown via a dotted line with an arrowhead. See Figure 4-12 and Figure 4-13.

Association

Conceptually, an association between two classes signifies that some sort of structural relationship exists between the classes.

In the UML, an association is shown by drawing a line between the classes that participate in the relationship. Associations may be unidirectional or bidirectional. Bidirectional association is shown with a simple line. Unidirectional association is shown with an arrow on one end.

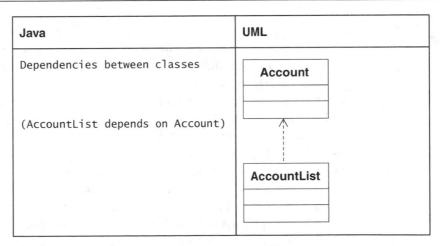

Java	UML
Dependencies between classes (AccountList depends on Account)	

Figure 4-12   Dependency between classes

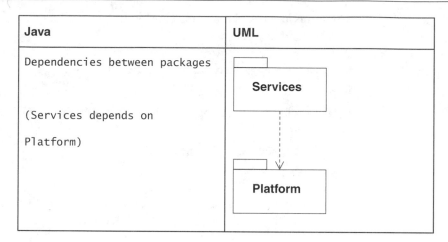

Java	UML
Dependencies between packages (Services depends on Platform)	Services Platform

Figure 4-13   Dependency between packages

A unidirectional association implies that an object of the class from which the arrow is originating (i.e., the class that has the nonarrowhead side of the association) may invoke methods on the class towards which the arrow is pointing. In Java, this manifests itself as an instance variable on the class that may invoke methods.

Figure 4-14 shows a unidirectional association example.

Most associations are of the unidirectional kind, but it is possible for some associations to be bidirectional. A bidirectional association simply means that either object in the association may invoke methods on the other. In Java, this results in an instance variable on each class based on the type of the other class.

A bidirectional association example is shown in Figure 4-15.

What about showing associations with primitive types, such as *int* or *boolean*? Clearly, it could be done that way if you are so inclined. In fact, you may start out showing associations with a large number of entities in the analysis phase, but as you proceed through design and implementation, and identify the significance of each association, the number may be reduced significantly. In practice, if it doesn't really add much value to understanding the design, aside from adding some visual clutter to the model, there really is no point in showing the relationship visually. It is preferable to use associations to show only relationships that are significant and nontrivial.

Each end of the association is a *role* in UML terminology and may be named. For example, consider that a person may have a bidirectional association with a company that is employing the person. In this case, the roles may be named employer and employee, respectively. From an implementation perspective in

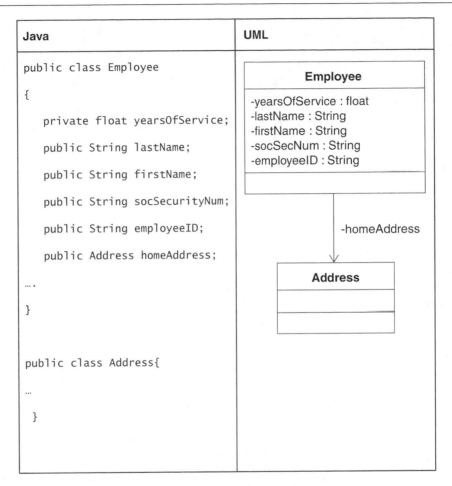

Java	UML
| ```
public class Employee

{

    private float yearsOfService;

    public String lastName;

    public String firstName;

    public String socSecurityNum;

    public String employeeID;

    public Address homeAddress;

....

}


public class Address{

...

    }
``` | |

Figure 4-14 An example of a unidirectional association

Java, the roles may be appropriate as the names of the instance variables in the respective classes. It is usually helpful to name a role if it adds value to understanding the model. If not, it is perfectly reasonable to leave it unnamed. In such a case, the role name can simply be based on the name of the class.

An example of roles on a bidirectional association is shown in Figure 4-16.

Of course, objects in a class may have multiple associations with objects in another class. For instance, a corporation typically has many employees and a person may work for more than one corporation. This is modeled by assigning a multiplicity to the role(s). Multiplicity may be depicted as a specific value (e.g., 0, 1, 7) or as a range (e.g., 0..1, 1..5, 1..*). An asterisk is used to indicate an
```

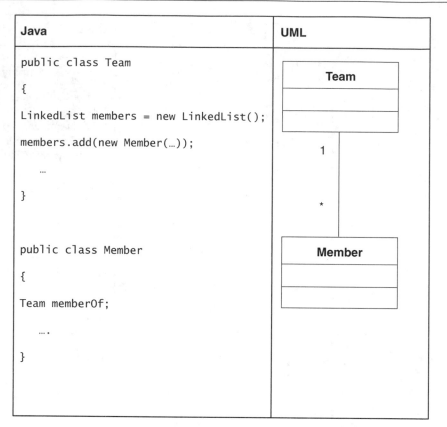

Java	UML
```public class Team{LinkedList members = new LinkedList();members.add(new Member(…)); …}public class Member{Team memberOf; ….}```	

Figure 4-15 An example of a bidirectional association

unlimited range. For example, "*" means zero or more or simply many, and "500..*" indicates 500 or more, up to an unlimited number.

In terms of Java implementation, multiplicity manifests itself as a multivalued instance variable. For example, assume that a corporation employs several persons, and a person can work for a maximum of three corporations. For the variable multiplicity without a fixed upper limit, this may translate to a *collection* representing the persons who work for a single corporation. For the person who works for three different corporations, this would result in an array of three elements.

A multiplicity example is shown in Figure 4-17.

Information relevant to the association roles cannot always reside with the classes involved in the association. For instance, it would be inappropriate to store the session between a shopper and the virtual shopping cart in either class. In such a case, an association class may be used to model this situation. See Figure 4-18.

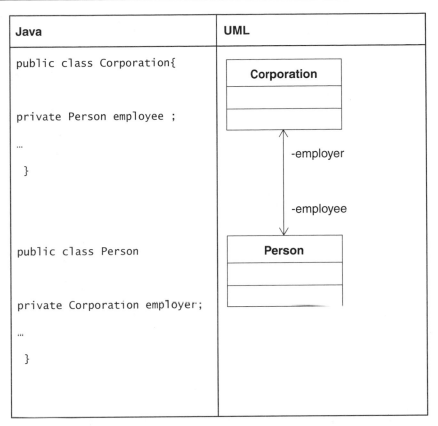

Java	UML

`public class Corporation{`
 	
`private Person employee ;`
 	
`...`
 	
`}`
 	
`public class Person`
 	
`private Corporation employer;`
 	
`...`
 	
`}`	

Figure 4-16   An example of roles on bidirectional association

Aggregation

Aggregation is a stronger form of an association. It is used to show a logical containment relationship, that is, a whole formed of parts. Although the parts may exist independently of the whole, their existence is primarily to form the whole. For example, a computer may be modeled as an aggregate of a motherboard, a CPU, an I/O controller, and so on. Note that the I/O controller may exist independently (e.g., in a computer store); however, its existence in the context of the whole is more appropriate.

Aggregation is modeled as an association with a hollow diamond at the class forming the whole. Because it is an association, an aggregation supports the concept of roles and multiplicity. In terms of implementation in Java, an aggregation maps to instance variables on a class.

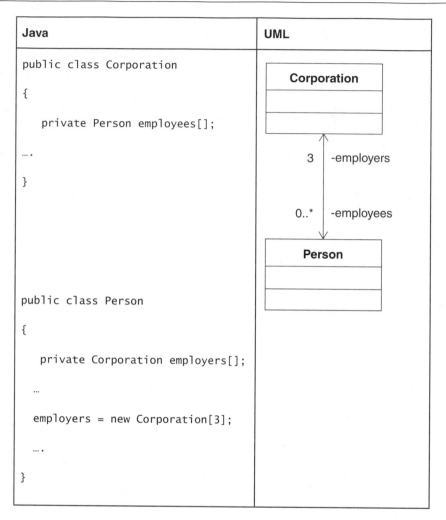

Java	UML

`public class Corporation`
 	
`{`
 	
`    private Person employees[];`
 	
`....`
 	
`}`
 	
`public class Person`
 	
`{`
 	
`    private Corporation employers[];`
 	
`    ...`
 	
`    employers = new Corporation[3];`
 	
`    ....`
 	
`}`	

Figure 4-17 An example of multiplicity

An example of an aggregation is shown in Figure 4-19.

The semantics and constraints of aggregation are not substantially different from those for basic association. In spite of this, everyone considers aggregation necessary.

Unlike association instances, instances of an aggregation cannot have cyclic links. That is, an object may not directly or indirectly be part of itself. For example, if an instance of A aggregates an instance of B, then that instance of B cannot itself aggregate that same instance of A.

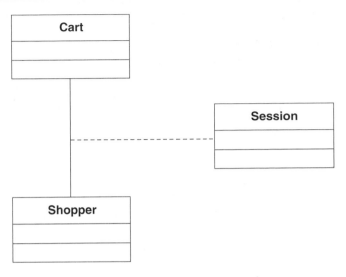

Figure 4-18 An association class

In general, unless you believe that using aggregation adds value or clarifies something, you should use association. (Composition, discussed next, is another alternative.)

Composition

Composition is another form of association and is similar to aggregation to some degree. However, it is less ambiguous.

Composition is appropriate for modeling situations that call for physical containment. It implies a much stronger whole-part coupling between the participants such that parts cannot exist without the whole. That is, parts share the life cycle of the whole. They are created when the whole comes to life and destroyed when the whole ceases to exist.

When working with an implementation language, such as C++, use of aggregation versus composition does map to different code. For example, aggregation implies pass by reference, whereas composition implies pass by value. However, this distinction is not applicable to Java. Hence, the code mapping of aggregation versus composition is the same even though you may still want to model them differently to communicate the intent of the design and highlight elements in an implementation independent fashion.

Composition is shown in the same way as aggregation except that the diamond is filled in.

Java	UML

``
public class Order
 	
{
 	
private OrderItem items[];
 	
private OrderDetails details;
 	
….
 	
}
``
	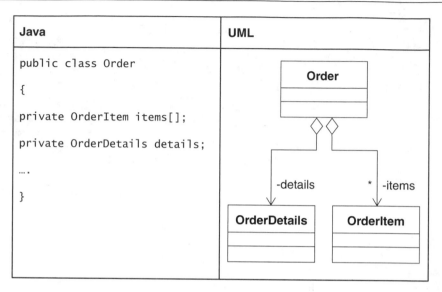

Figure 4-19   An aggregation example

Java	UML

``
public class Person
 	
{
 	
    private Person employer[];
 	
    private Person employee[];
 	
….
 	
}
``
	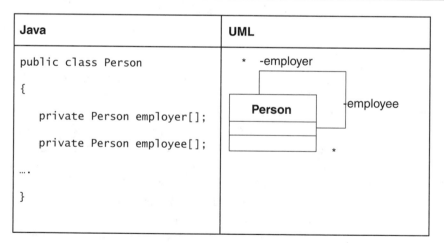

Figure 4-20   An example of a reflexive association

Reflexive Relationships

A class may have an association with itself. For example, if a person employs another person, the Person class may have an association with itself with the role names of employer and employee. Such a relationship is called a reflexive relationship.

This notation can be considered a modeling shorthand. Only one class icon rather than two is used to illustrate the relation. In Figure 4-20, it would be perfectly acceptable to show two separate Person class icons with the relation drawn between them. However, to do so consumes space on a diagram.

Summary

The use of the appropriate UML constructs can add significant value to the overall design. It can act as an aid in not only documenting the design but also making it more understandable.

In this chapter, we focused on the key concepts related to the class diagram. The key concepts discussed were

- Classes, attributes, and operations, and their relationship to Java implementation
- Package as a means of grouping things and its relation to Java
- Different kinds of relationships between classes and when to use which:
  - Association
  - Aggregation
  - Composition
- Inheritance representation in the UML
- The role of realization in the UML and how it relates to **extends** in the Java implementation language

Good modeling is not a trivial task. Like any other skill-based task, it requires significant effort and practice to become proficient in UML and modeling. In the next few chapters, we explore application of these concepts in the context of J2EE development.

Chapter 5

Overview of Activities

■

What Is a Software Development Process?

■

Overview of Popular Approaches to Software Development

■

Approach Used in This Book

■

Overview of Major Activities

■

Summary

Is software development an art or a science? The answer really depends on whom you talk to. But there is one thing about which everyone will agree: software continues to become bigger, more complex and harder to develop, and more difficult to manage.

In this chapter, we briefly explore some of the more popular approaches to software development and highlight their perceived strengths and weaknesses.

This is followed by a high-level overview of the approach we have chosen to follow for this book. The idea is to provide you with a roadmap for the rest of the book.

What Is a Software Development Process?

A software development process provides guidance on how to develop software successfully. Such guidance may cover the entire spectrum of activities associated with software development. The process might manifest itself in the form of proven approaches, best practices, guidelines, techniques, sequencing, and so on.

Whether formal or informal, the software development process ultimately employed has a profound impact on the success of a software project. An ad hoc approach might work well for a small project, but it might lead to chaos for a large project and hence greatly impact the overall schedule. Similarly, a bureaucratic software development process may lead to frustration and bog down even the best team.

Overview of Popular Approaches to Software Development

There are numerous processes for developing software. Some of the more prevalent/popular ones are discussed in the following sections.

The Just-Develop-It Approach

The just-develop-it approach is characterized by a general lack of formality and almost nonexistent process or ceremony surrounding software development activities. The software developer has the key role, which is perhaps differentiated by experience and expertise in the area. The sole focus of the development team is to complete the software project in the best way it can, using whatever means are afforded by the technologies at its disposal. Some up-front design work might be undertaken, but that is largely dependent on the initiative and preferences of the software developer who is responsible for the project.

In such an approach, the overall design of the software exists as part of the software. In other words, there is a one-to-one bidirectional mapping between the architecture, design, and implementation. The overall quality of the software is largely dependent on the developers involved in the project. Documentation, in general, is relatively unimportant. Instead, the project relies on the continued availability of the same or equally skilled developers, so they can continue to evolve or maintain the software.

Overall, this means that the software may range from an excellent piece of work that is highly flexible and evolvable to very poor quality software that is inflexible and unable to accommodate even the simplest changes in requirements. In a nutshell, the overall success rate is unpredictable at best and repeatability from one project to the next (or even from one project phase to the next) is mostly dependent on luck.

As it turns out, a large number of software development efforts today still rely on this development approach! Perhaps this is a manifestation of the compressed Internet delivery time pressures or simply the result of the software industry being in its infancy. Either way, the phenomenon is very real.

The Waterfall Process

The waterfall approach has been used extensively in the past and continues to be popular. The idea is to segment the development into sequential phases (e.g., requirements, analysis, design, implementation, test). This works well for small projects and for projects where the requirements are stable and relatively fixed, the problem domain is well understood, and the solution has been proven on similar projects in the past.

Figure 5-1 depicts the waterfall process.

The Iterative Process

Unfortunately, most software projects nowadays do not meet the criteria for utilizing the waterfall approach. Requirements are constantly changing; projects often break new ground by tackling novel problems and trying out cutting-edge technology, and so on. The iterative development approach, which is based on Boehm's spiral model, is primarily aimed at addressing these issues. The idea is to

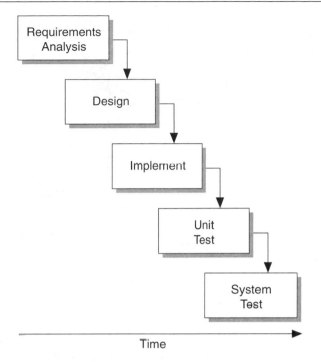

Time

Figure 5-1   The waterfall process

reduce risk early in the project by going through the identified sequence of activities (requirements, analysis, design, etc.) multiple times and revisiting each of the key activities in a planned manner. Each iteration ends with an executable release. Among other advantages, this approach permits early identification of issues with respect to inconsistent requirements, enables end user involvement and feedback, provides a higher confidence level in the state of the project, and so on.

Figure 5-2 depicts the iterative process graphically.

We discuss the iterative approach in further detail in the context of the other approaches explained in this chapter.

The Rational Unified Process

The Rational Unified Process (RUP) is an evolution of the *Objectory* process, which was acquired by Rational Software a few years ago and was merged with the *Rational Approach*. It has been enhanced over time via the incorporation of other aspects of software development as well as best practices identified by the software industry over the years.

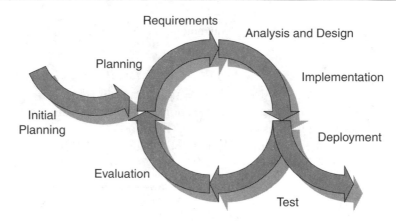

Figure 5-2 The iterative process (used with permission from Phillippe Kruchten, author of *The Rational Unified Process: An Introduction.* p. 7, Reading, MA: Addison-Wesley, 1999.)

At the heart of the RUP lie the software best practices:

■ *Develop software iteratively:* A major issue with traditional (i.e., waterfall) software development effort is the discovery of design defects late in the development cycle and the prohibitive cost to fix them at that stage. Iterative development follows a more continuous and cyclic process, allowing easier course corrections along the way. Thus, high risk issues can be focused on and the risk eliminated early on. Problems are identified continuously and can be overcome in a more cost-effective manner rather than being discovered at the very end of the effort when they can threaten the entire project.

■ *Manage requirements:* Requirements are often evolutionary in nature. That is, a project never starts with all its requirements already captured and outlined. Instead, the process is one of gradual identification, understanding, and refinement. As such, requirements need to be managed carefully to ensure project success.

■ *Use component-based architectures:* Component-based software offers the advantage of true modular development. Such modular development leads to better overall architecture. Components, whether in house or commercially obtained, also promote reuse both in "as is" and customized forms.

■ *Visually model software:* In the words of Grady Booch, "A model is a simplification of reality that completely describes a system from a particular perspective."[1] Building models leads to better understanding of the problem and improves communication about it, thereby making complex systems more manageable. Visual modeling is the preferred way to do modeling because it allows you to work at a higher level of abstraction.

- *Continuously verify software quality:* Studies have proven that the earlier you identify a problem, the cheaper it is to fix. In fact, studies have proven that fixing problems reported after the product is deployed are always several times costlier to fix. Continuous testing means early testing, which can be much more cost-effective. Such ongoing testing can also offer a more objective assessment of the true status of the project.

- *Control changes to software:* Today's large software projects are typically distributed across multiple geographical sites, involving several teams with a large number of developers. The probability of conflicting changes, resulting in chaos, is very high. Thus, there is a strong need to control changes for effective progress on the project.

The RUP has two basic dimensions. One RUP dimension groups activities logically according to the disciplines that are responsible for executing them. The RUP identifies six core disciplines:

- *Business modeling:* As the name suggests, the purpose of this discipline is to develop a model of the business. The idea is to better understand the overall business so the software application can fit into it more appropriately. Business modeling is most suitable in situations where a large amount of information is expected to be managed by the system, and a relatively large group of people is expected to use the system. A *business use case model* and a *business object model* are typically produced as part of the business modeling discipline.

- *Requirements:* The requirements discipline aims to develop a solid understanding of the requirements. The intent is to achieve agreement with customers as well as to provide guidance to developers. A use case model is produced as part of the requirements discipline. A user interface prototype may also be produced.

- *Analysis and Design:* Requirements captured in the requirements discipline are analyzed and transformed into the design in the analysis and design discipline. An architecture is developed to guide the remaining

---

1. Kruchten, P. *The Rational Unified Process: An Introduction.* Chapter 1 "Software Development Best Practices" by Grady Booch, p. 11, Reading, MA: Addison-Wesley, 1999.

development effort. Analysis and design models are developed as part of this discipline.

- *Implementation:* In this discipline, the design is transformed into the actual implementation code. A strategy is developed for layering and partitioning the system into subsystems. The end result is a set of implemented, unit tested components that form the product.

- *Test:* As is obvious from its name, the test discipline is all about verifying the system. Among other things, this typically means verifying that all requirements have been met, confirming that components work together as expected, and identifying any defects remaining in the product. The primary outputs of this discipline are a *test model* and a set of defects generated as a result of the testing.

- *Deployment:* The deployment discipline makes the product available to the end users. As such, it covers details such as packaging of the software, installation, user training, and distribution of the product.

There are also three supporting disciplines: *configuration and change management, project management,* and *environment.*

The other RUP dimension deals with giving structure to the iterations in a software project. The RUP groups the iterations into four phases. Each phase ends with a milestone that is a management-level decision point.

As Figure 5-3 shows, each phase (and each iteration within a phase) usually touches multiple disciplines. Depending on the specific iteration, a specific discipline may provide the emphasis for a phase, whereas the other disciplines play a minor role in the iteration. For instance, an earlier iteration is likely to spend more time in the requirements discipline, whereas a later iteration is likely to spend more time in the test discipline and a much smaller portion of time in the requirements discipline.

The four phases defined by the RUP are

- *Inception phase:* The inception phase revolves around the scoping of the project in terms of the product, understanding of the overall requirements, costs involved, and key risks. The emphasis during the inception phase is on creating a vision document, identifying an initial set of use cases and actors, developing a business case for the project, and developing a project plan showing the phases and planned iterations.

- *Elaboration phase:* The elaboration phase is perhaps the most significant phase. In this phase, the requirements are analyzed in detail, and an overall architecture is developed to carry the project through to completion. Stability in requirements and a stable overall architecture are basic expectations for the end of this phase. Emphasis is on developing a use case model, an analysis model, a design model, an architecture prototype, and a development plan.

- *Construction phase:* The focus of the construction phase is on design and implementation. This is achieved by evolving the initial prototype into the actual product. The key deliverable for the end of the construction phase is the product itself.

- *Transition phase:* In the transition phase, the product is readied for the users. This may involve fixing defects identified during beta testing, adding any missing capabilities, training end users, and so on. The final product is delivered to the customer at the end of the transition phase.

The RUP can also be customized to meet specific needs of an organization or project.

Figure 5-3 combines the various elements of the RUP and visually shows the relationships between phases and disciplines.

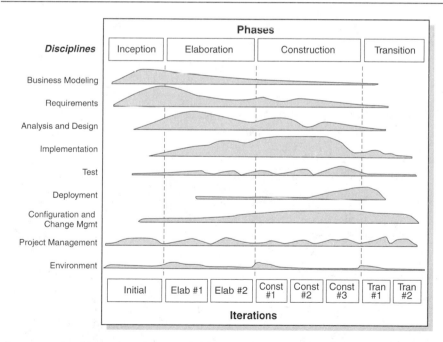

Figure 5-3 The Rational Unified Process (used with permission from Phillippe Kruchten, author of *The Rational Unified Process: An Introduction.* p. 23 [modified to reflect RUP terminology changes circa 2001], Reading, MA: Addison-Wesley, 1999.)

The ICONIX Process

The ICONIX process offers an approach that is similar to the RUP. This process emphasizes "robustness analysis" and formalizes that analysis into a robustness diagram. Robustness analysis revolves around analyzing use cases and establishing a first cut at the objects that participate in each use case. These objects are classified into control, boundary, and entity objects. Practically speaking, the difference is a matter of semantics. The RUP notion of use case analysis is essentially the same as ICONIX robustness analysis. In addition, the RUP addresses all aspects of the software development life cycle, whereas the ICONIX process focuses on analysis and design.

The OPEN Process

The Object-oriented Process, Environment, and Notation (OPEN) process was developed by the OPEN consortium. Like the RUP, it evolved from a merger of earlier efforts in the area. It is primarily intended for use in an object-oriented or component-based software development environment.

OPEN is defined as a process framework known as the OPEN Process Framework (OPF). OPF provides a set of components, which are divided into five groups: Work Units, Work Products, Producers, Stages, and Languages.

Producers are typically people. Producers work on Work Units and produce Work Products. Languages, from the Unified Modeling Language (UML) to Structured Query Language (SQL), are used for creating the Work Products. All this happens in the context of Stages, such as phases, milestones, and so on, which provide the organization for the Work Units.

Extreme Programming/Feature-Driven Development

Extreme Programming (XP), originally proposed by Kent Beck, has gained much attention lately. XP is often positioned as a "lightweight software development process" and in fact can be almost construed as an antiprocess in the traditional sense.

The main idea behind XP is to keep things as simple as possible to get the job done. XP activities are organized around four major undertakings: planning, designing, coding, and testing.

Planning is organized around a "Planning Game." Requirements are collected in the form of user stories, which can be used for discussion with customers and provide sufficient detail for estimates and scheduling trade-offs. Requirements are captured on index cards. This is followed by identifying a "metaphor" for the overall system, which provides the overall shared vocabulary for the team. Requirements are partitioned into small tasks, each of which can be implemented in a very short amount of time (weeks).

Because requirements can change rapidly, XP does not spend any time on up-front analysis. Instead, the design and coding begins immediately. In XP, the code is the design; hence, the design phase consists of discussing features with the customer, identifying the test cases for successful implementation, and then implementing the simplest solution that will meet the requirements. Developers always work in pairs and focus on implementing the tasks, doing any refactoring of existing code as required along the way. Integration with other parts of the system may take place several times a day.

Primary testing is centered on unit testing, and functional testing is dictated by the customer to determine acceptability of the software product.

Feature-Driven Development (FDD), developed by Jeff de Luca and Peter Coad, is based on XP. It primarily differs from XP in that FDD includes a requirement to develop a domain object model as part of an early design as a way to compensate for the relative absence of an overall architecture/design. FDD further constrains the definition of XP tasks to user-consumable features and elevates features to a central notion within the overall development process.

Approach Used in This Book

As you may have already deduced from the depth of the process descriptions given thus far, the approach in this book is largely based on the RUP.

The decision to do so was based on the following:

- The RUP is a proven process and is currently being used successfully in a large number of projects.

- We strongly believe that architecture, analysis, and design are essential to a project's long-term success. Unlike other processes, for example, FDD and XP, the RUP provides excellent coverage of these key aspects.

- There are enough similarities between the RUP and other processes (e.g., ICONIX) to make the work presented in this book useful to even those not using the RUP in its pure form.

- The RUP can be customized to suit specific needs.

Of course, this decision was not based, by any means, on an exhaustive comparison of the different approaches and was no doubt influenced by our own familiarity with the RUP.

We should point out that in this book, we have chosen to use a customized version of the RUP tailored for the needs of this specific book and case study. In

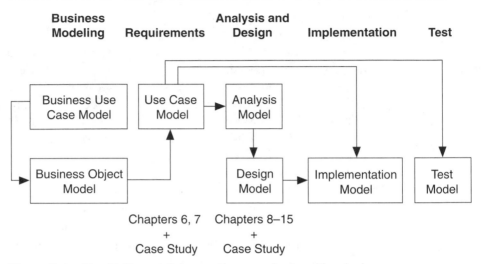

Figure 5-4   The RUP workflows, artifacts, and related book chapters

addition, we do not attempt to cover each and every artifact, deliverable, or element outlined in the RUP. This is primarily due to space and time limitations imposed by the book.

For instance, we condense what would realistically be done over several iterations with multiple increments, each into a seemingly single iteration. We also do not cover all disciplines identified in the RUP, limiting ourselves to those most directly relevant to illustrating specific aspects of analysis, design, and development.

Figure 5-4 graphically illustrates the relationship between the different RUP workflows, artifacts produced during the workflows, and how the chapters in this book relate to them.

Refer to the References section at the end of this book for additional sources of information about the RUP.

Overview of Major Activities

We limit our discussion in the book to some key activities. Each topic spans one or more chapters.

Chapter 6: Architecture

Chapter 6 introduces the notion of architecture and discusses some of the key concepts of architecture, such as decomposition, layering, and so on. These concepts are then applied and elaborated upon in the remaining chapters.

Chapter 7: Analyzing Customer Needs

Chapter 7 focuses on understanding what is required to be implemented. We start by capturing the requirements in the form of a use case model. This involves identification of actors and use cases and articulation of the requirements concisely in the form of sequence diagrams and activity diagrams.

Chapter 8: Creating the Design

Chapter 8 revolves around developing a high-level design. We start by developing a better understanding of the specific use cases. Each use case is refined using the concept of boundary, control, and entity classes, and the system responsibilities are distributed to these classes. Sequence diagrams are used to capture the refined use case scenarios, and collaboration diagrams are used to better understand the interactions. We also develop the initial class diagram representing the structural relationships in the model. As well, we start to identify the dependencies and packaging requirements.

Chapters 10–15: Detailed Design

Chapters 10–15 focus on bringing the Java 2 Platform, Enterprise Edition (J2EE) technologies and UML together. We use the design model developed in Chapter 9 as the starting point and evolve it as we cover specific technologies. For example, in Chapter 10, we partition the control classes further and evolve a subset of those classes into servlets. In Chapter 11, we introduce JavaServer Pages (JSP) and cover some of the presentation related aspects of the application.

In these chapters, we make use of class diagrams, interaction diagrams, statechart diagrams, and activity diagrams as well as component and deployment diagrams.

Chapter 16: Case Study

Chapter 16 recaps the various activities undertaken as part of the first iteration in Chapters 6–15. The idea is to provide a consolidated view of the case study used throughout the book. We fill in the holes using detailed UML diagrams for scenarios not covered in the rest of the book. We further talk about the second and subsequent iterations of the case study and highlight some of the key considerations in moving forward with the project.

Summary

There are various aspects of software development. Some of the key elements are architecture, understanding requirements, analysis and design, and implementation.

Over time, numerous approaches have been developed for software development. Although there are differences among the specific software development processes, there are also a lot of similarities. In this chapter, we highlighted some of the current popular processes.

To provide a framework for the discussions to come in the remaining chapters, we provided a high-level overview of the activities undertaken in Chapters 6–16.

Chapter 6

Architecture

Software architecture is one of those terms that everyone claims to understand but no one can define precisely—or at least, not precisely enough to satisfy everyone else.

This is partly because of the relatively short existence of the software profession itself and partly due to the newness of the concept of architecture in the context of software.

In this chapter, we take a closer look at software architecture and some of the key concepts involved in it.

What Is Software Architecture?

Most software architecture definitions involve references to one or more of the following:

- Static structure of the software. Static structure refers to how elements of software relate to each other.
- Dynamic structure of the software, meaning the relationships that change over the lifetime of the software and determine what the software looks like when it is running.
- Composition (or decomposition) of the software. This refers to the type of significant but smaller pieces, such as subsystems and modules, that can be part of the software.
- Components and interaction among them. This refers to the various pieces that make up the software and how they interact with each other.
- Layers and interaction among them. Layering allows imposition of a specific ordering or structure upon the software, thereby permitting and /or preventing certain relationships as deemed appropriate for the software.
- Organization of the physical software pieces to be deployed. The physical source code must be organized into appropriate types of deployable units, for example, .jar, .war, and .exe files, for optimal usage
- Constraints on the software. Limitations, either natural or self-imposed. For example, the requirement for software to be written in the Java language.

■ Rationale for the software. That is, why does the software look the way it does? This is important because from an architectural perspective, if something cannot be explained, then it isn't really part of the architecture.

■ Style that guides the software development and evolution.

■ Functionality of the software. In other words, what does the software do?

■ Set of significant decisions about the organization of the software system.

■ Other considerations such as reuse, performance, scalability, and so on.

The following definition perhaps best captures the essence of software architecture:

> The software architecture of a program or computing system is the structure or structures of the system, which comprise software components, the externally visible properties of those components, and the relationships among them [Bass 1997].

Software architecture is additionally concerned with:

> . . . usage, functionality, performance, resilience, reuse, comprehensibility, economic and technological constraints and trade-offs, and aesthetics [Kruchten 1999].

Some of these latter aspects of software architecture, of course, have a somewhat more ethereal nature and do not lend themselves easily to precise analysis as do structure and decomposition, for example.

It should be clear from the preceding definitions that architecture is multifaceted. As such, no single diagram or drawing can be viewed as representing the architecture of given software. Nor is architecture just a representation of the underlying infrastructure or the detailed design of the system.

Architecture is only concerned about the internal details of the software to the extent that these internal details are manifested externally (for example, how a component behaves when viewed from the outside).

Why Architecture?

Every piece of software ever created has architecture. The architecture exists regardless of whether the designer of the software created it knowingly or even knew what the term software architecture meant.

So, the real question is not whether your software needs to have architecture but whether you need to create it in a deliberate fashion.

The following list contains a few reasons why it is important to focus on software architecture:

- An ad hoc approach to software structure will eventually lead to a software system that is brittle and hard to add to because no consideration was given to the need to adapt to new or changed requirements.

- Decomposition of the software into smaller pieces makes the software easier to understand, manage, develop, and maintain. If done properly, it can also significantly improve reusability across projects.

- Software architecture aids in component-based software development.

- Performance can be managed by architecting the software properly from the start. Consider a project that requires a service throughout the software system. Whereas in a haphazard and unplanned version of the project, the same code may be redone over and over again leading to unpredictable performance, a properly architected software that provides the service via a single component would have more predictable performance.

- Better reuse can be achieved via proper architecture. Consider a product line requiring the same basic services with slight variations. With a layering approach, only the topmost layers may need to be replaced. Without layering, extensive changes may be necessary to support multiple products.

- Ill-conceived constraints can hamper the software evolution, for instance, a constraint to have a monolithic, nondistributed system because distributed software systems are harder to build.

- Failure to understand and identify beforehand how the software could be modified to accommodate more users and heavier data processing, provide newer services, take advantage of new technologies, and so on, can lead to a situation where the software has to be rewritten because the original architecture did not consider scalability and evolution needs. Availability and reliability of the software system are largely dependent on the scalability of the system.

- Having a documented architecture makes it easier to understand and communicate the intent and substance of the software system to the development team.

- Security built into the software, testability of the software, maintainability, and overall manageability of the software are also strongly influenced by the architecture of the software system.

Key Concepts in Enterprise Application Architecture

In this section, we discuss some concepts that are central to *arriving* at good software architecture. The notion of architecture, of course, is broader than the items discussed, but we focus on these because of their growing role in the development of large-scale software.

Decomposition

Decomposition refers to the partitioning of a system into smaller, logical pieces to make it easier to manage the complexity. Modules, subsystems, and components are all examples of decomposition.

Decomposition helps define and clarify interfaces between different pieces of a system. It can also be helpful in situations where you must integrate legacy or externally purchased applications.

Decomposition can also help with distribution of the software across multiple processors. The drawback, of course, is that inappropriate or over-decomposition can easily lead to serious performance degradation due to the communication overhead.

A side benefit of decomposition is that it provides a natural partitioning of the development tasks and makes them easier to distribute among a larger team.

In the Unified Modeling Language (UML), decomposition is modeled via packages, modules, and subsystems. Within the Java 2 Platform, Enterprise Edition (J2EE), decomposition can be accomplished via Web components and Enterprise JavaBeans (EJB) components.

Figure 6-1 shows a simple system decomposed into several subsystems.

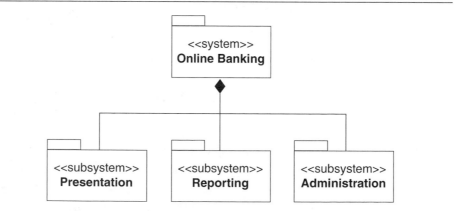

Figure 6-1   System composed of several subsystems

Components

A component is a cohesive unit of software that provides a related set of functions and services.

Components can be developed and delivered independently of other components; that is, they are inherently modular in nature, but are useful only in the context of a *component model*. A component model provides the underlying infrastructure for component composition, interaction, and so on. EJB, Java-Bean, and COM are examples of component models.

A component has well-defined interfaces that permit it to interact with other components. Components conforming to the same component model that offer the same interfaces can be substituted. In essence, the interfaces of a component provide the contracts between the component and the application.

It is possible for a component to contain other components.

Some reasons for using components include

- Compared to traditional software, components are easier to maintain and modify for future needs.
- Components have the potential to increase productivity in the software industry by allowing rapid assembly and completion of applications from prebuilt components.
- Applications built from components can potentially be more flexible. For example, it is easier to distribute applications to meet higher load and so on.
- Components that perform specific tasks can be bought and sold. These can be assembled together into larger applications. This reduces time to market,[1] overall resource requirements, expertise required, and so on.
- Components facilitate a natural partitioning of the software system into cohesive units.

Coarse-grained components map well to high-level subsystems arrived at via a functional decomposition of the system. As they are at a higher level of abstraction, coarse-grained components may have fewer well-defined dependencies. Coarse-grained components aim to deliver discrete and complete business capability. In the context of J2EE, single or multiple EJBs and associated Java classes may be used to implement a coarse-grained component. Examples of coarse-grained components include a warehouse module that keeps track of

---

1. On the other hand, this is a potential risk factor as well if you are relying on an external source to deliver a critical component.

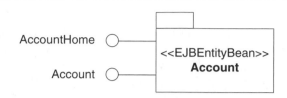

Figure 6-2   An EJB component as a UML subsystem

all aspects of items received and distributed, a life insurance policy processing module, a contact management module, and so on.

Fine-grained components, on the other hand, are comparable to traditional objects in functionality and scope. Unlike coarse-grained components, fine-grained components may have a large number of dependencies. In the Java arena, a fine-grained component maps to elements such as JavaBeans.

EJBs can be modeled as UML subsystems. See Figure 6-2 for one possible representation of an EJB component in the UML.

Given the importance of interfaces in terms of components and their relationships, it is useful to model these explicitly. A statechart diagram can be used to model the interface and the valid sequence of operations supported by the component.

Components also typically have complex behavior. It is usually helpful to explicitly model component behavior via an activity diagram or a statechart diagram to understand it in more detail.

We discuss both these modeling aspects in further detail in Chapter 12.

Frameworks

In its simplest form, a framework can refer to any piece of developed and tested software that is reused in multiple software development projects.

More formally, a framework provides a generalized architectural template that can be used to build applications within a specific domain. In other words, a framework permits you to specify, group together, and reuse elements to effectively build some specific software system.

Consider the example of a software company that builds some service software systems that always include customer billing and account management functionality. It could start each software system from scratch and rewrite the billing and account management portions. More realistically, the software company would be better off taking the billing/accounting pieces from one of its earlier implementations and developing a formal framework to provide the foundation for each new software system.

A framework can be used in two basic ways. In the first approach, the library approach, you use a framework for establishing a set of reusable components. In the alternate approach, a framework is used for creating a template for new projects or for defining the architecture of specific types of systems. Each approach has its advantages, and requires different levels of advance planning and effort.

The *library approach* consists of using a framework to create a set of reusable components and is the easier approach in the sense that it is very much like using a library. Referring back to the system with the billing and account management capabilities, you would simply take all the relevant classes, put them together, and create a framework containing the classes of interest. When it is time to implement your next system, it is simply a matter of using the framework and reusing the desired pieces within it to develop the billing and account management functionality.

In the *framework as template approach,* you create a framework that contains assembled pieces of your typical system. Creating a new system simply requires you to use the framework as the basis for the new application, and then implement abstract methods or use some other form of customization (e.g., subclassing) to implement the new software system. Clearly, this is more work than simply putting some classes into a loosely organized library, and it requires some advanced planning. However, it also yields superior results in terms of reuse because you use the framework to capture and reuse key, exceptionally scarce knowledge of the system architects. The template approach allows you to develop new systems faster because not only do you get the implementation code for the pieces, but you also get an authentic blueprint for putting it together in a consistent and usable manner. For instance, if you are putting together a framework for developing Internet-based applications, such a framework might provide pieces for security, simple query interactions, interactions involving transactions, user confirmation services, and so on along with instructions on supported configurations and how to quickly assemble the different pieces to create a new Internet application. *Brokat Financial Framework* by Brokat Technologies[2] is an example of such a commercial framework based on the J2EE technology that can be reused and rapidly extended to develop new financial applications.

Regardless of the approach, the end result of using frameworks is an increase in the relative amount of time you can spend on developing the features and functionality and less relative time spent on rehashing what you have already done. In the process, you also decrease the overall software development time because you create less new source code.

---

2. See www.brokat.com for details

Some considerations in developing a framework:

- *The framework should be simple to understand.* Deep inheritance hierarchies and inconsistent APIs and such make for poor frameworks. Remember, the idea is to get the user to start using the framework quickly and effectively.

- *Provide adequate documentation.* Keep in mind that others will use the framework you are developing over a long period of time. The more you can clarify the intent of the framework, document the assumptions, and show how you meant it to be used, the longer the framework will last.

- *Identify concrete framework extension mechanisms.* Frameworks grow over time to meet new needs. By providing built-in extension mechanisms or identifying the proper way of extending the framework, the framework will evolve into a more versatile and cohesive framework rather than deteriorate into a hodge-podge of code. For the Internet-based application framework example mentioned earlier, a consideration might be to identify framework extension points to easily support new connection types in the future, for example, wireless instead of line-based connections.

Patterns

A software pattern is a reusable design that has been captured, distilled, and abstracted out through experience and has been proven successful in solving specific types of problems.

Patterns are useful because:

- They convey proven knowledge captured through years of experience. Using patterns can reduce the overall risk of failure due to specific types of mistakes.

- They can help in solving difficult problems that have been encountered in similar situations.

- Use of well-established software patterns enhances communication within the team by providing the basic context for discussion among team members.

Software patterns are generally classified into, among others, the following categories: analysis patterns, architectural patterns, design patterns, and coding patterns. The primary difference between the categories of patterns is the level of abstraction.

For instance, architectural patterns deal with the structure of software systems, subsystems, or components and how they relate to each other. Design patterns, on the other hand, operate at the class and object level. They are based on proven solutions to problems that arise when designing software in a specific context.

Design patterns are typically classified into three broad categories:

- *Creational:* Creational design patterns provide solutions to configuration and initialization design problems. A *singleton* pattern, which provides for a pattern for restricting the class to a single instance, is an example of a creational design pattern.

- *Structural:* Structural design patterns solve design problems by structuring the interfaces and their class relationships in specific ways. Proxy pattern, discussed later in this section, is an example of a structural design pattern.

- *Behavioral:* Behavioral patterns identify ways in which a group of classes interact with each other to achieve a specific behavior. An example is the Observer pattern discussed later in this section.

Design patterns can be applied to existing elements within a design to improve a solution, or a new set of elements can be constructed using a design pattern to solve a problem that has been recognized through analysis.

Figure 6-3 shows a simple design pattern commonly referred to as the Proxy pattern. In this pattern, an object (Proxy) is essentially providing an indirect access mechanism to another object (RealSubject). This is identified via the association between the Proxy and the RealSubject. The Subject provides a common

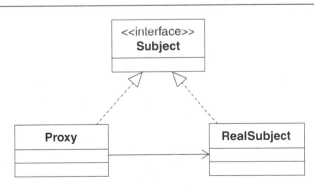

Figure 6-3   A design pattern

interface to Proxy and RealSubject, thereby allowing them to work closely. This relationship is captured via the common interface realization.

For instance, a Proxy may be useful in situations where access to the actual resource cannot be allowed due to security reasons.

We identify and refer to some existing and emerging patterns relevant to J2EE development in the J2EE technology chapters.

Patterns are represented in the UML using a *collaboration*. A collaboration is a description of a general arrangement of objects and links that interact within a context to implement a behavior. It has a static and a dynamic part. The static part describes the roles that objects and links may play in an instance of the collaboration. The dynamic part consists of one or more interactions that show message flows over time in the collaboration.

A *parameterized collaboration,* that is, a collaboration made of generic model elements, is used for design patterns that can be applied repeatedly. This is accomplished by binding the generic model elements in the parameterized collaboration to specific model elements when the collaboration is instantiated.

Collaboration supports specialization; hence, it is possible to create collaborations that inherit from other collaborations.

In the UML, the use of a collaboration is represented by a dashed ellipse. Relationships with classes participating in the collaboration are shown via a dashed line from the collaboration to the class.

Figure 6-4 shows a UML collaboration representation for the Subject-Observer pattern. The pattern is properly represented together with the structural specification in the form of a class diagram, and the behavioral specification is indicated using a sequence diagram or statechart diagram.

The class and sequence diagrams for the Subject-Observer design pattern are shown in Figure 6-5 and Figure 6-6, respectively.

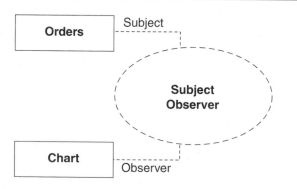

Figure 6-4   A collaboration representing the Subject-Observer pattern

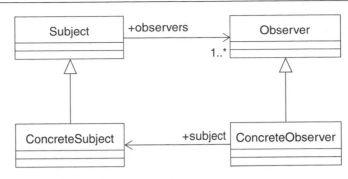

Figure 6-5   Class diagram for Subject-Observer pattern

The general idea is that observers register with a subject for notification when there is a change to the subject, and the observers are notified when there is a change so they can update their information accordingly. Consider this simple real-life example: You and several others are interested in updates to a specific product and have indicated this to the manufacturer by registering for updates. When the product is updated, you and the other observers are notified

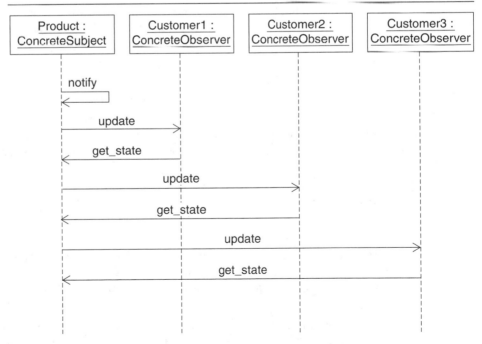

Figure 6-6   Sequence diagram illustrating the Subject-Observer pattern

of the change to the product. At that time, all observers can individually query the product to find out the details of the update.

Layering

Large-scale enterprise software can be complex and difficult to develop and manage. Layering is a pattern for decomposition. Decomposition leads to a logical partitioning of the system into subsystems and modules, and layers group and separate those subsystems, thereby constraining who can use the subsystems, components, and modules. Layers create separation of concerns within the software by abstracting specific types of functionality into functional layers and providing conceptual boundaries between sets of services.

The Rational Unified Process (RUP) identifies two common approaches to layering:

- Responsibility-driven layering
- Reuse-driven layering

In responsibility-driven layering, layers have well-defined responsibilities, meaning they fulfill a specific role in the overall scheme of things. Such layers are also referred to as *tiers*. See the next section for more details on tiers.

In reuse-driven layering, layers are crafted so as to provide the most reuse of elements of the system. In such a setup, layers typically provide services to other layers. This permits layers to be understood individually without necessitating understanding or significant prior knowledge of the layers above or below them, which leads to lower coupling between the layers.

For example, a software system may have, among other layers, a presentation services layer to provide capabilities that allow the display of information to the user and a general services layer to provide services such as logging, error handling, and so on.

A user should be able to use the presentation services capabilities without regard to the layers below it.

The relationship among layers is strictly hierarchical in nature. That is, a layer may rely on the layer below it, but not vice versa. From the standpoint of reducing coupling, it is also desirable to not have any dependencies between layers that are not immediate neighbors. Indeed, J2EE provides an example of layering itself, where the container is a layer built on top of the operating system.

Depending on the complexity of the software system, layers can also contain other sublayers. Layers should generally not bypass layers immediately below them to access other layers, but this is acceptable if the intermediate layers only act as bystanders, that is, simply pass along the request to the next layer and so on. For example, for services such as error reporting, it may make sense to directly access them throughout the application.

Layers are typically structured such that the lowest layer is most tightly coupled to the hardware and operating system. Middle layers provide the foundation for building a wide variety of software systems requiring similar capabilities. The top layer contains the software elements required for meeting slightly varying end user requirements, for example, specific business services available in the application to specific customers or customization of the application for European versus Asian customers.

Layers should be an important structural consideration in any enterprise application design. Generally speaking, smaller software systems will require fewer layers, whereas larger systems may require more layers. However, even large applications do not generally have layers in the double digits.

In the UML, layers are represented as a package with the <<layer>> stereotype. Figure 6-7 shows an example of a UML layered architecture. See Chapter 13 for additional discussion in the context of the sample application.

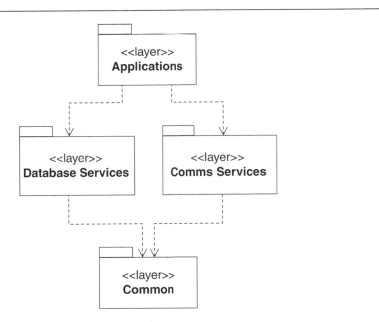

Figure 6-7   A layered architecture in UML

Tiers

Tiers are primarily concerned with distribution of a software system over multiple, separate processes. Processes may be physically distributed over multiple processors or reside on the same physical device.

Tiers can be mapped to responsibility-driven layers in which case a tier becomes synonymous with fulfilling a specific role within the system, such as presentation, business logic, data access, and so on.

Mainstream computing has evolved over time into the multitiered architectures in use today. In the early days of computing, mainframes and dumb terminals characterized the computing environment. Two-tiered, LAN-based client-server systems were the norm for a long time. And although n-tier architectures have been utilized in specific industries for a long time, it is only recently that n-tier architectures are becoming mainstream in the industry.

Tiered architectures are desirable from the point of view of increasing throughput, availability, or functionality of the system by increasing the overall, physical processing power. Tiered architectures can also play a role in separating out different areas of application concerns to improve overall maintainability.

Such distribution introduces

- Communication efficiency and reliability issues between tiers
- The need for identification and location of components in a distributed environment
- Security issues due to a potentially diverse and geographically distributed system
- Synchronization issues between tiers
- Failure recovery issues
- The need for additional interfaces to accommodate the tier architecture
- Additional resource needs due to the distributed nature of the software

As discussed earlier, one way to achieve distribution in an n-tier architecture is to align specific layers with each tier. J2EE follows this approach.

In the J2EE tiered architecture:

- Client tier is primarily concerned with user interaction.
- Presentation tier deals with presenting the results of business queries.
- Business tier contains the key business rules.
- Data tier provides the interface to the persistent data store.

The J2EE approach is shown graphically in Figure 6-8.

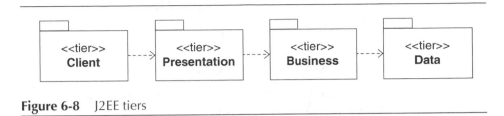

Figure 6-8 J2EE tiers

Approaches to Software Architecture

Numerous approaches to software architecture have been proposed and utilized over time. In this section, we highlight some published approaches to software architecture to provide you with a broader perspective.

Each of these approaches has its strong points and weaknesses as well as its advocates and critics.

The J2EE View of Architecture

Tiers + components + services are key to understanding the J2EE architectural philosophy.

Given that the J2EE is predominantly focused on providing a viable proposition for building large-scale enterprise applications that are scalable, it should come as no surprise that it advocates partitioning the application into multiple tiers. The J2EE platform provides mechanisms to decompose the system into relatively coarse-grained components. J2EE also advocates a services-based architecture that is characterized by a collection of cooperating and communicating services. The services rely on well-defined APIs for interoperability.

The J2EE official guidelines shy away from a strict recommendation of adherence to a layer-like hierarchical view of the tiers, opting instead for a more accommodating stance. The suggestion is to use the tiers and associated technologies if it makes sense for the specific situation. For example, it is perfectly appropriate to access the data tier directly from the presentation tier.

J2EE recommends using the Model-View-Controller (MVC)[3] architectural paradigm for developing enterprise applications. As discussed briefly in Chapter 2, the basic idea behind the MVC is to minimize the coupling among objects in a system by aligning them with a specific set of responsibilities in the area of

---

3. For more details and the J2EE perspective on the MVC paradigm, see java.sun.com/j2ee/blueprints/design_patterns/model_view_controller/index.html. Additional sources are listed in the References section at the end of this book.

the persistent data and associated rules (Model), presentation (View), and the application logic (Controller).

The 4+1 View Model of Architecture

The primary motivation behind using different views for architecture is to reduce the overall complexity.

A view is essentially a look at the model from a specific vantage point or perspective, such that only the details that are relevant and important are included and all else is ignored.

Originally proposed as the 4+1 View Model of Architecture [Kruchten 1995], it is now part of the RUP. It has been widely used as the basis for architectural analysis and design of systems.

The basic premise behind the 4+1 View of Model Architecture is that a software system can be modeled well with the following interlocking views:

- The *Logical View* models design packages, subsystems, and classes.
- The *Implementation View* describes the physical organization of the software, for example, executables, libraries, source code, and so on.
- The *Process View* is concerned with the concurrency aspects of the software. For example, processes, tasks, and threads that are part of the software system.
- The *Deployment View* focuses on the mapping of the executables onto physical nodes and computing hardware.
- The *Use Case View* is a special view in that it ties all other views together.

This list does not imply that there can be no other views. For instance, it would be reasonable and desirable to have a security or a transaction view for J2EE-based software.

Hofmeister et al.: Four Views of Architecture

Hofmeister, Nord, and Soni present a slightly different view for achieving software architecture [Hofmeister 2000] based on four views, some of which partially overlap the 4+1 Views discussed earlier:

- The *Conceptual View* is primarily concerned with conceptually sound decomposition of the system into very coarse-grained components called *capsules*.[4] These capsules interact with each other via conceptual connectors. Capsules and connectors form the basis for the eventual software system.

- The *Module View* deals with the realization of capsules and connectors. The coarse-grained components are mapped to actual subsystems and modules in the context of the specific technology to be employed for the project.

- The *Execution View* deals with the flow of control within the runtime system. This includes issues such as concurrency, distribution, and performance.

- The *Code View* embodies how the components are mapped to source files and executables as well as concerns such as build times and development tools.

Putting It All Together

Which comes first—software architecture or analysis? The answer, of course, partly depends on to whom you talk.

Architecture provides the blueprint for the software, but without proper analysis, the requisite understanding of the system—required for the blueprint—cannot be developed. Thus, it is very much an iterative process in that requirements form a key input into the software architecture, but there may be a need to adjust or clarify the requirements as the architect works through them to arrive at the architecture.

Defining a software architecture is very much an evolutionary process. Although an architect may want to start with some basic notions about what may be appropriate or inappropriate based on past experience, he cannot simply take the requirements and expect to arrive at the final architecture overnight. The architecture gradually takes shape as deliberate, informed decisions are made with specific requirements and trade-offs in mind.

It should be emphasized that the concepts discussed in this chapter are primarily tools at the disposal of an architect. Like all tools, they are useful only when used in the proper context rather than for the sake of using the concepts. For example, if no particular pattern exists to address the problem faced, it wouldn't make sense to alter the design so you could apply some patterns.

---

4. The concept of capsules is based on the concept of active objects called actors (which are to be distinguished from use case actors), proposed for real-time software systems [Selic 1994].

We further discuss aspects of architecture in their proper context, that is, alongside analysis and design as we face specific problems and address particular concerns.

Summary

Software architecture is an all-important but often neglected, or at least misunderstood, aspect of enterprise software development.

Software architecture is multifaceted and covers more than software structure. No single diagram can be used to describe software architecture.

Some key concepts in the area of software architecture are decomposition, layering, tiers, patterns, frameworks, and component-based software. These are essentially tools at the disposal of an architect rather than "must apply" concepts for all software projects.

Discovery of the software architecture is an evolutionary process and must be done in the context of the requirements and in conjunction with the analysis. This approach is followed in this book.

Chapter 7

Analyzing Customer Needs

In this chapter, we look into the need for software analysis and design and how to go about it.

To keep the examples relevant, we have chosen to use portions of the case study documented in Chapter 16. The case study describes the development of an online banking system. To get the most out of the examples, you should review the "HomeDirect Requirements" section in Chapter 16.

Why Software Analysis and Design?

Let's start by trying to answer a basic question: Why even talk about analysis and design? After all, analysis seems to have fallen off the favorites list of some developers[1] and has even been labeled as leading to nothing more than "analysis paralysis."

There is always the possibility that some teams may get bogged down in the analysis phase. However, skipping analysis and design altogether and jumping straight into implementation hardly appears to be the best alternative.

Suppose you want to go from Point A to Point B. If A and B are fairly close, and you are generally familiar with the area, it should be relatively straightforward to undertake the journey without bothering to look at a map and doing some advance planning.

On the other hand, if A and B happen to be a great distance apart, and you are dealing with uncharted territory, your chances of success are greatly improved if you do some prior planning.

Software development is no different. For small software projects using familiar technology in a comfortable domain, perhaps you can get by without analysis and design. But it is essential in large, unfamiliar territory type projects if you are to avoid the pitfalls and disasters to which a vast majority of projects fall victim.[2]

---

1. Extreme Programming (XP), for example, does not give much credence to analysis.

2. According to the Standish Group's Chaos Report, 1998; only "26 percent of software projects succeed."

Problem Analysis

Requirements come in all shapes and forms and from a variety of sources. For example, they may be presented in the form of written documents by an end user, via meetings with visionaries in the company, or via direct customer interaction and face-to-face visits.

Projects often fail because the requirements were not accurately understood. This is not too surprising in light of the fact that language, whether written or oral, is imprecise by nature and open to multiple interpretations. So, the first thing to do is to make sure the basic requirements are understood; that is, go beyond what is obvious and stated in the requirements document. It is only through such an approach that you can really identify the essential usage patterns for the software system you will be developing.

This is where use cases come in. You can apply use case modeling to develop a precise model of what is required of the system, and then utilize the use cases as the basis for driving other aspects of your enterprise system development. In effect, a use case acts as the string that binds the beads of a necklace together. Use cases bridge the gap between the end user and the requirements of the system. They can be used to establish tractability between functional requirements and the system implementation itself.

The analysis is best done in a group setting. It helps to have different people looking at the same requirements from their individual points of view. It is usually also helpful to have a domain expert take part in the discussions. Participation of the customer, or author of the requirements, is also beneficial so that you can gain firsthand knowledge of the intent. All this deliberation may save you a lot of rework later. Some techniques that can be used at this stage to get to the bottom of a problem include brainstorming sessions and fishbone diagrams.

When going through this stage, it is helpful to try to reduce duplicate requirements and distill the overall set of requirements into a smaller number. Avoid the temptation to do the design at the same time as gathering requirements. Requirement-creep (similar to feature-creep where features continue to grow way beyond the original intent) should also be avoided by exerting a vigorous attempt at traceability to the customer needs.

For a more thorough discussion of this topic, see *Object-Oriented Analysis and Design with Applications,* by Grady Booch, Addison-Wesley, 1994, and *Use Cases-Requirements in Context,* by Daryl Kulak et al., Addison-Wesley, 2000.

Use Case Modeling

Ivar Jacobson et al.[3] popularized the application of use cases for understanding the functional system requirements in the early 1990s. Later, use case notation was incorporated into the Unified Modeling Language (UML). It is seemingly simple in concept but highly useful, especially in understanding the functional requirements for large and complex systems.

In the context of this book, use cases are very important as the RUP is very much a use case-driven development process. Not only are use cases used to capture the requirements, but they also provide the foundation for activities from analysis through testing.

There are two fundamental concepts in use case modeling:

- *Actor:* An actor represents something (or someone) outside the system, typically a user of the system. Actors interact with the system, which results in some action by the system. Each distinct role is represented by an actor.
- *Use case:* A use case encapsulates a sequence of steps performed by the system on behalf of an actor. Use cases provide something of value to the actor. A use case consists of a primary sequence of events and may have one or more alternate sequences of events.

Requirements come in two primary flavors: *functional* and *nonfunctional*. Functional requirements, which are focused on what the system must be able to do, lend themselves easily to use case modeling. Nonfunctional requirements are focused on things such as usability and performance, and are harder to model using use cases.

Let's put use case modeling into practice by applying these concepts to the HomeDirect system case study—requirements of which are detailed in Chapter 16.

To get the most out of the remaining discussion, you should review the "HomeDirect Requirements" section in Chapter 16 before continuing on.

We will focus on the functional requirements to derive the use cases.

Identifying the Actors

Actors are usually easier to identify than use cases. The difficulty in identifying actors is twofold. First, it is easy to fall into the trap of creating multiple actors for the same role. Second, actors can be implicit in the requirements; that is,

---

3. Jacobson, Ivar, et al. *Object-Oriented Software Engineering*. Addison-Wesley, 1992.

they may not be identified as users of the system; and therefore, you must look beyond the obvious to find them.

As you read the description or gather requirements for a project, ask yourself a few important questions: Who will use this functionality? Who is supplying or obtaining information? Who can change the information? Are there any other systems that interact with the system being developed?

As we examine the HomeDirect related information, the following terms qualify as roles: customer, user, administrator, account holder, bank employee, vendor, HomeDirect service, the system, Mail system, LoansDirect system, Bills-Direct Service, and ACMEBank.

Based on the requirements and coupled with our common understanding of how online banking systems typically work, it is easy to establish that customer, user, and account holder almost definitely all refer to the same role. So, we can eliminate the redundant user and account holder. Vendor sounds like a customer, but is really more than a customer because, unlike a customer, it can also receive payments. Similarly, bank employee and administrator, although different roles within the bank (i.e., a bank employee may not necessarily be a HomeDirect administrator) almost certainly refer to the administrator role.

Recall that actors are outside the system. Suffice it to say that after similar reasoning with the remaining items on the list, we are left with a much shorter candidate actor list for the HomeDirect system:

- Customer
- Administrator
- Vendor
- Mail system
- LoansDirect system
- BillsDirect system

Finding the Use Cases

Use cases are always expressed from the perspective of the actor (that is, the user of the system). The idea is to capture a sequence of events performed by the system at the request of the actor, such that they yield some observable, valuable result to the actor.

Take a look at the "HomeDirect Requirements" section in Chapter 16, which deals with the transfer of funds. The following sequence of steps describes the transfer of funds:

1. The customer requests a funds transfer.

2. The system asks the user to identify the accounts between which funds are to be transferred and the transfer amount.

3. The customer selects the account to transfer funds from, the account to transfer funds to, and then indicates the amount of funds to transfer.

4. The system checks the account from which funds are to be transferred and confirms that sufficient funds are available.

5. The amount is debited to the account from which funds are to be transferred and credited to the account previously selected by the customer.

This is essentially the main sequence of events for a use case, which we will call "Transfer funds." An alternate sequence of steps in this case may detail the steps performed when insufficient funds are available.

An easy way to start discovering the use cases is to take each actor you have identified and try to identify the behavior or information the actor under consideration requires from the system. The challenge in discovering use cases is to avoid going to too fine a granularity, leading to a proliferation of use cases.

Applying this method to the HomeDirect case study and using the customer actor as the starting point yields the following raw list of candidate use cases: login, logout, change password, view account balances, list transactions, download transactions, transfer funds, add vendor, delete vendor, pay bills, check security account balances, browse securities, buy security, and sell security.

Recall that each use case must produce an observable result and provide something of value to the actor (i.e., the customer actor). The login and logout candidate use cases we have identified do produce observable results (i.e., successful login/logout), but there really is not much value in them for the customer. A HomeDirect customer would never just login or just logout. Most likely, a customer would login and logout in the context of performing some action, like paying bills or checking account balances. So login and logout are not good candidates for use cases.

In fact, login and logout form part of all use cases associated with the customer role. For instance, in the transfer funds use case detailed earlier, you would first login, transfer funds, and then having completed the transfer, logout.

The view account balances and browse security account summary look very similar in that both really just show you what is available in specific types of accounts. Perhaps it would be better to abstract them out as a browse account balances scenario, which applies to all types of accounts equally well.

Actors as well as use cases can utilize the inheritance relationship. So, another possibility would be to create a browse account balances use case, and then have two specializations, one focused on the investment accounts and the other on the remaining types of accounts. To keep it simple for now, we will just utilize a single use case, "Browse account balances."

Another set of use cases where some relationship likely exists is in the list transactions and download transactions. The only real difference between the two is that in the first, the list is displayed on screen, whereas the second "displays" the list in a file.

It is debatable whether add and delete vendor should be two separate use cases or lumped into a single use case called modify vendor list. You can even argue that they are really part of the pay bills use case. After all, would a customer really ever login to the HomeDirect system to just add a vendor? This may be a case where further clarification is needed. Some real-life online banking systems actually require the customer to add a vendor to the list at least several business days prior to making a first online payment. If such is the case, it is reasonable to expect a customer to login, add one or more vendors, and then logout without necessarily making a bill payment. For simplicity, we will use this as the clarification obtained from ACMEBank and model the use cases as a single "Modify vendor list" use case.

The refined list of candidate use cases follows:

- Change password
- Browse account balances
- List transactions
- Download transactions
- Transfer funds
- Edit profile
- Pay bill
- Buy security
- Sell security

The complete set of use cases for the HomeDirect system is documented in Chapter 16.

Use Case Diagrams

In the UML, actors are represented by a stick figure, and use cases are shown as ellipses. A use case diagram simply shows the structural relationships between the actors and the use cases, not the dynamic relationships. The relationship

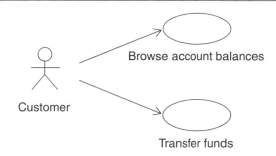

Figure 7-1   A simple use case diagram

between actors and use cases is shown via a directional association indicating the source of invocation. Figure 7-1 shows the Browse account and Transfer funds use cases for the HomeDirect system. Both are invoked by the customer.

Use Case Relationships

You may recall that we decided that login and logout do not meet the litmus test of being use cases because they do not provide something of value to the customer. They are really part of the various HomeDirect use cases, such as Browse account balances and Transfer funds. So, we somehow have to reuse the sequence of events required for login and logout.

The UML notation provides "include" and "extend" relationships, which can be used to model such reuse within use cases.

Include

An *include* relationship allows you to capture a common piece of functionality in a separate use case, and then "include" the use case in another use case via the include relationship. The include relationship is shown as a dependency relationship stereotyped as <<include>>. See Figure 7-2.

Extend

An *extend* relationship allows you to model optional behavior for a use case. That is, you can capture some behavior in a separate use case and, within another use case, indicate the exact points (called *extension points*) where the separate use case may optionally be invoked as part of the use case. An extend relationship is modeled as a dependency and stereotyped as <<extend>>. See Figure 7-3.

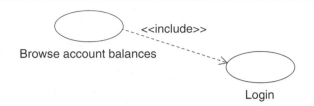

Figure 7-2 An example of an include relationship

Figure 7-4 shows another, more detailed use case diagram for the Browse account balances and List transactions use cases for the HomeDirect system.

Chapter 16 provides a complete use case model for the HomeDirect case study.

Typical problems encountered by those new to use cases revolve around the following:

- Creating use cases that are too coarse-grained. For instance, "Process order" may be too coarse if it represents "Create new order," "Submit order," and "Change order" from the user's perspective.

- Creating use cases that are too fine-grained. Continuing with the preceding order example, "Change zip code for order," might be an example of a fine-grained use case.

- Writing the use cases from a system perspective. For example, "Obtain catalog from database" versus "Browse catalog."

- Getting bogged down in extend versus include relationships. An extend relationship can easily be expressed as an include relationship, so choose one, and move on.

- Getting carried away with use case and actor generalizations. Neither is essential, at least not initially. Keep in mind that you can always add an

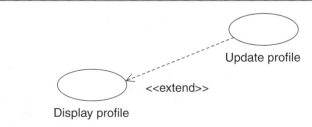

Figure 7-3 An example of an extend relationship

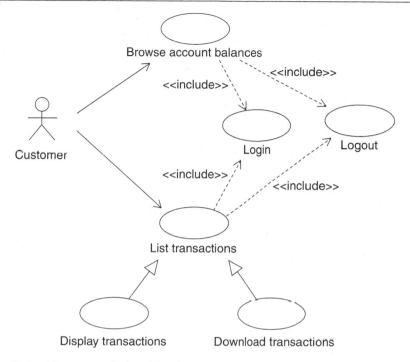

Figure 7-4 Use case relationships for HomeDirect

actor or use case generalization later in a subsequent iteration once you understand the details better.

Sequence Diagrams

A use case is still very much a textual description and is subject to interpretation. A sequence diagram is used to express the use case in more precise, technical terminology. This is achieved by depicting the use case in terms of interaction between the actor and the system.

A sequence diagram is a type of interaction diagram in the UML. The other kind of interaction diagram is called a *collaboration* diagram. Sequence diagrams capture a specific scenario, with a use case typically consisting of one or more scenarios (for example, main workflow and alternate workflows). The emphasis in a sequence diagram is on the time ordering of the interaction. Thus, the vertical axis represents the time dimension in a sequence diagram.

A sequence diagram utilizes the description of a use case. Figure 7-5 shows a sequence diagram for the Transfer funds use case discussed earlier. To create a sequence diagram, each step from the textual description for the use case is placed on the left side. Two vertical lines are used to show the lifeline of the actor and the system. The actor is represented by the actor stick figure symbol, and the system is simply shown as a rectangle.

The interactions between the actor and the system are shown as arrows, with the direction of the arrow indicating the direction of interaction. Specifically, a request from the actor to the system is shown as an arrow from the lifeline of the actor to the lifeline of the system, with the arrow pointing to the system lifeline. A response from the system to the actor is shown with an arrow drawn from the system lifeline to the actor lifeline and points to the actor.

The first arrow labeled "select accounts" routes back to the customer lifeline, indicating that the customer performs account selection at the start of the scenario. This is followed by a funds transfer request from the customer to the system, and so on.

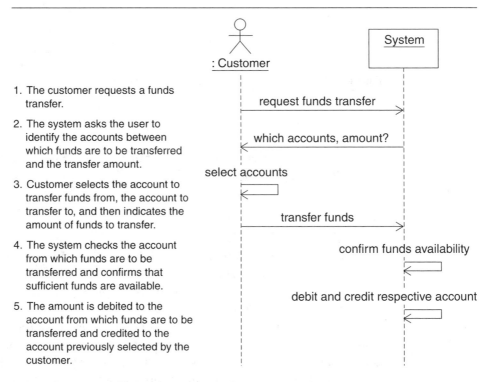

Figure 7-5 Transfer funds sequence diagram

Sequence diagrams simply show the dynamic interaction among participants in the scenario and do not show the structural relationship between them. If a use case has several flows, several sequence diagrams may be required to capture all aspects of the use case.

The question often comes up as to how complete the sequence diagrams should be. In this early phase of requirements' capture and analysis, the sequence diagrams, by necessity, are relatively simple and may be incomplete. This changes as you progress through use case analysis and refine these sequence diagrams with further details. It is useful to have the main flow of each use case captured as a sequence diagram; however, capturing each and every alternate flow, especially when there may be a large number of them, is not necessary. The main idea is to capture enough of them to have confidence that you have sufficient information for the next phase of the project.

Activity Diagrams

An alternate, and some would argue a more powerful, tool in the UML arsenal for such use case analysis is the UML activity diagram. For instance, activity diagrams can more easily show multiple paths taken as a result of actor decision and system exceptions. This is difficult to show in a sequence diagram as sequence diagrams are intended to show interaction among objects in the context of a single scenario.

An activity diagram is similar in concept to a flowchart and is useful for modeling workflow as well as illustrating dynamic behavior of a use case and the detailed design of an operation.

An activity diagram shows the flow of control for the use case from one *activity* to the next. An activity represents some action that takes place during the execution of the use case. This typically maps to some work that has to be done as part of the workflow or execution of an operation in the context of a class.

Activities are represented by a round-ended rectangle. An activity may be decomposed further into other activities, represented on another activity diagram.

Once an activity has completed, execution moves to the next state as determined by the available transitions on the activity. Activity diagrams also support decision points. In addition, it is possible to show parallel work required as part of an activity diagram by using the concept of synchronization bars.

A simple activity diagram representing the act of placing a phone call is shown in Figure 7-6.

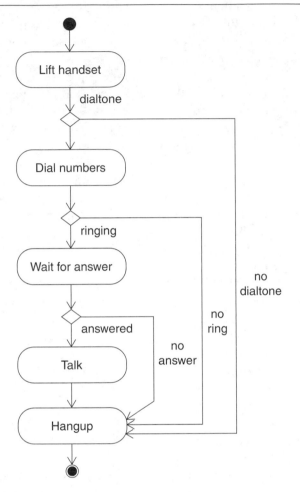

Figure 7-6   A simple activity diagram

Swim lanes can be used to show multiple objects on an activity diagram and how they work together to fulfill the overall use case.

Figure 7-7 shows an activity diagram for the Transfer funds scenario. The vertical lines indicate the boundary for the actors within the system. This is an initial activity diagram and does not show all the details, such as conditional activity, and so on.

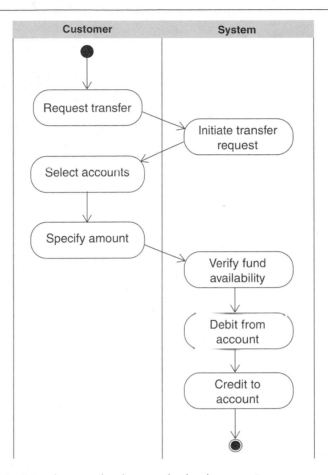

Figure 7-7   Activity diagram for the transfer funds scenario

Summary

Properly capturing requirements is essential to a system's success and its long-term viability. In the UML, use case modeling offers a simple yet powerful means of capturing your requirements.

In the use case model, actors are the primary instigators of use cases and represent entities outside the system. Use cases can be thought of as a sequence of steps required to achieve something useful to an actor. That is, a use case must yield something useful to the end user of the use case. Sequence diagrams and activity diagrams are useful for precisely identifying and understanding the behavior of a use case.

Chapter 8

Creating the Design

- Use Case Analysis

- Use Case Realizations

- Refined Use Case Description

- Sequence Diagrams

- Collaboration Diagrams

- Class Diagrams

- Coalescing the Analysis Classes

- Packaging

- Summary

Once you have captured the use cases, you should then analyze them further and begin the process of transforming requirements into system design. This involves developing a better understanding of the details of a use case via a refinement of the use case.

In this chapter, we discuss how to go from use cases to the initial design of the system.

Use Case Analysis

The initial exploration of the internal workings of the system is called *Use Case Analysis*. Use Case Analysis provides an initial, high-level definition of how internal elements interact in order to satisfy the system's functional requirements, and how they relate to each other statically. This activity can involve much trial and error before satisfactory solutions are created. For this reason, time should not be spent creating refined descriptions of internal elements. "Analysis classes," for which behaviors are often described abstractly using natural language, suffice. Analysis classes are not implemented in software. Rather, analysis classes are refined later in the overall design process into precisely defined design classes and subsystems.

Use Case Realizations

Thus far, our focus has been on capturing the requirements and making sure we understand what we need to build. Everything we have done is generic in that no consideration has been given to how we will actually design or implement our solution.

The same set of functional requirements can lead to vastly different systems that are functionally equivalent but are totally different in the way they solve specific problems. For example, the online banking system could be offered to the customer base as two different products: an application that actually dials into the banking system or a Web-based application that uses the Internet (perhaps

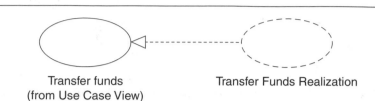

Transfer funds
(from Use Case View)
        Transfer Funds Realization

Figure 8-1   Use case realization for Transfer funds

the bank wants to market the direct dial version as a more upscale and secure version). The functional requirements are the same, but the implementations are vastly different for the two solutions.

Use case realizations can be used to carry forth the design of multiple implementations for the same set of requirements. They allow the same use case to be implemented in different ways while maintaining a link with the original requirements. Use case realizations therefore offer a concrete link through which you can trace back to the original requirement for all the different models that might exist for a given set of requirements.

We represent use case realizations graphically using a dotted-line ellipse. A Unified Modeling Language (UML) "realize" relationship is drawn between the realization and its use case. Figure 8-1 shows a use case realization for a Transfer funds use case.

Each use case realization can have object interaction diagrams and class diagrams associated with it. Each object interaction diagram we develop during Use Case Analysis shows the interactions between actors and instances of analysis classes that are needed to support one flow of events through a use case. The class diagrams illustrate the static structural relations between these internal system elements.

Refined Use Case Description

The Use Case Analysis process is often jump-started by taking the customer-consumable "black box" use case textual descriptions and adding "gray box" details that reveal some of the system's internal processing activities. The black box use case description might be sufficient from a customer perspective, but it certainly is not a sufficient level of detail to allow developers to implement the system.

As an example, consider the Transfer funds use case that was outlined in the previous chapter. Although the use case is accurate in that it covers the interaction that takes place, some details are missing. For example, how does the customer choose the account? Does the system provide a list of accounts? When the customer indicates the amount of funds, does it have to be a whole number or can it be in decimal format? How does the system verify that the account from which funds are to be transferred has sufficient funds? These kinds of questions facilitate refinement of the use cases during the Use Case Analysis phase.

The following sequence of events provides a more elaborate version of this use case:

1. The customer selects the transfer operation.
2. The account information is sent over the Internet to the system.
3. The system retrieves the customer's profile.
4. The system builds a list of accounts from the customer's profile and provides specific details about each account, such as the current balance, overdraft limit, and any fees that might apply to the transfer funds action. This information is displayed to the customer.
5. The customer selects the accounts to transfer funds between and the amount to transfer. Transfer amounts are allowed in any amount specified in dollars and cents.
6. The system verifies that the amount entered for the transfer is numerical and is a valid amount.
7. The system prompts the customer for confirmation prior to proceeding with the transaction.
8. Upon confirmation, the system begins the transfer funds transaction.
9. The system retrieves the current balance for the account from which funds are to be transferred.
10. The system subtracts the total amount of transfer from the account balance, along with any applicable fees, to confirm that sufficient funds are available.
11. The amount is debited to the account from which funds are to be transferred and credited to the account to which funds are being transferred.
12. The system logs the transfer in the daily transactions register and obtains a reference identification number.
13. The system provides the reference number to the customer, confirming that the transfer has taken place.

A more detailed sequence diagram for the updated use case is shown in Figure 8-2.

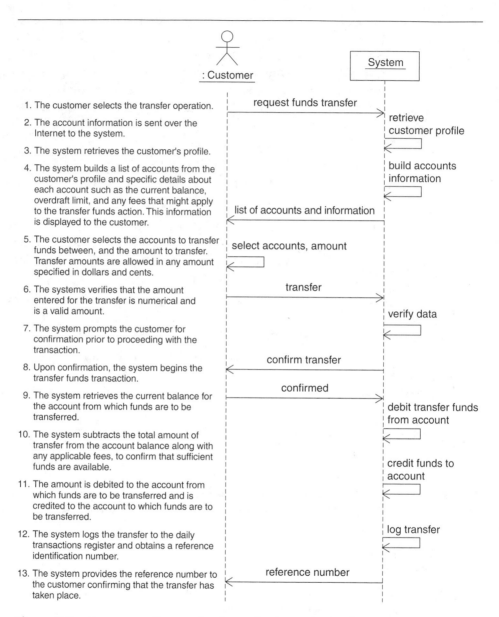

1. The customer selects the transfer operation.

2. The account information is sent over the Internet to the system.

3. The system retrieves the customer's profile.

4. The system builds a list of accounts from the customer's profile and specific details about each account such as the current balance, overdraft limit, and any fees that might apply to the transfer funds action. This information is displayed to the customer.

5. The customer selects the accounts to transfer funds between, and the amount to transfer. Transfer amounts are allowed in any amount specified in dollars and cents.

6. The systems verifies that the amount entered for the transfer is numerical and is a valid amount.

7. The system prompts the customer for confirmation prior to proceeding with the transaction.

8. Upon confirmation, the system begins the transfer funds transaction.

9. The system retrieves the current balance for the account from which funds are to be transferred.

10. The system subtracts the total amount of transfer from the account balance along with any applicable fees, to confirm that sufficient funds are available.

11. The amount is debited to the account from which funds are to be transferred and is credited to the account to which funds are to be transferred.

12. The system logs the transfer to the daily transactions register and obtains a reference identification number.

13. The system provides the reference number to the customer confirming that the transfer has taken place.

Figure 8-2 Sequence diagram for the revised transfer funds use case

Sequence Diagrams

Once gray-box details have been added to the textual use case description, more elaborate sequence diagrams can be created to reveal the internal workings of the system. Instead of showing the interaction between actors and a monolithic system, the system is split into analysis level objects. The responsibilities of the system are divided among the analysis level objects to achieve a finer grained sequence diagram.

There are three kinds of analysis objects, and each plays a specific role in the refined model of the system.

Boundary Objects

As the name suggests, boundary objects exist at the periphery of the system. They are on the front line, interacting with the outside world.

In the refined model, boundary objects represent all interactions between the system's inner workings and its surroundings. These include interaction with a user via a graphical user interface, interactions with other actors (such as those representing other systems), communications with devices, and so on. An example of a boundary object in the online banking example would be the user interface for the logon scenario.

One of the advantages of using boundary objects is that they serve to isolate and shield the rest of the system from external concerns.

Boundary objects are identified via the <<boundary>> stereotype. Alternately, a circle with a perpendicular T can be used as the icon representation of a boundary object. Boundary objects are transitional in nature and usually, though not always, only last for the lifetime of a use case. Generally speaking, each actor-use case interaction pair maps to a boundary object. This is shown in Figure 8-3.

Entity Objects

Entity objects represent information of significance to the system. They are usually persistent and exist for an extended duration. Their primary purpose is to represent and manage information within the system.

Key concepts within a system manifest themselves as entity objects in the model. For example, in the online banking case study, information about the customer, the accounts, and so on would be suitable for modeling as entity objects.

Entity objects are stereotyped as <<entity>> or shown as a circle with a tangential line at the bottom of the circle. Entity objects usually span multiple use cases and might even exist beyond the existence of the system itself. Information

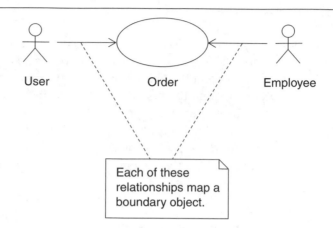

Figure 8-3 Each use case-actor relationship is a potential boundary object

needs vary radically between systems, and so do the number of entity objects in a use case or a system.

See Figure 8-4 for an example of a use case to entity mapping.

Control Objects

Control objects are used to model behavior within the system. Control objects do not necessarily implement the behavior, but may instead work with other objects to achieve the behavior of the use case.

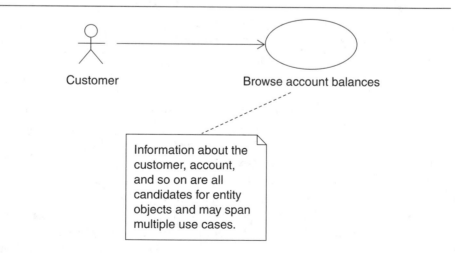

Figure 8-4 Entity objects and use cases

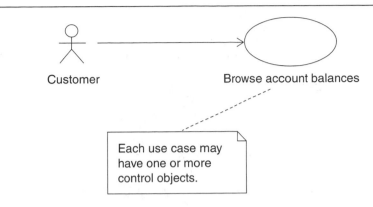

Figure 8-5   Control object and use case

The idea is to separate the behavior from the underlying information associated with the model, making it easier to deal independently with changes in either later on.

Control objects are usually transient in nature and cease to exist once the use case has been completed. They are identified via the <<control>> stereotype or as a circle with an arrow icon.

An example of a control object within the system may be an object that coordinates secure access to the online banking system. There may be one or more control objects per use case. The mapping is shown in Figure 8-5.

Figure 8-6 shows a composite view of the Transfer funds use case and the analysis objects identified for the use case thus far. Note the iconic representation of the boundary, control, and entity objects.

An updated version of the sequence diagram for the Transfer funds use case, this time with the system decomposed into analysis objects, is shown in Figure 8-7.

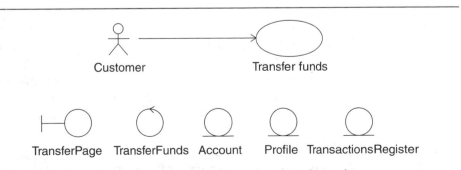

Figure 8-6   Transfer funds use case and associated analysis objects

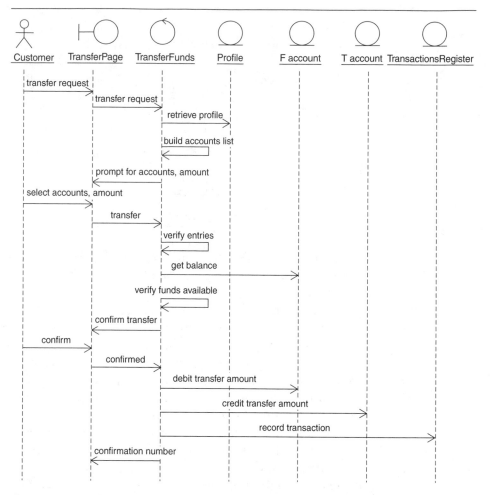

Figure 8-7 Refined sequence diagram for the transfer funds scenario

There are a few things to note in the refined sequence diagram shown in Figure 8-7. If you compare it to Figure 8-2 at the beginning of the chapter, the overall scope or detail of the sequence diagram has not changed. Instead, different pieces of the system are now collectively responsible for the same set of responsibilities. For instance, the interaction with the customer is the responsibility of the TransferPage[1] boundary object. The boundary object in turn interacts

---

1. The term "page" is used generically in this context. This may manifest itself as an HTML page, a client dialog, and so on at a later time.

with a controller that coordinates the activities within the use case. Several entity objects are involved in fulfilling the use case. It should be noted that a separate sequence diagram, perhaps involving interactions between a different set of objects, should be created for each significant complete path (flow of events) that can be taken through the use case. These paths, or scenarios, might be generated as the actors deviate from the most expected behavior or if exceptional conditions occur within the system. The collection of these sequence diagrams can be part of the same use case realization. They collectively show the possible internal interactions that can occur as the use case is performed.

Collaboration Diagrams

Collaboration diagrams are the other type of object interaction diagram in UML. Unlike sequence diagrams, which are focused on the time ordering of the interaction, collaboration diagram emphasis is on showing the relationships and

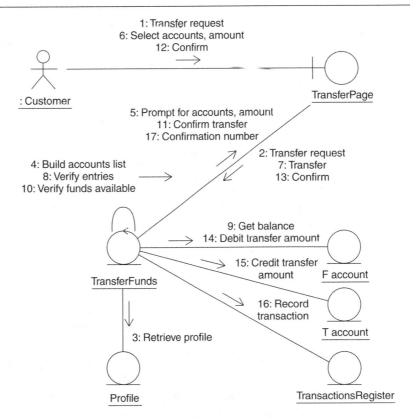

Figure 8-8 Transfer funds collaboration diagram

communication links among the participants. Collaboration diagrams provide a better picture of the overall interactions for a given class.

Sequence diagrams allow you to convey some information, for example, timing information, which cannot be conveyed via collaboration diagrams. Collaboration diagrams also tend to become difficult to comprehend once you exceed a few objects on the diagram, whereas sequence diagrams have proven to be capable of handling scenarios involving a large number of objects.

The preceding caveats aside, for all practical purposes, the distinction is really one of preference. It is relatively straightforward to derive a sequence diagram from a collaboration diagram and vice versa.

Figure 8-8 shows a collaboration diagram version of the sequence diagram for the Transfer funds use case shown in Figure 8-7.

Class Diagrams

Thus far, we have focused on identifying the analysis classes that participate in a use case and distributing the responsibilities of the use case to the identified classes. This has been done in the context of interaction diagrams, which primarily capture the dynamic behavior of a use case.

Classes often participate in several use cases, and it is equally important to understand their static relationships to ensure consistency across the system.

We now turn our attention to this aspect by defining the classes and their relationships more precisely based on the Use Case Analysis work done thus far. We use the Transfer funds use case as a means to illustrate these static relationships.

The UML class diagram is useful for capturing the static relationships between different structural elements. A single class diagram, referred to as the View of Participating Classes (VOPC) diagram, is created for each use case. The purpose of the VOPC diagram is to illustrate in a single diagram all aspects of the system architecture that are exercised by a specific use case.

All interaction diagrams created for the use case realization are examined for classes, operations, relations, and so on to be included on the VOPC.

As a first step, we identify and place all the classes that participate in the use case on a class diagram. Because we have already distributed the behavior of the use case to the classes, it is a relatively simple exercise to create *analysis operations* for the responsibilities assigned to the class. Each analysis operation maps to one of the system responsibilities borne by the analysis class. That is, there is a one-to-one mapping between each unique message in an analysis-level interaction diagram and an analysis operation.

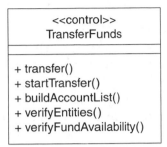

```
        <<control>>
        TransferFunds

    + transfer()
    + startTransfer()
    + buildAccountList()
    + verifyEntities()
    + verifyFundAvailability()
```

Figure 8-9   TransferFunds control class with analysis operations

It is important to note that these are analysis operations, meaning that these operations will most likely need to evolve as we continue with our analysis and design efforts.

Figure 8-9 shows the TransferFunds control class with analysis operations representing the responsibilities assigned to the class.

Another aspect of fleshing out each individual class is to identify attributes for the class. Attributes represent information that may be requested of the class by others or that may be required by the class itself to fulfill its responsibilities.

Attributes are often identified via requirements through knowledge of the domain and through an understanding of the information that is required to fulfill the responsibilities.

At this stage in the analysis, it is appropriate to identify attributes as generic types, such as number, string, and so on. The exact type can be sorted out at a later time as dictated by implementation parameters. Figure 8-10 shows the attributes for the customer Profile analysis class.

Keep in mind that information modeled as attributes should require only relatively simple behavior, such as *get* or *set* operations. If this is not the case or if two

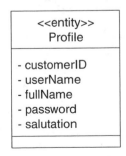

```
        <<entity>>
        Profile

    - customerID
    - userName
    - fullName
    - password
    - salutation
```

Figure 8-10   Customer Profile entity class with attributes

or more classes share the information, it is better to model that information as a separate class.

We complete the class diagram for the use case by identifying the relationships between the classes. The relationships we are specifically interested in are association and inheritance (see Chapter 3 for a discussion on association and aggregation).

A good starting point for identifying such relationships is the collaboration diagram. If there are links between classes on a collaboration diagram, a need for communication exists, so a relationship is warranted.

The direction of communication should also be identified. This may be unidirectional such that an instance of class A can send a message to class B but not vice versa, or bidirectional, meaning that either can send a message to the other party in the relationship. Each relationship should also be analyzed for multiplicity. For example, if up to four instances of a class can participate in an association, that end of the association should be identified with the multiplicity of 0..4.

It is always tempting to add additional relationships to the class diagram because you believe they are required or may be required down the road. Just remember that this analysis is use case driven and unless it is part of the use case, it would not make sense to add relationships.

Figure 8-11 shows the TransferFunds use case class diagram.

Some notes about the class diagram for the TransferFunds scenario: First, note that the controller does not need to keep references to the customer Profile and the TransactionsRegister for repeated access. Instead, these are

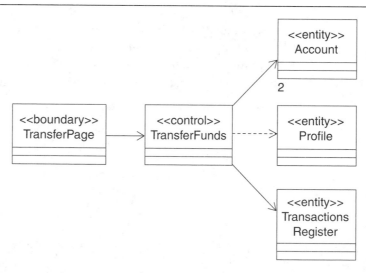

Figure 8-11   TransferFunds use case class diagram

retrieved each time based on the customer involved and upon completion of the transaction itself. As such, these relationships are captured as dependencies instead of associations. Second, in a transfer funds scenario, there are two accounts involved (from, to). This involvement of two accounts (as opposed to a simple account) is captured via a multiplicity of two for the TransferFund control class and the Account entity class.

Coalescing the Analysis Classes

Having analyzed all the use cases and having created the class diagrams for each use case, it is time to merge the various analysis classes to arrive at a unified analysis model. This is an important activity, as we want to arrive at a minimal set of classes and avoid unnecessary redundancy in the final analysis model.

The key task at this stage revolves around identifying classes that may be duplicated across use cases or masquerading in slight variations. For example, control classes that have similar behavior or represent the same concept across use cases should be merged. Entity classes that have the same attributes should also be merged, and their behavior combined into a single class.

Figure 8-12 shows the preliminary analysis model for the HomeDirect case study after an initial merge of the major use cases. Note the consolidation of the various control classes identified for several individual use cases into three control classes. The revised control classes were arrived at by merging control classes for closely related use cases (e.g., login, bills, etc.).

At this stage, things are still in flux as some details remain to be resolved. It is not uncommon to go through some reflection and walkthroughs to arrive at an analysis model that everyone is comfortable with.

For more details of specific scenarios and related issues, see Chapter 16.

Packaging

In the relatively simple HomeDirect online banking case study used in this book, we have identified about a dozen use cases. Each use case has in turn resulted in two, three, or more analysis classes, which easily adds up to 30+ classes just in the very first iteration. Clearly, as we delve deeper into the design and implementation, this number will likely increase.

Furthermore, as projects move to design and implementation, the team grows, and it becomes necessary to make arrangements so that work can be allotted, and everyone can work simultaneously.

This is where packaging comes in. It allows you to manage complexity by grouping *like* classes or *related* classes into separate packages.

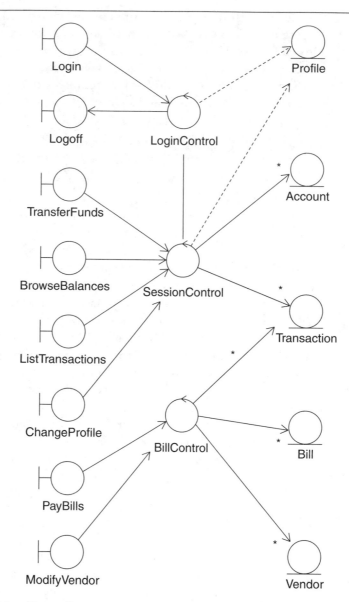

Figure 8-12 Class diagram representing a preliminary version of the merged analysis model

The argument for placing like classes in a package is that of convenience. You can easily locate all the classes that are similar in concept or purpose. If you were to group all your control classes in a package, for example, you would be using the first approach-grouping by likeness or similarity.

Grouping related classes has the advantage of the packages being somewhat more self-contained. If a team is responsible for delivering a specific set of functionality, they could develop, test, and deliver the package fairly independently.

In the UML, the folder icon represents a package. A package can contain model elements such as classes and interfaces. Packages can also be nested.

One of the key challenges in large and complex projects is to understand the dependencies between the various pieces of software. A dependency exists between packages if class X in package A depends on a class Y in package B. Thus, a change in class Y can potentially have a ripple effect on class X and any other classes that depend on it.

The role of packaging becomes more important as the size and complexity of the project increases because even the smallest ripple can have a dramatic effect when multiplied.

Package dependency is shown on a diagram by drawing a dashed arrow from the package that has the dependency to the package it has the dependency on. It is a good idea to adopt a convention of drawing all dependency arrows in the same direction (e.g., top to bottom, left to right, etc.). This makes it easier to understand the chain of dependencies.

Figure 8-13 shows a simple diagram involving packages. The approach taken is that of grouping like classes in packages.

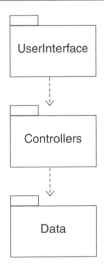

Figure 8-13   Package dependency

The package dependency diagrams for the HomeDirect case study are shown in Chapter 16.

Summary

Use Case Analysis provides an initial, high-level definition of how internal elements interact in order to satisfy the system's functional requirements and how they relate to each other statically. This is a fundamental activity on the way to design and development.

Use Case Analysis is supported via sequence diagrams. Instead of showing the interaction between actors and a monolithic system, the system is split into analysis level objects. The responsibilities of the system are divided among the analysis level objects, which are referred to as boundary, control, and entity objects, to achieve a finer grained sequence diagram. Collaboration diagrams are another aid in such analysis.

Once the dynamic behavior has been captured in the form of sequence diagrams and collaboration diagrams, class diagrams can be developed to capture the static relationships between the various elements participating in fulfilling the use case.

Packaging provides a convenient mechanism for managing complexity and allotment of team effort. Another critical aspect where packaging can be leveraged deals with understanding the impact of changes in the project via dependency analysis.

Chapter 9

Overview of J2EE Technologies

- The Big Picture

- Servlets

- JavaServer Pages (JSP)

- Enterprise JavaBeans (EJB)

- Session Beans

- Entity Beans

- Message-Driven Beans

- Assembly and Deployment

- Case Study

- Summary

Up to this point, we have focused on the Unified Modeling Language (UML) and analysis without giving much thought to the design details of these Java 2 Platform, Enterprise Edition (J2EE) technology components. Over the next few chapters, we'll switch gears and move the discussion to a more detailed level to discuss each of the major J2EE component types, highlighting the different roles the UML plays in dealing with them.

In this short chapter, we outline how the different J2EE technologies fit together, and then highlight the contents of the remaining chapters. This will allow you to develop a better understanding of the big picture and give you the opportunity to focus your attention only on those chapters that best suit your needs. Five different J2EE component types and technologies will be covered in the remaining chapters.

The Big Picture

Each of the J2EE technologies is intended for a specific purpose and ideally suited for solving specific types of challenges.

Figure 9-1 provides a 50,000-foot view of how the various technologies fit together.

The main point to note is that each technology is designed to be used in a specific tier, and each tier is designed to be very focused on the role that it plays in the overall J2EE application development paradigm. This limits the roles individual components can play, even though surpassing these limits may be feasible from a technology perspective.

Servlets

In Chapter 10, we examine these typically compact components. Servlets are most often used as a conduit for passing data back and forth between a Web client and an enterprise application running on a server. This is especially true when there are no specific presentation details required of the information being passed back.

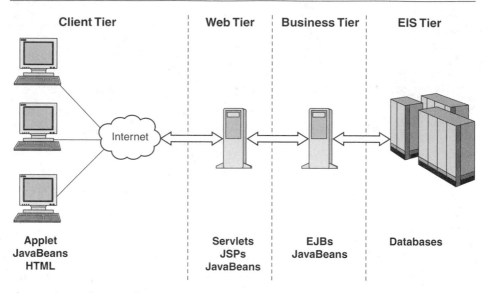

Figure 9-1 The J2EE big picture

Servlets come in two flavors: *GenericServlet* and *HttpServlet*. We discuss both servlet types to a necessary level of technology detail, and then talk about how to model them and gain the most from their UML representation, for example, via modeling of servlet-to-servlet communication, relationships, session management, and so on.

This chapter is equally applicable to both J2EE 1.3 (Servlet specification 2.3) and J2EE 1.2 (Servlet specification 2.2).

JavaServer Pages (JSP)

In Chapter 11, we look at the newer J2EE technology of JSP. The key advantage of JSP technology is that it allows for better separation of presentation content and logic, thereby simplifying development and maintenance.

Although JSPs get compiled into servlets, they are best suited to a role that is fundamentally different. We discuss this in the context of UML modeling of JSP to understand how to best model this hybrid technology and where to best utilize it.

Enterprise JavaBeans (EJB)

Chapters 13, 14, and 15 deal with the different types of EJB components. The chapters discuss these components for both J2EE 1.3 (EJB specification 2.0) and J2EE 1.2 (EJB specification 1.1).

Session Beans

In Chapter 12, we discuss this first type of EJB component. Because this is the first chapter that deals with EJBs, we cover several general details that apply to all EJB types; later chapters simply reference this one where necessary.

Session beans are currently the most often deployed EJB type, and they are often used as the main controller in an enterprise application, commonly tying servlets or JSPs to entity beans or other enterprise application components.

We discuss how to model their design with the UML, go into the technology details, and then discuss further how UML modeling can assist in the area of bean-to-bean relationships, session management, transactions, and so on.

Entity Beans

In Chapter 13, we highlight how entity EJBs help your enterprise application by providing more than just methods to access your database. UML modeling and more technology details are covered.

We also touch on why entity beans have a bright future and why EJB developers might be more compelled to use them nowadays with recent technology enhancements and improvements.

In addition, we cover EJB relationships in this chapter and discuss how the UML can simplify the task of dealing with more complex combinations of EJB components. We also talk briefly about the EJB Query Language, what Persistence Managers do, and how they both relate to the Abstract Persistent Schema.

Message-Driven Beans

In Chapter 14, we discuss these compact EJBs, which were newly introduced in J2EE 1.3. Intended for use with loosely coupled systems, we discuss the UML and technology details as well as give some insight on where to gain the most from using message-driven beans.

Assembly and Deployment

In Chapter 15, we discuss more of the eXtensible Markup Language (XML) deployment descriptor aspects as they apply to the various J2EE components.

We also cover how UML component and deployment diagrams can help in the whole enterprise application assembly and deployment process.

Case Study

In Chapter 16, we step through the HomeDirect example in further detail—parts of which we have been referring to throughout the chapters. Several use cases are elaborated fully and completed down to the implementation level. Also included is a discussion of some key decisions taken in the transition from analysis to implementation and trade-offs made in the process.

Summary

This chapter provided an overview of the J2EE technologies and components that will be covered in the remaining chapters of the book.

Specifically, we will cover servlets, JSPs, session beans, entity beans, and message-driven beans as well as assembly and deployment aspects applicable to these technologies.

The final chapter in the book provides a detailed case study that shows how to apply the UML to the sample project that has been used throughout the book.

Chapter 10

Servlets

❖ *Process Check:* *In this chapter, we focus on design as we progress through the Rational Unified Process (RUP) analysis and design discipline. We also discuss some aspects of implementation in the context of the servlet technology.*

Recall the control object TransferFunds from the discussion in Chapter 6. If you look closely at the final sequence diagram presented in Chapter 6, you'll notice two very distinct types of interactions performed by this class:

■ *Interactions with boundary objects to obtain information and perform some basic work*

■ *Interactions with entity objects*

Implementing a control class with a dual set of responsibilities and a large scope would make the control class less maintainable and less scalable. To make the control class more maintainable and scalable, it is preferable to partition the control class into two classes, one focused on the external interaction and the other responsible for carrying out the internal coordination and logic.

As it turns out, the externally focused part of TransferFunds evolves to a Java servlet. We introduce the servlet in the next section, and then discuss how you actually determine the responsibilities of the servlet in the context of the HomeDirect case study.

Introduction to Servlets

Historically speaking, servlets have been around longer and have seen much wider use than other Java 2 Platform, Enterprise Edition (J2EE) technologies. In the past, they tended to be large in size and complicated to maintain in comparison to the level of Web functionality they actually provided. Going forward, servlets will likely continue to see wide use for some time. However, their typical size is shrinking, and the level of complexity they tend to deal with is consistently becoming less.

The biggest benefit servlets offer developers is that they are designed specifically to process Hypertext Transfer Protocol (HTTP) requests coming from the Web client and pass back a suitable response. They perform this function well and require few resources to deliver this functionality.

In terms of structure, servlets are specialized Java classes that closely resemble the structure of Java applets, but they run on a Web server instead of a client.

An interesting point to note is that servlets can never have their own graphical user interface. Web servers host these components through the use of a Web container that manages all aspects of their life cycle.

Common Usage

Servlets have the distinction of being the most frequently used J2EE components currently found on the World Wide Web. As stated earlier, they typically involve a compact, lightweight architecture and design. They also tend to work well in cases where the requirements placed on this type of Web component are relatively small.

Most Web developers use servlets as the main point of entry to their server application from the Web client, and in this way, they are simply used as a conduit to pass information back and forth between the client and the server. Allowing client control to add or remove Web pages or files from the server can also be a good use for servlets, as long as the client has sufficient security clearance. Understandably, this usage is less frequently seen in practice.

Best Served Small

In theory, servlets are capable of doing just about anything possible that can be done with Java. The question arises as to why Web developers don't just build everything they need using these components. The problem is that building large servlets to handle complex Web interactions, transactions, database synchronization, and other internal logic is not a very scalable approach. Developers would spend most of their time working out the intricacies of low-level transactions, state management, connection pooling, and so on.

In the past, servlets were often built to perform most or all of the following tasks:

- Check and process user input
- Handle significant business logic
- Perform database queries, updates, and synchronization
- Handle complex Web transactions
- Generate dynamic Web page content as output
- Handle Web page forwarding

More advanced J2EE solutions make use of JavaServer Pages (JSP), Enterprise JavaBeans (EJB), and JavaBeans to split up and offload much of this work, often using new mechanisms built into J2EE to simplify the more difficult tasks for the developer. Servlets are then responsible for a more manageable set of tasks:

- Gathering and validating user input, but little or no actual processing
- Coordination of output, but with little or no direct generation of dynamic Web page content
- Minimal business logic

As you can see, servlets are best served small.

If constant demand for new Web site functionality did not exist, huge servlets could be built with all the accompanying aches and pains, and they might even stand a reasonable chance of being adequately maintained. However, the fact is that demands on Web sites keep increasing. Every service provider on the Web must continually update and upgrade to give their customers that new bit of data, that new cool feature, or that prized extra that differentiates their service from everyone else's service.

Unfortunately, the bigger servlets come at the cost of an increased challenge of providing adequate code maintenance, not to mention the increased risk of breaking some of the existing functionality. The blessing of a lightweight architecture at the outset can easily turn into a wretched curse later on if you are not careful.

J2EE Versions

The information in this chapter applies equally well to servlets using J2EE 1.3 or J2EE 1.2. The differences between these two specifications are insignificant with respect to the basic Unified Modeling Language (UML) modeling of these particular Web components.

Servlet Life Cycle

As stated earlier, servlets are deployed within a servlet container, which in turn is hosted by a Web server. The particular capabilities and level of compliance of the Web server determines which version of the servlet specification you need to be working with.

The basic behavior of a servlet involves a request-response type model derived from the way the HTTP works; thus, the inherent applicability as a Web component. This behavior is illustrated via a statechart diagram in Figure 10-1.

Servlets are built as Java classes that extend one of two basic servlet implementation classes: **HttpServlet** and **GenericServlet**. The former is the most often

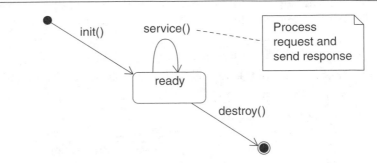

Figure 10-1   Servlet life cycle

used, yet slightly more complex of the two. Both servlet types employ the same basic life cycle.

Life Cycle Methods

The servlet life cycle makes use of three basic request handler methods, of which any or all can be implemented within the extended servlet class:

- **init:** Initializes the servlet
- **service:** Services the client request
- **destroy:** Destroys the servlet

Of these three methods, the **service** method is the most interesting because it actually does the majority of the necessary processing. It typically does the following:

- Receives the request from the client
- Reads the request data
- Writes the response headers
- Gets the writer or output stream object for the response
- Writes the response data

The **service** method is at the heart of the **GenericServlet** type. However, it is almost never overridden and instead is split into lower level HTTP request handlers when used with the **HttpServlet** type.

The **init** and **destroy** life cycle methods are always available to be overridden, but in several cases might not be used if the servlet has no specific objects or connections it needs to initialize or terminate.

A sequence diagram in Figure 10-2 shows a simple example of a servlet. This diagram applies to both the **GenericServlet** and **HttpServlet**. It highlights a simple example where a database query is made to formulate the response to the client. Note that the **service** method is further refined into a specific HTTP request in the case of **HttpServlet**.

Convenience Method

Besides the life cycle methods, servlets commonly make use of what are referred to as convenience methods. One such convenience method that applies for all servlets is **getServletInfo**, which returns a general info string about the particular servlet—normally author, version, usage, and so on.

Required Methods and Tagged Values

When building a servlet that extends the **GenericServlet** class, the **service** life cycle method must be implemented; otherwise, the servlet is invalid. All other methods are optional.

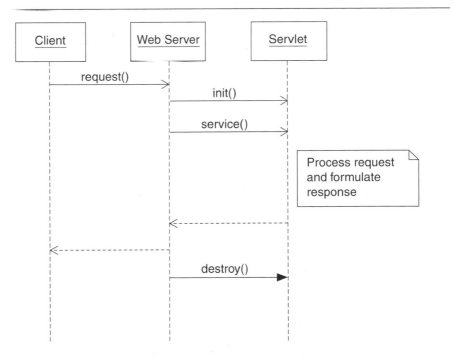

Figure 10-2   Sequence diagram showing servlet life cycle

Multiple threads may call a generic servlet instance's **service** method concurrently. To avoid this, the servlet can implement the **SingleThreadModel** interface, which is really a method of typing the servlet and indicating to the Web container that only a single thread should be allowed to call the method at any given time.

Implementing the **SingleThreadModel** can have a very significant effect on how the container decides to allocate resources when the servlet is deployed on the Web server, which can greatly impact the total number of concurrent servlet instances allowed.

Using this approach may be appropriate if you are dealing with a situation in which the servlet may need to alter information that is not thread safe or access resources that are not thread safe.

It is not recommended that you attempt to serialize any of the servlet methods other than by implementing this interface. The interface itself introduces no new methods.

Request Handling

Servlets are request-driven and have specific capabilities available to them that simplify handling of incoming requests.

Recall that a request to a servlet may consist of several pieces of data (for example, when a form consisting of several fields is filled in and submitted).

When the Web container receives a request intended for a servlet, it encapsulates the incoming data into a **ServletRequest** object (commonly referred to as the request object) and passes it on as a parameter to the servlet's **service** method. The servlet can then use the methods available in the **ServletRequest** interface to query the request object. Some of the queries are contained in the following list:

- **getCharacterEncoding** obtains information about the encoding format used for the request.
- **isSecure** finds out if the request was made over a secure channel.
- **getParameterNames** obtains a list of all parameter names in the request.
- **getRemoteAddr** determines the IP address of the client that sent the request.
- **getParameter** is used to retrieve the first parameter value associated with a named parameter type.
- **getParameterValues** is used to retrieve multiple parameter values associated with a named parameter type.

```
HttpSession session = request.getSession(true);
:
:
// obtain the values for UserID and password
String loginID = rquest.getParameter ("USERID");
String loginPassword = request.getParameter ("PASSWORD");
:
```

Figure 10-3   Using the request object

Several other methods are provided for querying different aspects of the request object. See **javax.servlet.ServletRequest**[1] for more information. A specialized version, **HttpServletRequest**, for HTTP based servlet requests is also available. See **javax.servlet.http.HttpServletRequest** for more information.

Figure 10-3 shows a simple usage scenario involving a request object.

Response Generation

A request generally warrants a response, and servlets are no exception in this regard.

Servlets make use of **ServletResponse** to simplify this common task. The **ServletResponse** object, commonly referred to as the response object, is in fact provided to a servlet alongside the request object as a parameter to the **service** method.

Output can be written in either binary or character format by obtaining a handle to either a **ServletOutputStream** object or a **PrintWriter** object, respectively. Some of the other methods provided by the **ServletResponse** interface are contained in the following list:

- **getOutputStream** obtains the handle to a **ServletOutputStream** object for binary data.
- **getWriter** obtains the handle to a PrintWriter object for character data.
- **setBufferSize** can be used to establish the buffer size for the response to enable better performance tuning.
- **flushBuffer** flushes the current contents of the buffer.

---

1. If you are new to Java or unsure about this reference, see the "Conventions" section in the Preface of this book.

For more information, see **javax.servlet.ResponseObject** and **javax.servlet. ServletOutputStream**.

An HTTP specific response object is also available and provides additional capabilities related to HTTP response header formulation. See **javax.servlet. http.HttpServletResponse** for more information.

Figure 10-4 shows a simple usage scenario involving a response object.

Alternatives for Response Generation

If you take a good look at Figure 10-4, you will see several HTML tags involved in the generation of output from the servlet. This represents only one approach for generation of dynamic output.

Another similar but more structured approach is to use libraries of HTML files to generate common headers and footers for the necessary response Web pages, with the dynamic portion of the page still generated much like what was shown in Figure 10-4.

A third and cleaner approach is to use the power of JSP and JavaBeans whenever possible. In this approach, the servlet simply needs to forward to a JSP page that contains all of the necessary presentation information and use JSP technology and JavaBeans to fill in the dynamic content portions of the page. Other than the forward, the servlet has little else to do with presentation except perhaps coordinating the necessary items for the JSP page to successfully do its work.

We discuss this approach further in Chapter 11.

```
PrintWriter out;
:
// set content type
response.setContentType("text/html");
:
out = response.getWriter();
out.println("<HTML><HEAD><TITLE>");
:
out.println("Login Unsuccessful");
:
out.flush();
out.close();
```

Figure 10-4   Generating the response

HTTP Request Handlers

The **HttpServlet** class extends the **GenericServlet** class and therefore inherits all of the standard servlet capabilities. In addition to the basic servlet life cycle methods and convenience method, the more complex **HttpServlet** class adds methods to aid in the processing of HTTP requests. These commonly used handler methods are

- **doGet:** Handles HTTP GET requests
- **doPost:** Handles HTTP POST requests

In the case of **doGet**, there is an additional method used for conditional HTTP GET support (the different HTTP request types are explained later in this section). The **getLastModified** method is like HTTP GET, but only returns content if it has changed since a specified time. This method can only be used if **doGet** has also been overridden and is intended to be used in cases where you are dealing with content that does not change much from request to request.

Advanced Handler Methods

There are several advanced handler methods that are defined as well:

- **doPut:** Handles HTTP PUT requests
- **doDelete:** Handles HTTP DELETE requests
- **doOptions:** Handles HTTP OPTIONS requests
- **doTrace:** Handles HTTP TRACE requests

Unlike the **GenericServlet** class, servlets based on **HttpServlet** have almost no valid reason to override the **service** method. Instead, you typically override these request handlers, which the base **service** method implementation calls when appropriate. The **doOptions** and **doTrace** methods also have virtually no valid reason to be overridden and are present only for full HTTP support. An **HttpServlet** must override at least one method, which usually means one of the remaining life cycle methods or request handlers.

Quick Guide to HTTP Requests

For the most commonly used request handler methods, the following list provides a quick guide of what the HTTP requests are for:

- **GET:** A call to get information from the server and return it in a response to the client. The method processing this call must not have any side effects, so it can be repeated safely again and again. A GET call is typically used when a servlet URL is accessed directly from a Web browser or via a forward from a form on an HTML or JSP page. A GET call shows the data being passed to the servlet as part of the displayed URL on most Web browsers. In certain cases, this might not be very desirable from a security perspective.

- **POST:** A call to allow the client to send data to the server. The method processing this call is allowed to cause side effects, such as updating of data stored on the server. A POST call can be used instead of a GET when forwarding from a form on an HTML or JSP page. Unlike GET, the use of POST hides from view any data being passed to the servlet. Some developers choose to process GET and POST exactly the same, or simply ignore one or the other if they do not want that particular call to be supported.

- **PUT:** This call is similar to POST, but allows the client to place an actual file on a server instead of just sending data. It is also allowed to cause side effects, just like POST. Although available, the use of a PUT call is not very common.

- **DELETE:** This call is similar to PUT, but allows the client to remove a file or Web page from the server. It is also allowed to cause side effects in the same way as PUT. Although available, the use of a DELETE call is not very common.

There is another request not specifically mentioned in the preceding list called HTTP HEAD. This request, although valid in the context of the **HttpServlet** class itself, is actually handled internally by making a call to the **doGet** method, which you might have overridden. It differs in that it only returns the response headers that result from processing **doGet** and none of the actual response data.

The RequestDispatcher Interface

Given the simplicity of servlets, it makes sense to keep each servlet focused on a specific task, and then set up multiple servlets to collaboratively achieve a more complex task. Servlets can take care of the mechanical aspects of such collaborative efforts easily by implementing the **RequestDispatcher** interface.

The **RequestDispatcher** interface provides two key capabilities:

- **forward:** This method allows a servlet to forward a request to another Web component. The servlet forwarding the request may process the request in some way prior to the forwarding. Forward can effectively be used to achieve servlet chaining where each link in the chain produces some output that can be merged with the original request data, and then be used as the input to the next servlet in the chain. This is essentially similar to the concept of pipes in the UNIX world.

  Note that the term "redirect" is sometimes used interchangeably with "forward," intending the same meaning. However, this should not be confused with the **sendRedirect** method found on the servlet response. A **sendRedirect** call does not guarantee preservation of the request data when it forwards to a new page, so it does not allow for the same servlet chaining capabilities.

- **include:** This method permits the contents of another Web component to be included in the response from the calling servlet. The first servlet simply includes the other servlet at the appropriate point in the output, and the output from the servlet being included is added to the output stream. This is similar in concept to Server Side Includes (SSI).[2]

Modeling Servlets in UML

The **GenericServlet** class is usually modeled as a standard Java class with the **<<Generic_Servlet>>** stereotype applied. The presence of the stereotype allows for the servlet to be represented in a compact form and still be easily distinguished as a generic servlet without the need to show the inheritance tree on the same diagram. A generic servlet can include any of the life cycle methods or the convenience method discussed earlier.

A more expanded view of the servlet class showing the inheritance from the **GenericServlet** class can also be used. In most cases, though, the more compact stereotyped class view is sufficient. The compact and expanded representations of the servlet are shown in Figure 10-5.

If the servlet implements the **SingleThreadModel** interface, which controls serialization of the **service** method, the servlet can be shown with the interface

---

2. SSI allows embedding of special tags into an HTML document. The tags are understood by the Web server and are translated dynamically as the HTML document is served to the browser. JSPs build on this idea.

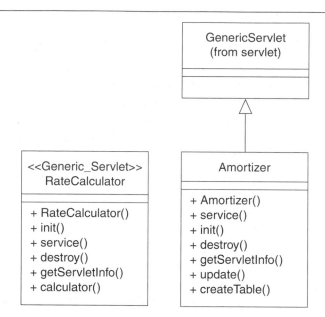

Figure 10-5 Compact and full representation of a generic servlet

to highlight this aspect. Optionally, the servlet can be tagged with *{Single ThreadServlet=True}* instead to clearly identify this on the diagram in a somewhat more compact format.

An example of a servlet that implements the **SingleThreadModel** is shown in Figure 10-6.

The **HttpServlet** class is modeled similarly to **GenericServlet**, but with the **<<Http_Servlet>>** stereotype applied. It can also include the life cycle methods, the convenience method, and any of the HTTP request handlers previously discussed.

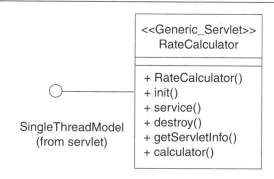

Figure 10-6 Servlet supporting the SingleThreadModel

The **SingleThreadModel** details as well as the tagged value for **SingleThread-Servlet** apply in the **HttpServlet** class exactly the same way as they did for **Generic-Servlet**. As stated earlier, you should not attempt to serialize any of the servlet methods other than by implementing this interface. This interface does not introduce any new methods.

Modeling Other Servlet Aspects

Other aspects of servlets that warrant modeling are servlet forward, servlet include, ServletContext, and Servlet Session Management. The following sections discuss these aspects in more detail.

Servlet Forward

Servlet **forward** is a special kind of relationship, and modeling it explicitly can help clarify the overall application logic. For example, it can shed light on the flow of the processing logic. In complicated **forward** chains, the relationship may be indicative of some algorithm being implemented. Two specific approaches help to identify the overall application logic in this regard.

First, on the class diagram, label the relationships between the servlets that invoke **forward** on other Web components with the <<forward>> relationship. An example is shown in Figure 10-7.

For more complicated servlet chaining, an activity diagram can be used to show the overall interaction. If desired, request and response objects with attributes appropriately updated at specific points can be shown to demonstrate the overall algorithm. See Figure 10-8.

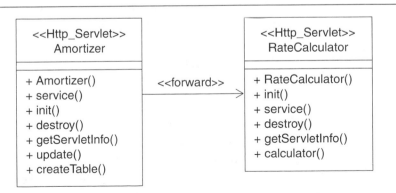

Figure 10-7   Modeling servlet forwarding on a class diagram

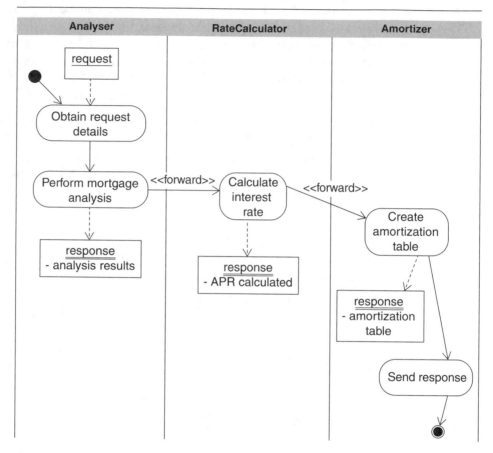

Figure 10-8 Modeling servlet forwarding with activity diagram

In this case, we have labeled the transition with the <<forward>> stereotype to emphasize that it represents a forward relationship between the elements involved. The comments shown for each occurrence of the response object identify what happens as the request and response objects pass through the chain.

Servlet Include

Include is another significant and special relationship as it affects the results produced by a servlet. In fact, **include** may be used as a means to structure and organize the overall output in a modular fashion. Servlet **include** relationships are modeled in the same fashion as the **forward** relationship, that is, as a unidirectional association stereotyped <<include>>. The direction of the association is from the including servlet to the resource being included. An example is shown in Figure 10-9. In the example, a servlet responsible for creating a mortgage amortization table includes header and footer servlets whose sole purpose is to generate the page header and footer, respectively.

ServletContext

Each servlet runs in some environment. The **ServletContext** provides information about the environment the servlet is running in. A servlet can belong to only one **ServletContext** as determined by the administrator. Typically, one **ServletContext** is associated with each Web application deployed in a container. In the case of distributed containers, one **ServletContext** is associated with one Web application per virtual machine.

The **ServletContext** interface can be used by servlets to store and retrieve information and share information among servlets. A servlet obtains the **Servlet-Context** it is running in by using the **getServletContext** method.

Some of the basic services provided by the **ServletContext** interface are

- **setAttribute:** Stores information in the context
- **getAttribute:** Retrieves information stored in the **ServletContext**

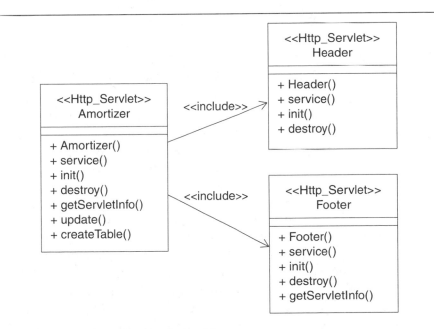

Figure 10-9   Servlet include relationship

- **getAttributeNames:** Obtains the names of attributes in the context
- **removeAttribute:** Removes an attribute in the context

An approach similar to the one discussed for servlet forwarding and shown in Figure 10-8 can be employed to model servlet interactions with the **Servlet-Context**.

Servlet Session Management

Given the stateless nature of the HTTP protocol, managing repeat interaction and dialog with the same client (such as that required for an ongoing shopping session) poses some serious challenges. There are various means of overcoming these challenges:

- *Hidden fields:* Hidden fields are embedded within the page displayed to the client. These fields are sent back to the client each time a new request is made, thereby permitting client identification each time a client makes a request.
- *Dynamic URL rewriting:* Extra information is added to each URL the client clicks on. This extra information is used to uniquely identify each client for the duration of the client session, for example, adding a "?sessionid=97859" to the end of each URL the client clicks to identify that the request is associated with session id 97859.
- *Cookies:* Stored information can later be passed back to the client repeatedly. The Web server provides the cookie to the browser. Cookies are one of the more popular means of setting up a servlet session.
- *Server-side session object:* Cookies and URL encoding suffer from limitations on how much information can be sent back with each request. In server-side session management, the session information is maintained on the server in a *session* object and can be accessed as required. Server-side session objects are expensive to use, so it is best to use them sparingly.

The Java Servlet Application Programming Interface (API) provides abstractions that directly support some of the session management techniques discussed in the preceding list.

The core abstraction provided by the servlet API is the *HTTP session,* which facilitates handling of multiple requests from the same user.

Figure 10-10 gives an example of servlet session management.

Activity diagrams can be used to model the servlet and session interaction. This is similar to the approach discussed for servlet forwarding and shown in Figure 10-8.

```
import.javax.servlet.http.*;

...
// locate a session object
HttpSession theSession = request.getSession (true);

...
// add data to the session object
theSession.putValue("Session.id", "98579");

...
// get the data for the session object
sessionid = theSession.getValue("Session.ID");
```

Figure 10-10   Servlet session usage

Servlet Deployment and Web Archives

A descriptor based on XML is used in the deployment of servlets on a Web server. The compiled servlet class, additional supporting Java classes, and the deployment descriptor are packaged together into a Web archive file, also known as a ".war" file.

The deployment descriptor is an XML-based file that contains specific configuration and deployment information for use by the servlet container.

Figure 10-11 shows an example of a vanilla XML deployment descriptor for an **HttpServlet**. Additional required fields in the descriptor are filled in during configuration and deployment on the Web server.

We discuss servlet deployment descriptors and Web archive files and their role in the context of modeling in Chapter 15.

```
<?xml version="1.0" encoding="UTF-8"?>
<!DOCTYPE web-app PUBLIC "- / / Sun Microsystems, Inc.
/ / DTD Web Application 2.2
/ / EN" "http: / / java.sun.com/j2ee/dtds/web-app_2_2.dtd">
<web-app>
  <servlet>
    <servlet-name>LoginServlet</servlet-name>
    <servlet-class>LoginServlet</servlet-class>
  </servlet>
</web-app>
```

Figure 10-11   A simple vanilla XML deployment descriptor for a sample HttpServlet

Identifying Servlets in Enterprise Applications

Now that you have become intimately familiar with servlets, it is time to return to building the HomeDirect online banking example.

At the beginning of this chapter, we identified the need to evolve the control object in the Transfer funds use case by splitting it into two, one focused on the external interaction and the other focused on the internal interaction.

Of course, the question remains: How do you actually arrive at this division of responsibilities? The answer is partly based on understanding what a servlet is capable of doing and the rest on judgment and experience. In general, the role of the servlet is that of a coordinator between the boundary objects and the rest of the system. All the interaction between the boundary object and the composite control class belongs in the new servlet. How you split the interaction that is shown between the control object and the entity objects is somewhat less clear. The key factor to remember is that the servlet is primarily a coordinator; and hence, it should only take on lightweight responsibilities, which could include initiating some business logic. However, actual business logic, computations, interaction with entity objects, and so on would all fall outside of these responsibilities.

With this in mind, let's take another look at the interactions involving the control object as shown in Figure 10-12.

If we look at all of the control object responsibilities, we see that the lower half is comprised of several actions that together form a complete transaction. We decide to separate this part and have it be handled by an internally focused control object, leaving the rest to be taken care of by a servlet. Figure 10-13 shows the result of this division of duties.

In this scenario, the servlet is an example of what the RUP calls a *front component*. A front component is typically a servlet or a JSP that is primarily responsible for processing user input but is not itself responsible for presentation. Rather, it acts simply as an entry point to the application and as a coordinator with other components. Note that the term "TransferPage" is used to generically represent a user interface. We might decide to make this a static HTML page or something more dynamic.

We discuss what to do with the other, internal focused control object in the next chapter.

Of the two types of servlets discussed, an **HttpServlet** appears ideally suited to take on the external interaction role due to the Web-based nature of the HomeDirect interface.

Figure 10-14 expands further on this scenario. There are really two customer actions involved in this use case. The first is where the customer decides

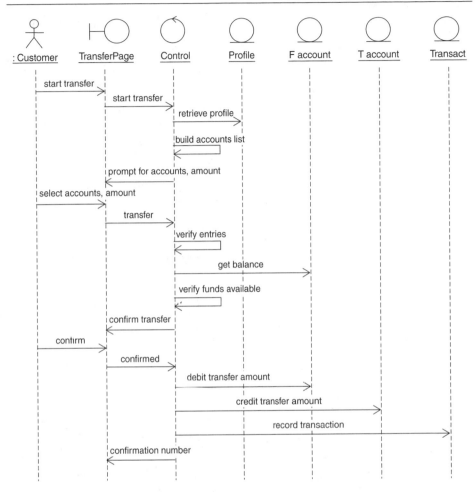

Figure 10-12   Control object interactions

to do a transfer action. This invokes MainServlet, which coordinates the retrieval of the pertinent accounts data and displays this via the TransferPage boundary object. The customer then selects the desired accounts and enters the amount to transfer. Control at this point is forwarded to a secondary TransferServlet, which coordinates the actual transfer action via the internally focused control object.

Figure 10-15 shows the details of the servlets for this example. We purposely have the servlets handling as little processing as possible, offloading most of the

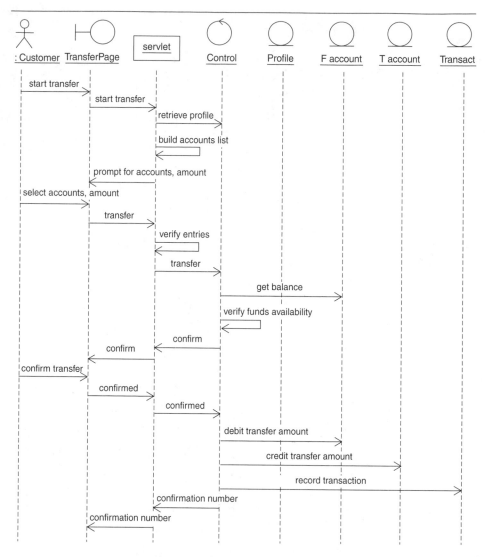

Figure 10-13 Division of responsibilities between the servlet and internal control

work to the other J2EE components, which we discuss in more detail in later chapters covering JSP and EJB technology.

The decision to split up the servlet responsibilities will vary depending on specific needs. In this case, our preference was to minimize the responsibilities of the MainServlet to being a coordinator only. A secondary level of servlets was therefore developed to handle the details of individual use cases.

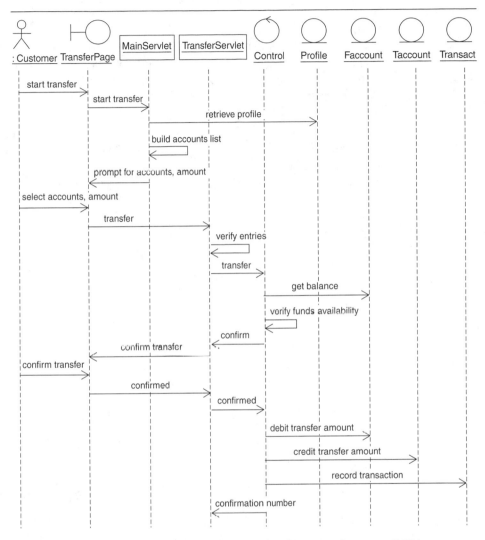

Figure 10-14 MainServlet and TransferServlet division of responsibilities

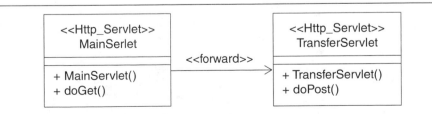

Figure 10-15 MainServlet and TransferServlet details

Summary

Servlets have a lightweight architecture and are ideally suited for request-response paradigms. Servlets are like ordinary Java classes with the exception that specific life cycle methods must exist in the servlet. Specific HTTP request handler methods are used for **HttpServlet**. Two types of servlets, **GenericServlet** and **HttpServlet**, are defined in the J2EE.

Servlets are modeled as stereotyped Java classes. UML modeling techniques can bring special focus on some aspects of servlets, such as forwarding, including, and session management by servlets.

An XML deployment descriptor is required for deploying a servlet.

Chapter 11

JavaServer Pages

- Introduction to JSP

- Anatomy of a JSP

- Tag Libraries

- JSP and the UML

- JSP in Enterprise Applications

- Summary

❖ **Process Check:**
In this chapter,
we focus on
design as we
progress through
the Rational
Unified Process
(RUP) analysis
and design disci-
pline. We also
discuss aspects
of implementa-
tion in the con-
text of the JSP
technology.

Until a few years ago, the term thin client *was unheard of. That changed with the advent of the Web browser and the subsequent rush to create sophisticated Web-based applications in virtually every industry.*

Thin clients, as we all know, utilize a markup language for presentation. Sophisticated server-side applications written in languages such as Java are thus used to generate the markup language for presentation to the client.

This intermingling of the programming side of the application with the presentation side has some drawbacks:

- *Presentation can change frequently. This means a lot of recompilation and rebuilding for reasons that have nothing to do with the application logic.*

- *The presentation has to be* coded *in the context of the programming language using constructs such as* println. *This means the presentation layout is not as readily intelligible as it is encoded within the application programming language and cannot really be previewed until runtime. From the servlet designer perspective, it is equally hard to read line after line of HTML code embedded within* println *statements.*

- *In most large organizations, the Web presentation developer role is distinct from the software developer role. This coupling has created a drawback such that the Web developers now must understand the programming side to create the presentation layout, and they can no longer use specialized tools available to them for developing the presentation.*

The JavaServer Pages (JSP) technology was conceived specifically to address these issues.

Introduction to JSP

Like servlets, JSP is a type of Java 2 Platform, Enterprise Edition (J2EE) Web component. JSP is similar to server-side scripting technology, but there is a key difference—JSP is compiled, whereas scripts are interpreted. JSP allows a program to be embedded in HTML documents, which can later be parsed by a Web server. JSP utilizes the Java Servlet technology to achieve server-side processing.

A JSP consists of Java code embedded within a structured document such as HTML or XML. The idea is to use the markup language for the static portions of the presentation and embed special tags within the page to markup the dynamic content. The tags are also used to process incoming requests from a client and generate responses as a result. When a JSP is requested, the JSP code is processed on the server, and the combined results of the processing and the static HTML page are sent back to the client.

Use of JSP allows the presentation code to be easily maintained as regular HTML code and shields the Web developer from having to deal with an unfamiliar language and tools.

Some may argue that because Java is still embedded within a JSP, the separation of presentation from business logic is not a reality. The key point to keep in mind is that it is a difference of perspective. In servlets, the presentation side is forced to absolutely live in the software development world, whereas JSPs are presentation-centric components with carefully packaged Java pieces embedded within them to handle the dynamic aspects.

Typical Uses of JSP

The JSP specification provides the JSP with the same capabilities as the servlet, and it is indeed possible to create a very confusing but legal JSP that has all the code normally put in a servlet. Similarly, it is equally possible to totally ignore the JSP technology and use servlets exclusively.

The proper usage is a combination of the two. The idea is to leverage the JSP for presentation-centric tasks and utilize the servlets where logic is paramount. A JSP is ideally suited for use in situations where dynamic content must be presented to the client. In general, JSP should be focused on presentation, and any Java code embedded within the JSP should primarily be for communication with servlets and/or other control/data entities.

A JSP does consume extra system resources (e.g., requires compilation), so it should not be used where presentation content is static. A plain HTML page should be used in such situations.

Model 1 and Model 2 Architectures

Two architectures, generally referred to as *Model 1* and *Model 2,* were especially dominant in the JSP developer community when JSPs were first introduced. Today, most development efforts make use of Model 2; however, there are still some simpler cases where a Model 1 approach has merit.

Model 1 architecture is simple in that it involves using JSPs for presentation as well as the business logic. The advantage of this approach lies in its simplicity and its ease of implementation. Unfortunately, Model 1 can quickly lead to bloated and brittle code that is hard to manage and evolve.

Model 2 architecture follows the Model-View-Controller (MVC) paradigm. It is more programmer friendly as it involves using one or more servlets as controllers. Requests are received by the frontline servlet(s), and then redirected to JSPs as warranted and required. The key to success with Model 2 is identifying the right number of servlets required to fulfill the tasks (extreme cases being a single servlet for everything and a servlet for each use case or possible action!). Another key element of this strategy is the use of JavaBeans as the model. The JavaBean acts as the "communication" vehicle between the controller servlet(s) and the JSPs. The controller fills in the JavaBean based on the request, and the JSP can then compose the actual page using values from the JavaBean. In this case, the JSP typically uses the *jsp:useBean* tag to access the JavaBean. Model 2 provides a cleaner separation of the presentation from the logic. Although the Model 2 approach is harder to implement, code developed using the Model 2 approach is easier to manage.

Some developers erroneously believe that Model 1 is obsolete and has essentially been displaced by Model 2. In fact, you can employ either of the two models depending on what you are trying to achieve. Deciding between the two models should be driven by the following guidelines:

- *Model 1:* Use this model when you are trying to build a simple Web application that does not have significant processing requirements.
- *Model 2:* Use this model when requests typically kick off extensive processing, which can result in diverse responses.

In the end, though, the best approach is to use whichever model you are comfortable with and whatever works for your development team and style.[1]

---

1. You might also come across references to Model 1.5. This is similar to Model 1 except that most of the logic is placed in the JavaBean instead of the JSP. See the References section at the end of the book for additional sources of information.

JSP versus Servlet

All JSPs are compiled into servlets and then executed within the servlet container environment. So, from a technical perspective, JSPs and servlets are quite similar in capabilities and what they can be used for.

The following list contains some key JSP advantages over servlets:

- JSPs are presentation-centric and offer a more natural development paradigm to Web presentation developers.
- JSPs make it possible to separate presentation from content (we discuss this further in the context of JSP tags and tag libraries in the "Tag Libraries" section). This means a project's presentation development can proceed in parallel with that of the logic.
- JSPs help in organizing the physical aspect of a Web application.

JSPs are compiled automatically, typically as part of the standard deployment process. Servlets, on the other hand, are a bit more manual in nature and require a manual compile step whenever they are changed unless your server tools or development environment takes care of this for you.

JSPs are often preferred over servlets if the presentation is expected to change frequently. Servlets, on the other hand, are preferred for more complex logical tasks, as they are typically easier to debug during the development process. This is primarily because you actually see the code for the servlet you are executing. Because a JSP is automatically compiled to servlet code for you, the code that is executed is in a different form than the code you originally provided in the JSP, which makes JSPs a little harder to debug. However, if you are just having the JSP do presentation tasks, this usually isn't a big problem.

The servlet versus JSP consideration is not always an either-or scenario in the context of a specific software system. It is reasonable to have a mix of both to achieve a balanced system. For example, you may want to use a servlet as a controller such that the requests get handled by the servlet. Once the servlet has taken care of the request processing (either directly or by working with other elements of the software such as EJBs), it could forward the results on to a JSP to display the results to the user.

Anatomy of a JSP

A JSP consists of two basic items: template data and JSP elements. Template data provides the static aspects, and JSP elements are used for the dynamic aspects of a JSP.

Template Data

Template data refers to the static HTML or XML content of the JSP. Although it is essential for the JSP presentation, it is relatively uninteresting from a JSP programming point of view.

Aside from the usual substitutions, such as those based on quoting and escape sequences, the template data is written verbatim as part of the JSP response.

JSP Elements

JSP elements represent the portion of the JSP that gets translated and compiled into a servlet by the JSP compiler. In syntax, JSP elements are similar to HTML elements in that they have a begin and an end tag (for example, *<B>* bold text *</B>*).

There are three types of JSP elements defined in the JSP specification: directive elements, action elements, and scripting elements.

Directive Elements

Directive elements provide global information for the translation phase. These directives are general in nature, that is, not related to a specific request and thus do not directly impact the output to the client.

Directive elements take the following form:

```
<% @directive-name directive-attribute="attribute-value" other-
attribute-value-pairs … %>
```

An example of a directive element follows:

```
<% include file="Header.jsp" %>
```

A page directive and its attributes provide a convenient mechanism for instructing the environment on the configuration of various things, such as libraries to be imported, content type of the page, buffer size, and so on. With the exception of the import attribute, other page attributes can only be defined once in the JSP.

Action Elements

Unlike directive elements, action elements come into play during the request-processing phase. JSP actions elements are written using an XML syntax in one of the following two formats:

```
<prefix:tag attribute=value attribute-value-list…/>
```

or

```
<prefix: tag attribute=value attribute-value-list> body
</prefix:tag>
```

The idea is to establish an association between tags and have a "tag handler" defined for each tag, which gets invoked to handle the tag when the tag is encountered. Tag handlers are essentially pieces of code, for example:

```
<jsp:forward page="/errorPage" />
```

Actions prefixed with "jsp" are standard actions. Some standard actions are

- Include responses sent by other JSPs
- Forward requests to others
- Query and update properties of a JavaBean residing on the server

Actions may create objects that are made available to scripting elements via certain variables.

Scripting Elements
Scripting elements bring everything together in a JSP. These elements can be declarations used for defining variables and methods, blocks of code called scriptlets, and expressions for evaluation during request processing.

Declarations
Declarations define variables and methods. The syntax for declarations is <%! Declaration %> where *declaration* can be a variable or a function, for example:

```
<%! private static MyLoginCount=0;   %>
```

Expressions
Expressions are evaluated during the request-processing phase of the JSP, and the results are converted to a string and intermixed with the template data. The result is placed in the same place where the expression was located in the JSP page.

The syntax of expressions is <% = Some expression %>.

In the XML syntax, the same is expressed as:

```
<jsp:expression>Some expression</jsp:expression>
```

For example:

```
Login Count: <%= results %>
```

Scriptlets

A scriptlet is a mini "script" of code embedded within the JSP. It can contain, among other things, declaration of variables and methods, expressions, and statements. Like expressions, scriptlets get executed at request-processing time, and any resulting output is placed in the response object.

The syntax for declaring scriptlets is <% Java Code %>.

The XML equivalent is

```
<jsp:scriptlet>Java Code</jsp:scriptlet>
```

For example:

```
:
<% int guessNum = request.getParameter("GUESS");
if (guessNum == WinningNum) { %>
Congrats, you win!!!
<% }
else
{ %>
Sorry, try again.
<% }  %>
:
```

Objects Accessible to a JSP Implicitly

Each JSP has access to some objects without explicitly declaring them in the JSP. These objects are created by the container for use within JSPs and can be assumed to exist by the JSP developers.

These implicit objects are

- *request:* Represents the incoming request that initiated the processing
- *response:* Represents the response to the current request
- *pageContext:* Provides access to page attributes and convenience methods
- *session:* Session object for the current client
- *application:* Identifies the associated **ServletContext**
- *out:* Object for writing to the output stream
- *config:* Identifies the associated servlet config for the JSP

- *page:* Similar to **this** in the context of the current JSP
- *exception:* Identifies the exception that led to the error page

Tag Libraries

One of the challenges in meeting the objectives of the JSP technology is to minimize the programming logic complexity to which content developers are exposed.

The JSP 1.1 specification introduced a new capability for creating custom JSP tag libraries, which allow for the reduction of complexity. The idea is for the developer to provide simple and easy to use custom tags that can be used by the content developers to invoke complex logic.

A Tag Handler Class

A custom tag is composed of a tag handler class. The tag handler class is responsible for telling the system what should be done when a specific tag is encountered. The class file contains the actual Java code that is executed during the request.

Tags can optionally have one or more attributes and a body, but neither is required. The simplest tag is one without a body or attributes; the most complex tag has a body as well as one or more attributes.

The following list shows examples of a tag without a body, a tag without a body but with attributes, and a tag with attributes and a body:

- A tag without a body:

```
<mytaglib:MyTag/>
```

- A tag without a body but with an attribute:

```
<mytaglib:MyTag count="11"/>
```

- A tag with a body and an attribute:

```
<mytaglib:MyTag count="10">
This is the body. It can contain actions, directives and other
things
</mytaglib:MyTag>
```

For tags without a body, the tag handler class must implement the **doStart-Tag** method. Tags without a body are useful when you just want relatively fixed content (that is, something that is not very customizable from one reference in the tag to another) accessible to the content developer.

Attributes can be used with tags without a body to facilitate customization of the results. In such cases, the tag handler class must also implement a setter method corresponding to the attribute name and be prefixed with "set". This permits the setting of the relevant attribute(s) prior to the call to the **doStartTag** method, thereby allowing different results based on the value of the attributes.

For tags with a body, the tag handler class must also implement the **doEnd-Tag** method. The **doEndTag** generally does nothing more than instruct the system to continue on; however, it is possible for it to take other actions, such as abort the execution of the JSP.

The code example in Figure 11-1 shows a tag handler class for a tag without a body.

A Tag Library Descriptor

Tags are organized into tag libraries. The tag library descriptor (.tld) file contains the list of tag names and names of associated tag handler classes.

A tag library descriptor example is shown in Figure 11-2.

Figure 11-3 shows how a custom tag is used from within a JSP.

```
import java.io.*;
import javax.servlet.jsp.*;
import javax.servlet.jsp.tagext.*;

public class MyTag extends TagSupport
{
public int doStartTag()
    {
    try {
      JspWriter out = pageContext.getOut();
      out.print("A simple tag example");
       } catch IOException e)
           {
           //handle exception
           }
    return (SKIP_BODY);
    }
    }
```

Figure 11-1　An example of a simple tag handler class

```
<?xml version="1.0" encoding="ISO-8859-1" ?>
<!DOCTYPE taglib PUBLIC "-//Sun Microsystems, Inc.//DTD JSP
Tag Library 1.2//EN" "http://java.sun.com/j2ee/dtd/web-
jsptaglibrary_1_2.dtd">

<taglib>
  <tlibversion>1.1</tlibversion>
  <jspversion>1.2</jspversion>
  <shortname>example</shortname>

 <tag>
   <name>BlankLine</name>
   <tagclass>com.taglib.homedirect.BlankLine</tagclass>
   <bodycontent>EMPTY</bodycontent>

    <info>Inserts a blank line
    </info>
 </tag>
</taglib>
```

Figure 11-2   Tag library descriptor example

```
<%@ taglib uri="MyUtils-taglib.tld">
<%<html>
...
<utils:BlankLine />
<!--inserts a blank line-->
...
</html>
```

Figure 11-3   Using a custom tag from within a JSP

JSP and the UML

Modeling of JSP in the UML is somewhat complicated by the fact that a JSP is really a hybrid between a Web page for the client side and some logic that executes on the server side.

JSPs can of course be modeled as a single class in the logical view; however, this means an unclear separation of responsibilities between the client and the server sides and results in some confusion. For example, how do you establish whether an operation will be executed on the client or the server? You also do not know what kind of relationships make sense for such a class and in what context they are meaningful.

Modeling a JSP as a single class also defeats an objective of modeling, namely to clearly identify the architecturally significant pieces within the model in their appropriate context.

To get around this limitation, we use UML extension mechanisms to partition each JSP into two conceptual elements:[2]

- *<<ClientPage>>*: This represents the behavior of the JSP on the client side, that is, the externally visible presentation aspects of the JSP. Client pages have associations with client-side resources, such as other client pages, applets, JavaBeans, and such.

- *<<ServerPage>>*: This represents the behavior of the JSP on the server side. It primarily focuses on the internal logic associated with processing a request and providing a response. Server pages have relationships with other server-side resources, such as external systems, databases, and controllers in the system.

The relationship between a client page and a server page is also special and is defined as a <<Build>> relationship where the server page builds a client page. When a server page builds a client page, the result is an HTML or XML stream that is sent to the browser through which the request was originated. The build relationship between a server page and client page is shown in Figure 11-4.

A reminder about the icons used in the diagram in Figure 11-4. As you may recall from our discussion in Chapter 3, UML allows the use of stereotypes or icons for representing model elements. The icons used in the diagram[3] and in subsequent chapters take advantage of this facility.

ServerPage   ClientPage

Figure 11-4   Server page and client page

---

2. Originally proposed in *Building Web Applications with UML* [Connallen, 99].

3. These icons are based on the Web Application Extension icons as supported in Rational Rose.

Modeling Client-Side Relationships

The conceptual client page of a JSP can have relationships with several types of entities in addition to the associated server page:

- *Other client pages:* A client page may have incoming or outgoing <<link>> relationships with other client pages in the model.
- *Applets:* A client page may have applets associated with it. An applet is modeled as a class with the <<Java Applet>> stereotype. Relationships between a client page and an applet are modeled as an aggregation relationship or as a plain association.
- *Forms:* Forms are a common mechanism for accepting input via a browser. A form is modeled as a class with the <<Form>> stereotype. Input fields on a form map to attributes on the class. Forms are really a part of the client page, so this relationship is modeled as an aggregation relationship with the client page. Forms do not exist independently from a client page.

Figure 11-5 shows an example of JSP client page relationships.

Modeling Server-Side Relationships

Server-side JSP relationships fall into the following categories:

- *Other server pages:* A server page may be associated with other server pages. Such relationships are modeled as either <<forward>> or <<include>> relationships.

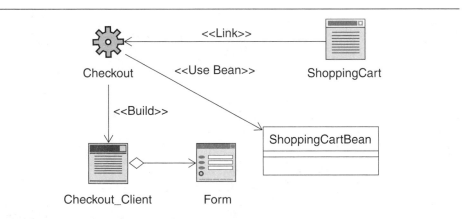

Figure 11-5   Client page relationships

- *Servlets:* Servlets are comparable to JSP behavior in this context. As such, they are modeled via the approach used for other server pages (outlined in the preceding bullet item).

- *Implicit objects accessible to the server page:* The objects that are utilized by the server page manifest themselves as unidirectional associations between the server page and the implicit object classes.

- *JavaBeans:* A page may access, or use, JavaBeans. In such situations, the relationship is modeled as an association relationship stereotyped as <<Use Bean>>. This represents a jsp:useBean tag in the JSP. By having this relationship, the JavaBean can be accessed from within the JSP.

- *Other classes:* A server page may have other classes that are important for showing the full scope of the server page. Relationships with such classes are shown using associations as required.

- *Dependency on other classes or libraries:* A server page may import other classes and libraries required to achieve its functionality. Such relationships are modeled as dependency relationships using the usual UML notation of a dashed line with an arrowhead.

- *Taglibs:* A server page may use custom defined tag libraries. You model this relationship by showing a dependency relationship from the server page to the tag library descriptor file. Optionally, the tag library descriptor can show dependency on the associated tag handler classes.

- *Enterprise JavaBeans (EJBs):* A server page may invoke methods on an EJB. This relationship is modeled as a directional association from the server page to the EJB Home and Remote interfaces for the subsystem representing the EJB.

Figure 11-6 shows an example of JSP server page relationships. In this example, the user begins at the PayBills JSP. Upon entry of the necessary bill payment details, the BillForm is submitted to the BillServlet, which coordinates with the control component to actually perform the bill payment transaction. Note how the BillPayer JSP includes the Banner and Footer JSPs. This is an example of what the RUP terms a *presentation component*. This approach is useful because it provides for a template-like approach to the user interface. Directives are used to include other JSPs and HTML pages to provide a consistent yet dynamic user interface throughout.

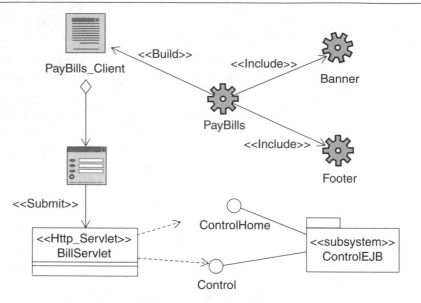

Figure 11-6   Server page relationships

JSP in Enterprise Applications

In Chapter 8, we discussed the use of boundary objects to capture and isolate interaction between a use case and external entities such as with other subsystems and with users. JSPs provide an effective yet simple vehicle for the interaction of the latter type, that is, with users of the system.

For instance, consider the HomeDirect use cases identified in Chapter 16. Each use case that interacts with the customer actor means that some sort of user interface is required. There is also some form of interface required for the Login/Logout use cases, which are included by the other use cases.

To understand how JSPs are used in enterprise apps, let's start with the Login use case. A login Web page, representing the login boundary object, would be appropriate for presentation to the user when the user attempts to use the banking system initially and initiates the Login use case. Additionally, there is a need for the user to enter a username and password via the Web page for validation by the system.

A controller is also required for the Login use case, as identified via the login control object during the analysis. Because we want to have the ability to change the presentation easily, we have chosen to follow the Model 2 architecture for our application and will use the JSPs primarily for presentation rather than as replacements for servlets.

In light of this decision, we will create a servlet to handle the processing of the login form. Although use case control objects often merge at design time, this use case acts as a "gatekeeper" of sorts in the sense that none of the other use cases can be executed until this one is successful. Given this prerequisite, it is appropriate to keep the login validation isolated from the rest of the application.

Figure 11-7 shows the overall structure of the Login use case.

Let's take a quick walkthrough to clarify what is occurring in Figure 11-7. The Login.jsp is the entry point into the use case. It builds the login client, which includes a LoginForm to allow the user to enter information. When the form is filled in and submitted by the user, the LoginServlet processes it by interacting with the appropriate entity objects to verify the information entered (we discuss the entity objects mapping to the solution domain in Chapter 13). If the login fails, the login servlet displays an error message, and then restarts at Login.jsp. If the login is successful, it is forwarded to another entity (not shown).

Note the use of Banner.jsp and Footer.jsp. Although we could have included the information directly into individual JSPs, we have chosen this approach as it

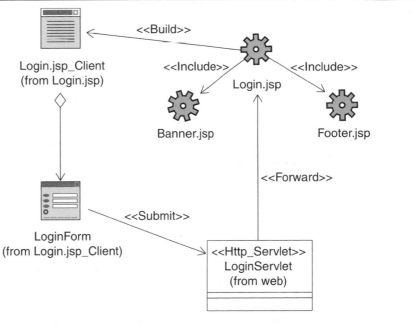

Figure 11-7   Login use case design

permits better reuse across the entire application and also serves to keep these details isolated.

A common technique in Model 2 is to use a JavaBean as a means of passing information between a servlet and a JSP. The idea is for the servlet to obtain and set the information in a JavaBean, and then forward the request on to the JSP. The JSP in turn uses the JavaBean to obtain and publish the information to the end user of the information. We use this technique for communication between the centralized controller for the remaining use cases and the various pages for displaying the results to the end user.

Figure 11-8 shows an example of this technique in the context of the List transactions use case.

In the figure, Main.jsp provides the anchor page for invoking the various commands available to HomeDirect users. Any commands invoked by the user are submitted to the MainServlet, which then coordinates the activities with the control and entity objects (not shown but discussed in detail in Chapter 12 and Chapter 13, respectively). When MainServlet has gathered all the information required for the response, it places the information in the JavaBean and forwards

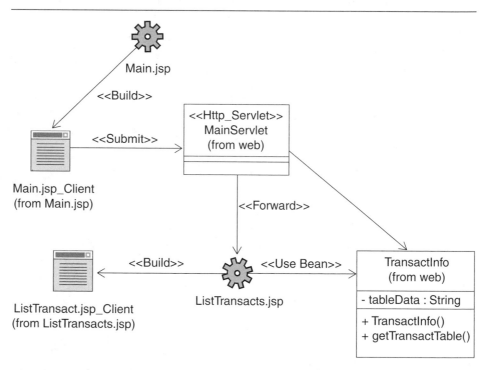

Figure 11-8 Using JavaBeans to share information

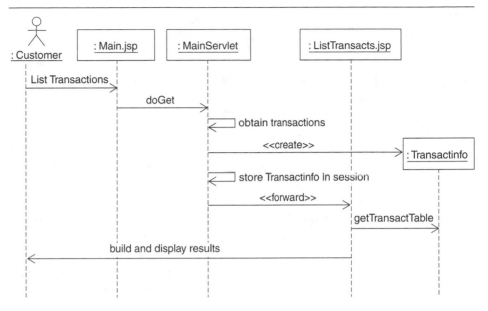

Figure 11-9   Sequence diagram detailing the login scenario

the request on to the JSP. The JSP then accesses the bean using the jsp:useBean tag and publishes it to the end user.

Figure 11-9 illustrates the dynamics associated with this scenario via a sequence diagram.

The code fragment associated with setting up the TransactInfo bean for use by the ListTransacts.jsp is shown in Figure 11-10.

```
// Get the user session
HttpSession session = request.getSession(true);
...
// Find collection of transacts
...
// Create bean to pass info to JSP page
TransactInfo transactInfo = new TransactInfo(transacts);
session.setAttribute("TransactInfo", transactInfo);
...
// Forward to next JSP page
RequestDispatcher dispatcher =
getServletContext().getRequestDispatcher("/ListTransacts.jsp");
dispatcher.forward(request, response);
```

Figure 11-10   Using a JavaBean to share information with a JSP

Summary

JSPs are intended to separate content from presentation. They are conceptually very similar to servlets. JSPs are essentially similar to a server-side scripting technology, the key difference being that JSPs are compiled, whereas scripts are interpreted.

Although a JSP is equivalent to a servlet, a JSP is not intended as a replacement for a servlet. Two development paradigms, generally referred to as Model 1 and Model 2, provide the underpinnings for effective use of servlets and JSPs.

A JSP consists of Java code embedded within a structured document such as HTML or XML. Tags are used to mark up specific pieces of JSP code. Users can also create their own tag libraries in the form of taglib libraries.

In the UML, JSPs and associated technology relationships are modeled by stereotyping existing UML constructs. A JSP is modeled as being composed of two distinct conceptual elements: the client page and the server page. The relationship between the client page and the server page is modeled as a build relationship. Client and server pages can also have relationships with other client and server pages.

Chapter 12

Session Beans

❖ **Process Check:**
Once again our
focus is on
design as we
progress through
the Rational
Unified Process
(RUP) analysis
and design disci-
pline. We also
discuss some
aspects of imple-
mentation in the
context of the
EJB technology.

In Chapter 10, we decided to evolve the control object into a pair of servlets and have another control object focus on the internal interaction and business logic. That internal interaction and business logic is the domain of a specific type of Enterprise JavaBeans (EJB) known as a session bean.

In this chapter, we start with a general discussion of EJB, and then look at how session beans are modeled in the Unified Modeling Language (UML). We later dig into the key technological aspects of session beans, and then finish with a discussion of where they fit into our evolving HomeDirect online banking example.

Introduction to Enterprise JavaBeans

The EJB specification is at the very core of the Java 2 Platform, Enterprise Edition (J2EE) platform. It defines a comprehensive component model for building scalable, distributed server-based enterprise Java application components.

The main ideas behind the EJB specification are to:

- Enable third parties, such as application server vendors, to provide as much of the commonly required underlying infrastructure (such as distributed communication, security, transactions, etc.) as possible in a uniform manner, thereby significantly simplifying the task of the distributed application developer.

- Provide the means to create reusable components that can be shared across platforms to reduce the overall development effort.

- Provide a blueprint for the implementation of Enterprise Java applications.

- Provide a model for the development of Enterprise Java applications such that the development, assembly, and deployment aspects are decoupled.

In order to deliver on this vision, EJBs rely on several key concepts:

- *Container:* Rather than deploying directly onto the application server, EJBs are deployed within a container. A container provides the execution environment for EJBs, manages its life cycle, and provides additional services. (We discussed the container concept in Chapter 2.)

- *Proxy pattern:* Rather than a monolithic component, EJBs take an approach based on the proxy pattern. The idea is to separate out the component into client and remote objects. Thus, an EJB user only sees the client object represented by the EJB interfaces, and the remote object is free to change implementation details, such as network location, underlying transport, and so on, as required.

- *Deployment descriptor:* To facilitate a decoupling of the development from deployment, that is, to enable customization of the component post-development, EJBs use the concept of a deployment descriptor. The deployment descriptor acts as a means of declarative customization of the EJB without requiring modification to the EJB code itself.

Using EJBs just because you think they are cool or because everyone else is using them can get you in trouble down the road. There may be perfectly good solutions to the problem you are trying to tackle that do not require EJBs.

The following list contains some possible reasons to consider using EJBs:

- You need to support multiple client types, for example, a Java application and browser-based front end. In this situation, the use of EJBs makes sense because you can put the business logic and data in a set of EJB components that can be accessed by multiple client types.

- Multiple sources need to access and update data in a concurrent fashion. EJBs provide built-in capabilities to address this issue.

- Your application requires the use of database transactions. This capability is built into EJBs and you can expect to see enhanced support in this area.

- Your application requires fine-grained security such as the ability to restrict access at the class operation level. This is again provided by EJBs.

- Your application must be scalable to a very large number of users. EJBs are designed for building large-scale distributed systems, so using EJBs will make the task of adding additional servers much easier.

- High availability is required or will be required for the application. If you anticipate the need for zero or very little downtime, you will probably require some kind of redundancy mechanism. This is not directly supported as such by EJBs, but coupled with a good application server, it becomes easier to achieve this with EJB technology.

There are currently three different kinds of EJBs. We now focus our attention on EJBs known as session beans.

EJB Views and the UML

Structurally, EJBs consist of a main Java class, often called the *implementation* class or the *bean* class, and two interfaces: Home and Remote. In the case of entity beans (discussed in Chapter 13), there is also a *primary key* class. The relationships between these items, as well as the particular J2EE base objects these items extend and implement, give the EJB its particular functionality and usefulness as a J2EE component.

All EJBs make use of a deployment descriptor to hold additional information pertaining to the component. This includes information like transaction settings on business methods, settings for the bean type, security settings, and more.

EJB component types are deployed within an EJB container with the help of a deployment utility. An EJB server hosts the EJB container. An EJB server is often referred to as an enterprise application server, or most commonly as an application server. The particular capabilities and level of compliance of the EJB server determine which version of the EJB specification you need to be working with.

Representing an Enterprise JavaBean in UML

Given UML's breadth, it should not come as a surprise that there are seemingly multiple potential ways to represent an EJB in the UML. Obvious candidates appear to be the two UML constructs: *class* and *component.*

A UML class is deficient in that unlike an EJB, a class is typically fine-grained. In addition, a class does not offer a very self-contained representation of an EJB by itself and requires additional modeling support (such as packaging) to achieve that.

You could possibly merge the different elements that make up an EJB and represent them as a single UML class, for example, in a fashion similar to that shown in Figure 12-1. In such a case, the class would need to have several different compartments, each containing design information pertaining to a different aspect of the complete EJB.

This approach might first appear to present a more compact EJB model, but the large number of necessary compartments can make working with this representation harder to understand and more prone to error. It also exposes far more information to an EJB client than is necessary or desirable.

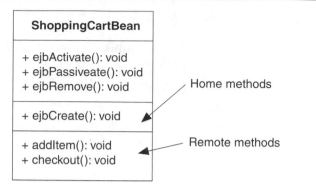

Figure 12-1 Example of a class-based EJB representation

Similarly, although the UML has the notion of *component,* it is not quite the same as an EJB component. The UML component is more closely associated with implementation, for example, representing a physical artifact such as a source code file. Furthermore, UML components are not typically modeled during analysis and design.[1]

Another approach[2] is to use something that combines the capabilities of a class (more precisely, a *classifier* in general) as well as a package, namely a *subsystem*. As mentioned in Chapter 4, a subsystem is essentially a group of UML elements that represent a behavioral unit in a model. It can have interfaces as well as operations. Subsystems, unlike components, are typically significant from an analysis and design perspective and do not suffer from the fine-grained nature of classes.

Given the sound rationale for using a subsystem for representing an EJB, the advantages it offers, and the fact that this approach is likely to become the de facto standard, we have chosen to use the subsystem construct to represent EJBs in this book.

It is best to look at EJBs from different perspectives relevant to specific roles (e.g., user, developer, etc.). Let's take a look at these different views of an EJB. We'll discuss session beans and technology details thereafter to elaborate further on these views.

---

1. Note that UML 1.4 will change the notion of a UML component and bring it closer to the J2EE definition of a component.

2. Proposed by the UML EJB mapping team in response to JSR 26, Sun Community Process (available at java.sun.com). For a good discussion of the rationale for this approach, see *Modeling Components and Frameworks with UML* by Cris Kobryn, Communications of the ACM, October 2000.

Client View

The client view of an EJB includes what the client can access, which consists of the Home and Remote interfaces. In a UML class diagram, the client view of an EJB is represented by a UML subsystem for reasons discussed earlier.

An advantage of using the subsystem approach is the ability to expose those aspects that are of particular relevance or hide irrelevant details. Figure 12-2 gives an example of a client view showing elements inside the subsystem. Note the specific stereotypes shown on the different elements. The stereotypes indicate that the UML constructs have been extended in their meaning to support special needs of the J2EE architecture. Such stereotyping also offers a simple and compact means of identifying the specific role played by a specific model element that is part of an EJB.

In practice, it is often desired to just use one of the more compact representations of the UML subsystem for the client view. This has the advantage of avoiding unnecessary clutter in your model diagrams. In this case, the preferred client view representation is shown in Figure 12-3.

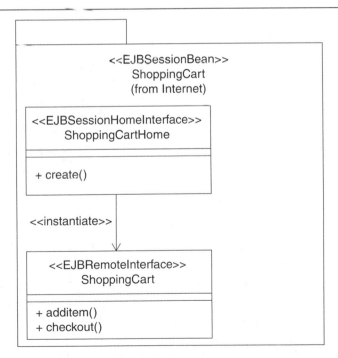

Figure 12-2   Full client view representation of a session bean in a UML class diagram

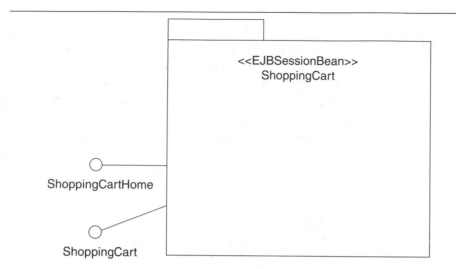

Figure 12-3 Compact client view representation of a session bean in a UML class diagram

Internal View

The internal view of an EJB includes all components of the client view, the implementation class and its associated relationships, and any other classes the user may have added to the design of the EJB. In a UML class diagram, these elements appear as normal classes and interfaces.

The client view is the façade for an EJB. The internal view of an EJB is obtained by exposing the UML package contents completely, as shown in Figure 12-4.

Session Beans

The areas we have discussed thus far apply equally well to all EJBs. Now we'll focus our attention specifically on the session bean type of EJB.

Session beans were the first EJB type to receive wide adoption and general use. In many J2EE development projects today, session beans are the only EJB type actually being used. This is likely to change in the future as the EJB specification enhances existing capabilities and introduces additional bean types, and as enterprise application servers improve their support for both the currently existing and newly defined types.

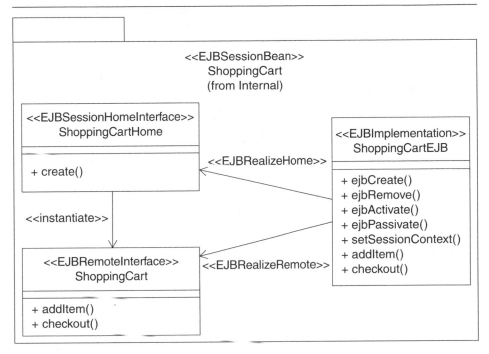

Figure 12-4   Internal view representation of a session bean in a UML class diagram

Popular Beans

Session beans are currently used primarily to handle client transactions or, as the name implies, client sessions.

The key advantages of using session beans are

- Built-in transaction management capabilities
- Built-in state management capabilities

The beauty of using EJB components is that many additional benefits, such as automated resource management, concurrency, and security, are also provided by the EJB container.

Every time you shop at a Web site built on the J2EE platform, there is a high likelihood that a session bean is handling much of the state and transaction management aspects of your shopping experience. Likewise, when dealing with your online trading brokerage, an Internet banking account, or any number of services you can imagine on the Web, session beans are most often being used to handle your transactions.

J2EE Versions

The topics covered in this chapter apply equally well to session beans using J2EE 1.3 as well as J2EE 1.2. There are very few differences between the two specifications with respect to session beans, and from a UML modeling point of view, they are essentially identical. As you will see in later chapters, there are other EJB component types where this is not necessarily the case.

Types of Session Beans and Conversational State

Session beans are designed to handle as many of the low-level state and transactional aspects of a client session as possible. However, there are several levels of control that Web developers may choose from to determine how much of the EJB container capabilities they want to use, and how much they still want to code manually.

Session beans come in two major varieties, *stateful* and *stateless*. This determines whether or not the component can retain what is known as *conversational state*.

Conversational state is defined as the data describing the conversation represented by a specific client pairing with a session object.

If the session bean retains this state, it provides the client with the ability to work with a particular session object, leave for some arbitrary amount of time (seconds, minutes, hours, days, etc.), and then return at a later time and pick up exactly where he or she left off with the same session object. This is called a *stateful session bean*.

In the opposite case, a client works with a given session object, and then leaves for some random amount of time. Immediately upon leaving, the session object is dropped and no conversational state is retained. If the client returns, a new session object is created and everything starts from the beginning. This is called a *stateless session bean*.

Because stateless session beans take up less system resources, they tend to be deployed more often than the stateful variety. As the requirements and client expectations for a session bean grow and EJB containers provide more efficient resource management capabilities, it becomes more compelling to use stateful session beans and reap the additional benefits.

The most common characteristics for a stateful session bean include

- Created for use by one client only
- Callable by a unique identifier
- Retain state across methods and transactions
- Retain state through instance passivation
- May implement session synchronization

The most common characteristics for a stateless session bean include

- Created for use by many clients, one at a time
- No unique identifier; usually part of a bean pool
- No state kept across methods and transactions
- No state kept through instance passivation
- Cannot implement session synchronization

Modeling Session Bean Conversational State

UML statechart diagrams can be used effectively to model the conversational state of a stateful session bean. Such modeling is useful in understanding the overall flow of the conversation and helps simplify the design of the bean business logic.

An example is shown in Figure 12-5.

This example depicts the conversational state for a TravelReservations bean, a version of which is commonly encountered on most Web-based flight reservations portals.

Making flight reservations involves several steps including setting up user preferences, such as the number of seats required, desired flight times, airline preferences, price range, and so on. The user then typically provides a pair of dates and to/from cities, which are used as the outbound (starting city to destination) and return (inbound) segments.

The user is presented with the flight selections for the outbound segment and asked to choose a flight. The process continues until the user has identified suitable flights and decides to have the ticket issued or start over with different dates. A successful scenario leading to the issuance of a ticket is shown in Figure 12-6.

As you can see from this statechart and sequence diagram, the use of the statechart to model the conversational state makes the TravelReservations bean easier to comprehend and implement. For instance, it is easy to see that the user can only set up the preference prior to initiating the request for suitable flights.

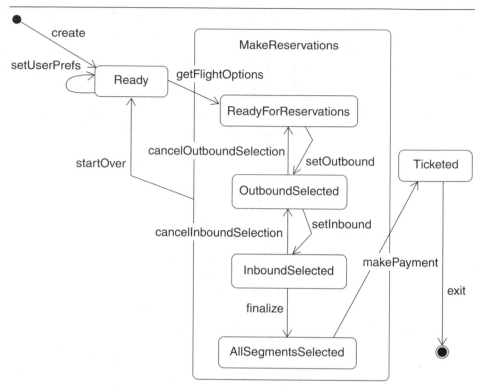

Figure 12-5 Modeling session bean conversational state

Any change in the user preferences requires the user to start over. This may or may not have been the design intent but modeling the conversational state in this fashion makes this very obvious.

Each of the states has specific implications for the data. That is, the states explicitly identify the data required by the session bean as it moves through the conversational states. For example, when the session bean is in the *Ready* state, it does not have any information related to the flight segments. Similarly, when the session bean is in the *AllSegmentsSelected* state, you know that it must have complete and valid information related to all flight segments.

Instance Passivation

Passivation is a useful feature the EJB container provides specifically for stateful session beans. Passivation occurs when the EJB is not currently in the middle of a client transaction, and the EJB server decides it needs to swap out the bean to

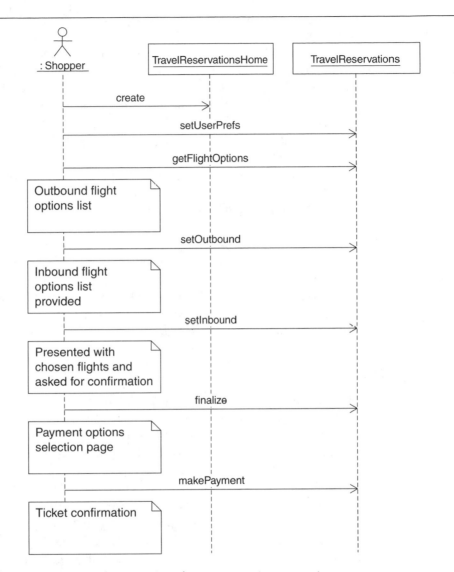

Figure 12-6 TravelReservations bean reservation scenario

free up some memory or other system resources. The swapped out EJB can then be activated again, usually on the next client interaction that requires it.

For stateful session beans, the client is always returned to the same unique session object once it is activated again. Only the particular client that initially created this session object can do so. This is necessary to retain the conversational state as well as to provide security for the information the client has placed within the particular session object.

In the stateless case, instance passivation is not specifically needed because it is inherent in the way the EJB container works for beans of this type. When the client is finished with this type of session object, it is cleaned and released back to a bean pool. The next time the session object is activated, it is used by whichever client session needs it at the time, but note that the session object has effectively been recycled to appear as good as new each time. While in the bean pool, these objects are still in an active state, and if the EJB server decides it needs to free up some resources, it just removes some of the idle session beans from the pool, effectively destroying them. So passivation in this case is really just destruction, which is okay because there is really no conversational state to hold on to.

Using the bean pool concept allows for many more clients to be handled than there are session beans available; however, keep in mind the limitations that this case can impose, especially for longer and more involved Web transactions. You don't want to choose stateless beans only to find that the amount of reinitialization time required by the session bean greatly outweighs any resource benefits you otherwise gain.

Cleanup and Removal

There are limits to the amount of time a session bean can hold on to resources on the EJB server without doing any useful work. For example, perhaps the client left the Web site to do something else and forgot to come back, or the network may be down, or the session object is holding information for a shopping cart that the client never came back to purchase after a given number of days. For such cases, the EJB container uses a bean removal mechanism.

Removal can occur for all session bean types. This is usually the result of a session bean either being in the passivation state for longer than the EJB timeout setting allows, or the EJB server is starving for resources and needs to destroy some idle beans. In very odd cases, this can also be the result of an EJB server failure or crash, so Web developers need to design their session beans to be able to withstand this scenario.

For stateful sessions, Web client scenarios like those previously described will typically result in removal. If the Web client that created the session object never comes back, the session must be destroyed because no one else can ever make use of it.

For stateless sessions, the reasons for removal are tied more to the particular EJB server implementation. In this case, the server might notice that the pool of session beans is underused, and that some other components being hosted need more system resources. So in this case, the size of the session bean pool would be condensed as required.

It is important to note that removal of a session object can never occur while a client is in the middle of using it. Removal can only happen while in the passivation or idle state. Of course a server crash or other catastrophic failure can give you the rough equivalent of removal, but this is clearly undesirable.

Transactions

Consider the Transfer funds use case discussed in earlier chapters. The use case boils down to debiting one account and crediting the equivalent amount to another account.

A problem arises when a failure occurs after the funds have been debited from the first account but not yet credited to the second account. This is problematic because, in general, you would want both the debit and credit to take place or, if one failed, neither to take place. In other words, the set of activities is closely tied to each other, and you want them to be carried out as if they were a single *unit-of-work*.[3] This unit-of-work is commonly referred to as a *business transaction* or simply *transaction*.

Another reason for transactions is the inherent distributed nature of enterprise software and the need to not only minimize exception handling logic in the client, but also to have it applied consistently without repetitious coding in multiple tiers. For example, exceptions do not offer a lot of information about the state of the requested activity. Use of transactions avoids reliance on exception handling to determine the future course of action.

Systems are generally expected to use transactions that follow the *ACID* principles:

- *Atomic:* Transactions must execute completely or not at all. Transactions successfully completed are *committed* (data updated); otherwise, the entire transaction is *rolledback.*

- *Consistent:* Proactively ensure that the system is in a consistent state. For example, in the case of the Transfer funds use case, if the transaction fails for whatever reason, the system retains consistency by reverting back to the state prior to the start of the failed transaction. If the transaction completes successfully, the consistency check requires that the balance of the

---

3. From Richard Monson-Haefel's *Enterprise JavaBeans,* O'Reilly Press, 1999. Recommended reading.

debited account and the balance of the credited amount be adjusted exactly by the transfer amount.

- *Isolated:* While the transaction is executing, the data being accessed by the transaction cannot be interfered with or accessed by another process or transaction until after the transaction is complete.

- *Durable:* Changes made as a result of the transaction are written to permanent data store. This allows recovery of the system without loss of committed transactions in the case of system crashes.

The ACID principles can serve as a guiding light in the design of session beans. A properly designed bean should meet the ACID test. You can compare a session bean design against each of the principles to see whether it complies.

Transaction Demarcation

Session beans are designed primarily to be transactional in nature. Business methods defined in the session bean are executed either as transactional methods or not, depending on the attributes set in the deployment descriptor for the bean. When a method is defined as being transactional, it must be called with a transaction context, which is either provided by the client using the session or by the EJB container itself.

A transaction context provides access to specific calls used to indicate critical points in the processing of a transaction. Depending on the demarcation type used, these calls are either made manually by the developer of the EJB or automatically by the EJB container. They are usually referred to as delimiters, or transaction demarcation methods:

- **begin:** Indicates the transaction is about to begin processing.

- **commit:** Indicates the transaction completed successfully and should now be committed to the database.

- **rollback:** Indicates the transaction failed for some reason and should not be committed. An effective **rollback** implies that the session object is returned to the state it was in before transaction processing started.

The transaction context can be used within a single business method or across any number of session bean calls. Note that the transactions must be flat, meaning a transaction cannot be nested within another in a session bean.

Bean-Managed Transactions

The first type of transaction demarcation is referred to as bean-managed transaction demarcation. This is also commonly referred to as client-managed or bean-managed transactions. In any case, this setting in the deployment descriptor implies that a client will write its own transaction handling code, possibly making use of the **javax.transaction.UserTransaction** interface, and demarcate the transaction by making the appropriate **begin**, **commit**, and **rollback** calls as necessary.

This type of demarcation provides the most control to the user, but in many cases where the transactional needs are fairly standard, this could cause the EJB developer to do more work than is necessary. In fact, it could eliminate one of the primary benefits for using a session bean in the first place.

Having transactional boundaries that cross more than a single business method can be a reason for using bean-managed transactions.

Container-Managed Transactions

In most cases, clients prefer to have the EJB container take care of these transaction demarcation calls. In the case of container-managed transactions, the container knows how and when to invoke the **begin** and **commit** requests as well as when to perform some standard processing to effectively do a **rollback** operation when it becomes necessary.

Using this method causes the EJB developer to have less control over what is actually done at different points during the transaction. But the major benefit is that low-level transaction details are taken care of for you, and this in itself is usually reason enough to use session beans in this mode of operation.

In some cases, the EJB developer might determine there is still some special processing that needs to be done just when the transaction is about to start or just after it completes. In this case, the developer can still choose to use container-managed transactions while at the same time make use of the special methods called out by the **SessionSynchronization** interface.

The SessionSynchronization Interface

With container-managed transaction demarcation, the EJB developer has the additional choice of implementing the **SessionSynchronization** interface. This choice is only valid for session beans. In this case, the EJB container still makes the demarcation calls for you, but it also provides you with access to overload the following three methods in your bean class:

- **afterBegin:** Issued immediately after the **begin** call for the transaction being made and before any part of the business method actually executes.

- **beforeCompletion:** Issued immediately after a **commit** call for the transaction being made and before the **commit** is actually performed on the transaction. This is the last point where a session can decide to **rollback** the transaction just before it completes.

- **afterCompletion:** Issued after a **commit** call for the transaction being made and immediately after the **commit** is actually performed on the transaction. This method provides a boolean argument that determines if the **commit** call actually succeeded or not.

In this way, the session bean can use the advantages provided by the EJB container of already knowing how to make the transaction demarcation calls, but at the same time allow the session bean to handle specific situations in a nonstandard fashion. All three of the methods shown in Figure 12-7 are treated like any other session bean life cycle method.

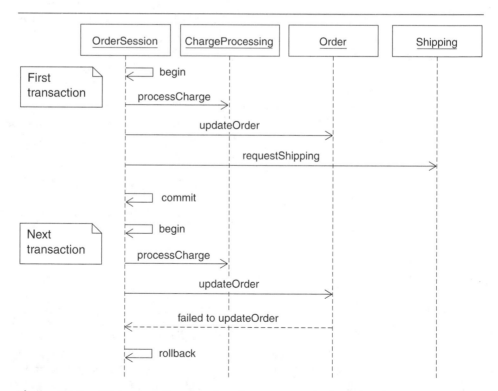

Figure 12-7   Sequence diagram showing some typical session bean transactions

Note that in Figure 12-7 the **begin/commit/rollback** operations are not invoked on the OrderSession EJB itself, but are shown as such for brevity. The methods are in fact defined by the userTransaction object obtained from the ejbContext object. The ejbContext object provides methods that can be used by an EJB to access the runtime environment details from the container in which it is running.

Limitations for Stateless Session Beans

Note that for stateless session beans, both bean-managed and container-manager transaction demarcation are possible, but implementing the **SessionSynchronization** interface is specifically not allowed in this case. Also, there is an inherent limitation where session objects that do not retain conversational state cannot possibly allow for transactions to span more than one business method. For these reasons, we find in practice that stateless session beans can only really be used successfully when the transactions involved are relatively small and simple. Transactions that are more complicated demand the full capability of a stateful session bean.

Transaction Attributes

As mentioned earlier, for container-managed demarcation, a transaction attribute is associated with each EJB method and is indicated in the deployment descriptor for the EJB. These values instruct the EJB container on how it should manage the client transaction whenever a given EJB method is called. Just about all user-defined methods in the EJB require this value, whereas several of the inherited methods that are always found in an EJB cannot use this setting.

Transaction attribute settings basically tell the EJB container whether you want to run the method in the client's transaction, create a new transaction, or run the method with no transaction. Running within a transaction implies that you are running with a transaction context. This context is specifically required for cases where your EJB method requires access to resource managers or where the persistent state of the EJB is also involved.

For session beans, transaction attributes are used with all of the business methods added to the Remote interface. The following list contains the relevant values and their meaning:

- **NotSupported:** This method is run without a transaction context. If one has been passed in, it is ignored for the life of the method call and restored upon completion.
- **Required:** This method is run with a transaction context. If none has been supplied, a new one is created to use during the method call.

- **Supported:** If the method is called without a context, it works just like **Not-Supported**. If called with a context, it runs exactly like the **Required** case.

- **RequiresNew:** This method is run with a new transaction context created and used during the call. If one has been passed in, it is ignored for the life of the method call, and the new context is used instead and is restored upon completion.

- **Mandatory:** This method is run with a transaction context. If none has been passed in, an exception is thrown.

- **Never:** This method is run without a transaction context. If one is supplied, an exception is thrown.

Modeling Transactions

EJB transactions may be bean-managed or container-managed. Although both utilize the same approach at a micro level, that is, from the perspective of what is happening underneath the covers, the visibility and control at the bean developer level is different.

In the case of bean-managed transactions, the transaction boundaries can be made obvious by showing the use of the appropriate operations in a sequence or collaboration diagram. For an example, see Figure 12-7.

But no such possibility exists for container-managed transactions, as the identification of a transaction is of a declarative nature.

One possible approach that can be used consistently across both types of transactions is to use sequence diagram messages with appropriate stereotypes to identify the transaction requirements.

Session Bean Technology

For the client, a session bean is seen as an object that implements some particular business logic that the client needs and typically is involved with some sort of transactional or state management requirements. Any given session object is only ever available to a single client; however, as you have just seen, session objects can be recycled and reused if they are stateless.

Home Interface

Every session bean needs to provide a Home interface. This is the interface used by the client program to invoke the basic bean life cycle methods. The Home interface of every session bean must define at least one method, **create<METHOD>**, which creates an instance of the session object, where **<METHOD>** can be any method name using **create** as the prefix plus any combination of arguments.

For stateful session beans, any number of these **create** methods can be defined with any valid number of argument combinations. For stateless sessions, there can only be a single **create** method with nothing else added to the name, and it must take no arguments.

For both session bean types, there are also **remove** life cycle methods that are already present in the base EJB interfaces; therefore, they don't need to be defined again.

An example of session bean Home interface code follows:

```
package com.homedirect.ejb.control;

import java.rmi.RemoteException;
import javax.ejb.*;

import com.homedirect.ejb.profile.Profile;

public interface ControlHome extends javax.ejb.EJBHome
{
    public com.homedirect.ejb.control.Control create()
        throws java.rmi.RemoteException,
        javax.ejb.CreateException;
}
```

Remote Interface

Every session bean also needs to provide a Remote interface. This is the interface used by the client program to invoke all of the specific business methods that the session bean has been built to support. Just about any method names and arguments can be used, but of course it's a good idea to stay away from names that already have an alternate meaning in the implementation class.

Both types of session beans require a Remote interface and the details for both are similar.

An example of session bean Remote interface code follows:

```
package com.homedirect.ejb.control;

import java.rmi.RemoteException;
import javax.ejb.*;
...
public interface Control extends javax.ejb.EJBObject
{
 public Profile getProfile() throws java.rmi.RemoteException;
```

```
 public void setProfile(Profile profile) throws
java.rmi.RemoteException;
…
 public String TransferFunds(    String fromAccount,
                                 String toAccount,
                                 long lAmount)
 throws java.rmi.RemoteException, AccountException,
GeneratorException;
…
}
```

Implementation Class

Additionally, each session bean has an implementation class or session bean class. It consists of the actual implementations for all methods called out in the Home interface and the Remote interface as well as the required session bean life cycle methods.

The implementation class must contain these methods:

- **ejbCreate<METHOD>:** For every **create** method called out in the Home interface, there must be a matching method in the implementation class that differs only in that the prefix used on the method name is **ejbCreate** instead of **create**. Arguments must also match, but note that the return types are different. This method is often minimal in size, perhaps performing just a few simple initialization steps for the EJB.

- **ejbRemove:** This method must exist with no arguments and gets called when one of the interface **remove** methods is invoked or when the EJB container initiates a remove action on its own. This method does any final cleanup of the EJB—the opposite of the initialization steps.

- **setSessionContext:** This method must exist and is called by the EJB container to allow the session bean to store the session context information in a local instance variable. In most cases, this method consists of just one line to store the context.

- **Business methods:** All business methods defined in the Remote interface must have an exact match in the bean class in terms of method name and arguments. The bulk of the logic for the EJB will exist in these methods. Accessor methods, like simple gets and sets, also fall into this category.

- **ejbPassivate/ejbActivate:** Because they are inherited from an interface, these methods must always be present for all session beans, but should actually be implemented only for stateful session beans. They are called during instance passivation/activation actions. Often these methods will be left empty unless some special initialization/cleanup routine is needed for when the EJB is passivated or activated later on.

There can be additional methods in the session bean class that are there simply as utilities to assist in supporting all of the other bean methods that are present. The session bean class is also the place where you would typically store all of your instance variables to hold specific information about the session object. In addition, the implementation class is also where the **SessionContext** field is kept. An example of a session bean implementation class follows:

```
package com.homedirect.ejb.control;

import java.rmi.RemoteException;
...
public class ControlEJB implements javax.ejb.SessionBean
{
    // EJB context
    public javax.ejb.SessionContext EJB_Context;

    // Private fields
    private Profile profile = null;
    ...
    // Lifecycle methods
    public void ejbCreate()
    {
        accountHome = LookupHome.getAccountHome();
        ...
    }
    // Other lifecycle methods

    // Business methods
    public Profile getProfile()
    {
        return profile;
    }
public String TransferFunds(String fromAccount,
                    String toAccount,
                    long lAmount)
            throws AccountException, GeneratorException
    {  // logic for TransferFunds
    }
...
}
```

Modeling Interface Behavior

One of the challenges in component-based development is understanding how to properly use the component. Although the interfaces of components, such as EJBs, do define services provided by the component by exposing the relevant methods, not every combination or ordering of the methods is valid.

For example, consider the Remote interface defined for a ShoppingCart session bean as shown in Figure 12-8.

Now consider the sequence diagram shown in Figure 12-9.

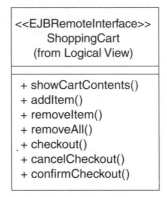

Figure 12-8   ShoppingCart session bean Remote interface

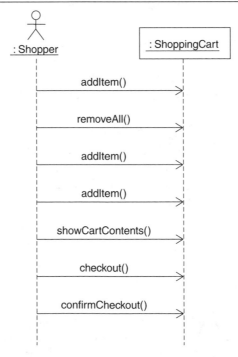

Figure 12-9   Sequence diagram showing usage of session bean

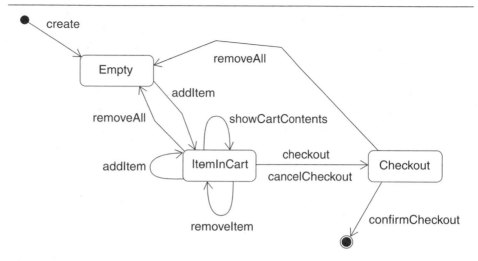

Figure 12-10   Statechart diagram for the ShoppingCart remote interface

The sequence diagram shows how the session bean will be used. But in order to confirm that the bean can in fact be used in this way, you would need to read written documentation for the bean or perhaps go through all the usage scenarios for the bean or examine the source of the code itself.

A simple way to communicate how the bean is intended to be used is to use a statechart diagram to model and document the interface[4]. A statechart for the ShoppingCart Remote interface is shown in Figure 12-10.

This statechart specifies all valid sequences in which this session bean can be used. If you evaluate the sequence diagram in Figure 12-9 against the statechart, it is easy to see that the sequence diagram contains a valid scenario. On the other hand, it is also easy to see that if the same sequence diagram were modified so that it contained an *addItem()* message between the *checkout()* and *confirmCheckout()* messages, it would be an invalid scenario based on this specific implementation of the ShoppingCart.

Session Bean Life Cycle

The session bean life cycle includes all of the concepts discussed thus far in this chapter. Figure 12-11 shows a UML state diagram for the stateful session bean life cycle. Figure 12-12 shows the significantly different (and simple) life cycle for a stateless session bean.

---

4. Based on [Selic 1994].

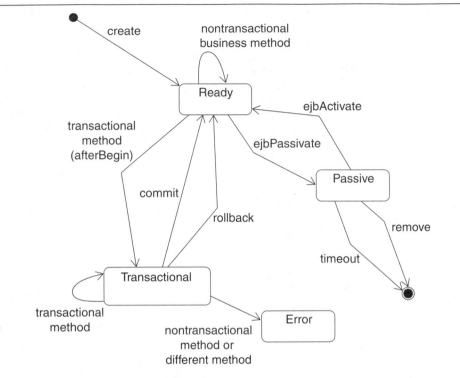

Figure 12-11 Stateful session bean life cycle

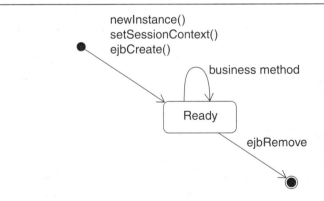

Figure 12-12 Stateless session bean life cycle

Session Bean Common Scenarios

A standard scenario for using a session bean is for the client to proceed as follows:

1. Call the **javax.rmi.PortableRemoteObject.narrow(...)** method to get a reference to the Home interface.

2. Using the Home interface reference, call the desired **create** method for the session object. A reference to the Remote interface for the session is returned.

3. Invoke any number of business methods using the Remote interface reference.

4. Call **remove** on either the Home interface or the Remote interface.

Some UML sequence diagrams showing the typical usage for a couple of different session beans are illustrated in the following figures. Figure 12-13 shows a common scenario for a stateless session bean. Figure 12-14 shows a more complicated scenario inherent in a stateful session bean. Both are shown using container-managed transaction demarcation.

The example in Figure 12-13 shows a successful transaction with boundaries across a single business method. Note also that the client in this case only deals with the interfaces and doesn't know, or need to know, any details of the implementation class. The physical location of the implementation class has no impact on the client. This provides great flexibility in that the implementation can be updated at a later date without affecting the client. The client is only impacted if the interfaces themselves change.

The example in Figure 12-14 shows two successful transactions in the session, each with single business method boundaries. Also note it is implied that the client waited a long time with no call after the first result, causing the passivation sequence to occur.

Modeling Session Bean Relationships

A session bean can have relationships with other components and classes, for example, JavaBeans, other session beans, servlets, and so on. Modeling of such relationships is discussed in this section.

Session Beans and Plain Java Classes

A session bean is just a pattern application to a set of Java classes, and there is nothing inherently unique about the individual elements that collectively make

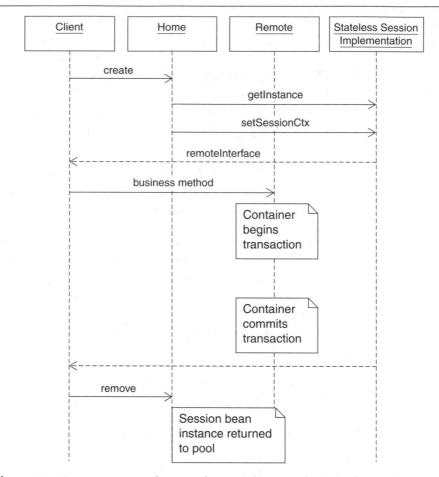

Figure 12-13 A sequence diagram showing the typical usage of a stateless session bean

up a session bean. As such, the relationships between a session bean element and other Java classes are quite ordinary. For instance, an EJB implementation class could utilize a number of Java classes to fulfill its needs. In such cases, a session bean would invoke methods on a Java class just as another Java class would.

Figure 12-15 shows an example of modeling a session bean and other Java classes.

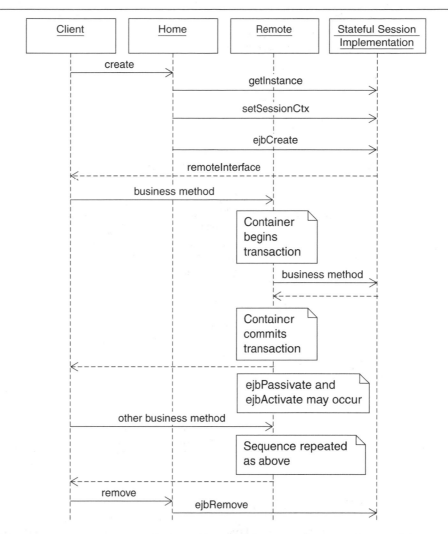

Figure 12-14 A sequence diagram showing the typical usage of a stateful session bean

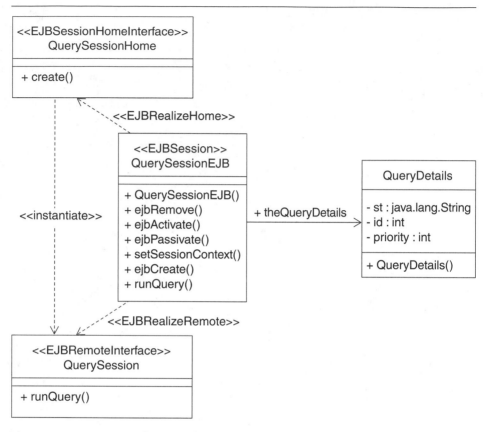

Figure 12-15   Session bean and Java classes

Session Beans and JavaBeans

Session beans and JavaBeans can be used together in various fashions. For example, a JavaBean may be used as a way of exchanging information between session beans and other JavaBeans in an enterprise application.

An interesting pattern[5] is to use a JavaBean as an accessor to a session bean. This has the advantage of providing a very simple interface to the client yet hides the full power of the EJB architecture behind the simple JavaBean.

5. Outlined in *Using JavaBeans as Accessors to Enterprise JavaBeans* by Andre Tost, October, 1999, published by IBM Developerworks.

Session Beans and Servlets

Servlets are often used as intermediaries between session beans and the user interface. For example, a servlet gets invoked to handle the incoming HTTP request. The servlet in turn calls upon a session bean to perform some specific tasks.

In such a situation, it is the servlet that invokes the session bean. As such, the servlet may also be responsible for locating the session bean on behalf of the client and instantiating the bean to handle incoming requests.

On a class diagram, such relationships are shown as dependencies or unidirectional associations from a servlet to a session bean. If the servlet doesn't need to be associated with the same session bean over time (e.g., a stateless session bean instance that is different each time), a dependency is appropriate for modeling the relationship. Otherwise, a unidirectional association would better serve the modeling.

An example is shown in Figure 12-16. Optionally, a servlet to session bean association may be stereotyped as <<instantiates>> to clearly identify that the servlet uses the session Home interface to create the session bean.

Some J2EE practitioners have argued[6] that servlets, rather than processing the request and response, should primarily focus on identifying and instantiating the appropriate session beans suitable for the task at hand, and then simply forward the request and response objects onward for the session bean to process. The argument is that it makes sense to use servlets when you are dealing with a Web browser, but as the clients become diverse, it makes sense to make the presentation logic client-agnostic and independent.

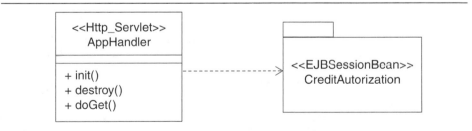

Figure 12-16   Servlet and session bean relationships

6. See, for example, "Presentation Logic and EJBs: Using session beans to help bridge the Java-HTML gap" by Michael Lacy, Java Developers Journal, May, 2000.

Session Bean and JavaServer Pages (JSP)

A JSP relationship with a session bean is essentially similar to that of a servlet and a session bean. An example is shown in Figure 12-17.

However, even though a JSP gets compiled into a servlet, it is generally preferred to use a JSP for presentation aspects and not embed detailed logic within the JSP as you would in a servlet. One approach is to use a JSP to call upon a servlet, which is then responsible for interacting with the session and/or entity beans.

Session-to-Session Relationships

A session bean may need to interact with other session beans to fulfill its responsibilities. For instance, you may use a stateful session bean to manage the subcontractor order placement session, and the stateful session bean may need to interact with a stateless session bean to obtain authorization for accepting the order.

As another example, consider a possible implementation of a shopping session. The user shopping session may be managed by a session bean, which has a one-to-one relationship with a cart bean.

Such relationships are modeled as association or dependencies between session beans. If a session bean needs to retain information about the other bean for an extended period of time, that is, in between business methods, the appropriate method is to use an association. Otherwise, a dependency is sufficient.

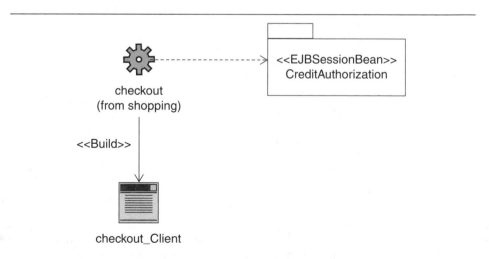

Figure 12-17   JSP and session bean relationship

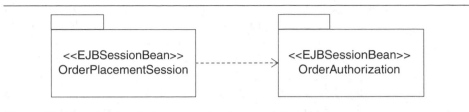

Figure 12-18 Session bean-to-session bean relationship

Using bean-to-bean relationships of this sort is sometimes referred to as session bean chaining. Session bean chaining involving a single stateful session bean and multiple stateless session beans is reasonable; however, caution is warranted if you are chaining several stateful session beans together. Due to the stateful nature of the session beans, it may take significant effort to set up the chain, so recovering from failure in the chain can be very time-consuming.

Figure 12-18 shows an example of a session bean-to-session bean relationship.

Session Bean Inheritance

The current version of the EJB specification does not specify a mechanism for EJB component inheritance. That is, subclassing of an entire EJB at once, such that you benefit from the interfaces as well as the implementation class. Some server vendors may support such EJB inheritance, but use caution if portability is a consideration.

The current recommendation is to subclass the Home and Remote interfaces and the implementation class separately, and then use them as the basis for creating new session beans.

Managing Performance

The decision to use EJB components in an enterprise application brings with it many benefits, as previously described. However, one area which you always need to keep an eye on when dealing with EJBs is their affect on the overall performance of the enterprise application.

EJBs in general make use of Remote Method Invocation (RMI) under the covers to effectively arrive at the separation of interface and implementation. The benefit is easier development of distributed applications and the ability to split the EJB workload over any number of different machines. Your enterprise application might have a session EJB instance running on one machine, whereas the entity objects and databases are somewhere else. By using EJBs with this remote capability automatically built in, the developer doesn't need to know how everything will eventually be deployed.

The drawback to this scheme is that a remote call is always more expensive, both time- and resource-wise, as compared to a call to a local object. As far as J2EE 1.2 is concerned, there are no alternatives to remote access. However, J2EE 1.3 is expected to support the concept of a *local client,* which we discuss in "The Local Client" section below.

Minimizing Remote Calls

So if remote calls are expensive, and there is no way around using them, how do you maximize your performance?

The primary rule to follow is to keep the number of EJB calls that you need to make to an absolute minimum. For example, if your session bean has three different tasks it needs to handle to support a request from a servlet, these should be rolled together into a single business method on the session bean for the servlet to call. Often this means that internally all this new business method does is call the other three methods directly. The point is you have now dropped the number of remote calls necessary to support this task by two.

The use of JavaBeans, as described earlier, can assist in lowering the total number of necessary remote calls as well.

In addition, different application servers also offer several different mechanisms to preallocate and pool resources, tune settings, and balance server loads to try to maximize the overall performance of your application.

The Local Client

Up to this point, it has been assumed that we are always dealing with a remote client. J2EE 1.3 introduces the concept of the local client for both session beans and entity beans.

The local client was introduced as a way to improve performance when the required EJB components are known to exist locally, running on the same Java Virtual Machine. When referring to the local client, there are several differences that apply:

- Remote client becomes local client
- Remote interface becomes local interface
- Home interface becomes local Home interface

- The objects that implement these two interfaces must be Java objects that are local to the client.
- The arguments and results of all methods on these interfaces are now passed by reference instead of by value.

By choosing to implement using the local client approach, you are potentially limiting the ability to split up the processing of significant portions of your enterprise application over multiple servers. In most cases, this drawback is greatly superseded by the gain in performance this approach can have. This approach might be suitable as a starting point. However, if you choose to follow the local client approach, it is a good idea to minimize the number of calls made to local EJB components in preparation for the day they need to be transformed into remote EJB components.

The local client is also recommended for most cases involving EJB-to-EJB relationships. However, the local client will not be valid to use in cases where target EJBs exist in different Java archive files or where a different transport mechanism is used to communicate with a non-Java implementation.

Keep in mind that at the time of this writing the local client approach is still not finalized. However, it is generally expected that this new feature will be carried over to the final version of the J2EE 1.3 specification.

Identifying Session Beans in Enterprise Applications

In the previous chapter, we split up the control object behavior into externally focused servlets and an internally focused control object with the main responsibility for business logic and handling interactions with entity objects.

Based on the discussion so far, you can probably already see that the session bean concept is ideally suited for being that internally focused control object.

In the context of using the session bean for the internally focused control object in the Transfer funds scenario, there are several details left to sort out:

- Is the session bean responsible for a single act, that is, to transfer funds, or does it have other responsibilities?
- Is this a stateless or stateful session bean?
- What kind of transactions does it have?
- Should it employ container-managed transactions or bean-managed transactions?

We could make it a single purpose EJB focused on just transferring funds, but recall from our earlier discussions that the EJBs are less granular in nature than a single operation. One way to determine this is to ask whether it would make sense for you to buy or sell the EJB as a component so it could be used by another similar enterprise Java application. Clearly, Transfer funds would not stand by itself as a whole component, but if you consider a session bean that handles the business logic required to support a banking customer's requests, packaging the functionality as a component makes more sense. So, during this first pass, we decide that Transfer funds, at least in this case, is one of several responsibilities of a session bean that handles a banking session.

The stateful versus stateless decision is not always easy. As a general rule of thumb, if the session bean needs to remember a significant number of items during the course of a complete transaction and those items are not already being held in a database object, it needs to have conversational state and should be a stateful session bean.

In this specific case, the request to transfer funds involves only a few pieces of data, namely the amount to transfer and the accounts involved. Some might argue that all of the account data should be held in the session bean as well to prevent having to gather this information every time. In fact, this usually isn't necessary or even desirable because this data is readily accessible through entity objects. You would run the risk of using data that is out of date if you did this, or you would be dealing with data synchronization issues that were otherwise unnecessary.

So in this case, we'll use the stateless session bean.

The next question is whether bean-managed or container-managed transactions are desired. The general answer is container-managed unless the particular application server you are working with somehow prevents you from accomplishing what you need or if your needs fall outside of any normal transaction processing. We are not doing anything strange or unusual in this scenario, so we'll use container-managed transactions.

Also keep in mind that each call to an EJB is potentially a remote network call, which is much more costly than just a function call. We want to minimize the number of calls required to accomplish each customer request for best performance. In the Transfer funds scenario, it is not practical to have several interactions with the session bean to transfer funds. Rather, this should be limited to a single request to transfer funds.

Based on the preceding discussion and choices, the revised sequence diagram for the Transfer funds use case is shown in Figure 12-19.

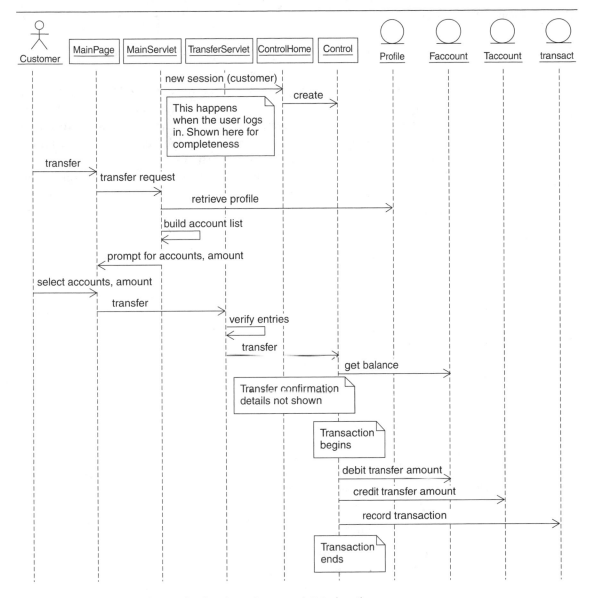

Figure 12-19   Revised Transfer funds with control EJB details

Summary

The EJB specification is an important part of the J2EE platform and defines a comprehensive component model for building scalable, distributed server-based enterprise Java application components.

EJB can potentially be represented in various ways in the UML. The approach taken in this book is to model an EJB as a *subsystem* because a subsystem offers the best of both a class and a package. There are three types of EJBs supported in the latest version of the EJB specification.

Session beans are currently the most commonly deployed EJB type. Conversational state and instance passivation are important concepts for session beans. There are two flavors of session beans: stateful and stateless. These have several key differences in their structure and behavior. Session beans also support transactions that can be bean-managed or container-managed.

There are various considerations in developing EJBs in general and session beans in particular. The use of UML modeling helps identify the issues and clarify potential solutions.

Chapter 13
Entity Beans

❖ *Process Check:*
We continue
with our design
as we progress
through the
Rational Unified
Process (RUP)
analysis and
design disci-
pline. We also
discuss some
implementation
specifics in the
context of the
Enterprise Java-
Beans (EJB)
technology.

In Chapter 12, we discussed how to model and design session beans using the Unified Modeling Language (UML), and then gave an overview of session beans at the technology level. We completed the chapter by showing where they fit into our evolving HomeDirect online banking example.

In this chapter, we focus solely on entity beans using a similar approach, again looking at the UML aspects as well as the technology level.

Introduction to Entity Beans

Entity beans are Java 2 Platform, Enterprise Edition (J2EE) components that have been designed specifically to represent data in a persistent store, which is typically a database. These business objects are primarily involved in the manipulation of this data to better match the needs of its clients, so there is more to the typical entity bean than just providing database accessor methods.

Generally speaking, data required by the client should come from entity beans rather than building separate data access objects. By using these EJBs, access and synchronization with the database are already provided for you. As a valuable plus, entity beans automatically provide the ability to share both state and behavior across multiple clients concurrently. They also provide other built-in features, like mechanisms to recover from a system crash.

Coarse-Grained Business Objects

Entity beans can provide much added value to enterprise applications, especially in systems dealing with complex data manipulations. However, just like other EJBs, there is a certain amount of overhead associated with using entity beans. As such, they are best suited to represent what we'll call coarse-grained business objects.

Coarse-grained objects are often those that represent a single logical record in a database, typically involving data that can exist completely on its own and still make sense. For example, a customer order would likely be something well suited to be represented by an entity bean. An individual item within the order is likely to be identified as more of a fine-grained object because the information provided by the individual item possibly has little value when taken outside the context of a customer order.

Identifying whether an object is coarse- or fine-grained is really dependent on the type of data you are dealing with and the enterprise application you are trying to build. For example, even a single customer order might be too fine-grained for you to consider. You might be more interested in the collection of every order a particular customer has made within a certain period. Maybe specific items in an order are more significant for you, and your entity bean is used instead to track complicated shipping details or return information for that item alone.

Figure 13-1 shows an example where it makes more sense for the single items to be identified within the context of the complete customer order, so they are pulled in as part of it.

Increasing Popularity

Historically, entity beans have seen less adoption in the industry when compared to session beans. There are several reasons for this:

- Data access methods are generally easier to write than good transaction management code, so entity beans are sometimes viewed as less critical to use than session beans.

- Like any new technology, the perceived added value has to greatly outweigh the cost of learning how to use it effectively. It can be argued that

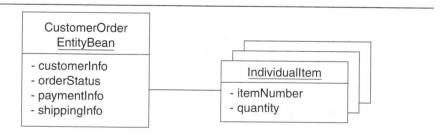

Figure 13-1 Customer order entity bean with individual items included

entity beans are more difficult to implement correctly than other EJB types and offer fewer direct benefits.

■ Entity bean support by some application servers has been problematic or poorly documented in the past.

■ Entity beans can have a significant impact on performance, especially when they are improperly used in the design (e.g., fine-grained).

■ The final details of the database to be used with an enterprise application are often not known until late in the development cycle.

Most of these issues are gradually being overcome by a better understanding of how to employ entity beans, by better overall support now being offered by J2EE compliant application servers, and by some technology improvements being incorporated in the J2EE 1.3 release.

Entity bean use is gradually increasing as these issues are being addressed and a greater overall understanding of appropriate and inappropriate entity bean design strategies is being developed.

J2EE Versions

As is the case with all EJB component types, entity beans are deployed with the help of an EJB container, which in turn is hosted by an application server. The particular capabilities and level of J2EE compliance of the server determines which version of the EJB specification you need to be working with.

For the rest of this chapter, all points pertain equally well to both J2EE 1.2 and J2EE 1.3 except where noted.

Entity Bean Views and the UML

Structurally, entity beans consist of a main Java class, often called the implementation class or the entity bean class, and two interfaces: Home and Remote. It also has a primary key class that contains methods for operating on the primary key for a single database table, or some compound set, depending on the data the EJB is intended to represent. The relationships between these items, as well as the particular J2EE base objects these items extend and implement, give the entity bean its particular functionality and usefulness as an EJB component.

Entity beans, like all EJBs, make use of a deployment descriptor to hold additional information pertaining to the component. This includes transaction settings on business methods, relationships with other entity beans, persistent field settings, and so on.

Let's take a look at the different views an entity bean has. We'll dive into the technology details thereafter to further explain these views.

Client View

The client view of an entity bean includes everything the client can call directly, which consists of the Home and Remote interface and the primary key class. As discussed in the previous chapter, in a UML class diagram, we represent the client view of an entity bean via a UML subsystem. An example is shown in Figure 13-2.

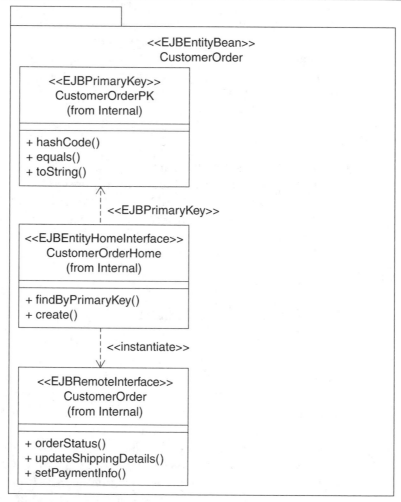

Figure 13-2 Full client view representation of an entity bean in a UML class diagram

An advantage of using the subsystem approach is the ability to expose those aspects that are of particular relevance in a specific situation or hide irrelevant details. Figure 13-2 provides an example of client view elements inside the subsystem. Note the specific stereotypes shown on the different elements. The stereotypes indicate that the UML constructs have been extended in their meaning to support special needs of the J2EE architecture. Such stereotyping also offers a simple and compact means of identifying the specific role played by a specific model element that is part of an EJB. The compact client view representation is shown in Figure 13-3.

Internal View

The internal view of an entity bean includes all components of the client view, the implementation class and its associated relationships, and any additional classes users add to the design of their entity bean. In a UML class diagram, these components appear as normal classes and interfaces.

The internal view is useful if you are interested in the details of the implementation. For example, the developer of the entity bean might find the internal view appropriate. However, aside from the additional details visible, the internal view is essentially equivalent to the client view of the entity bean, as shown in Figure 13-4.

Let's now spend some time digging through the technology aspects of entity beans.

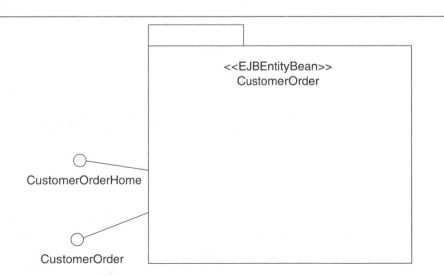

Figure 13-3 Compact client view representation of an entity bean in a UML class diagram

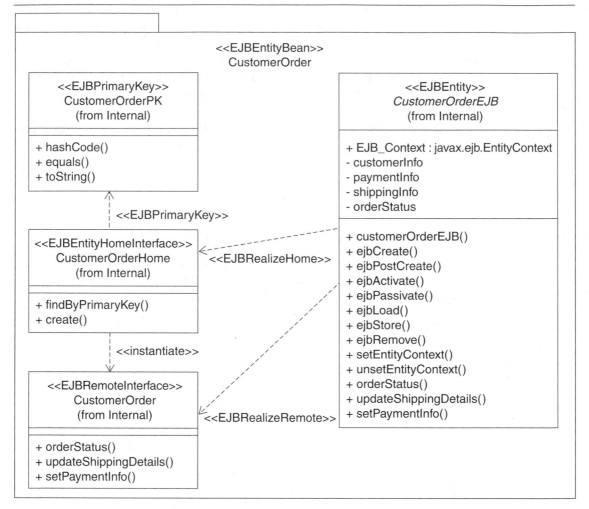

Figure 13-4 Internal view representation of an entity bean in a UML class diagram.

Persistence

Whenever an application is manipulating data, one of its considerations is ensuring longevity of the data beyond the immediate operation. Persistence refers to the activity of ensuring that the changes to data are saved appropriately.

Persistence services are what entity beans are all about, so it is important to understand the differences between the two persistence mechanisms these EJBs can use.

One mechanism is *container-managed persistence*. The goal for the majority of entity beans you deploy should be to use this mode of operation as frequently as possible. By letting the EJB container manage the persistence, all database access and synchronization is automatically handled for you. Because this is achieved using prebuilt and tested container capabilities, you get high quality persistence support without having to implement and test all the associated infrastructure code.

The other mechanism is *bean-managed persistence*. In this mode you are still using an entity bean, but you also have to code your own data access and synchronization calls. If you decide to use this approach, it is recommended that you use a separate object, typically referred to as a *data access object*. You would tie the methods in such an object to the **ejbLoad/ejbStore** methods that exist in the entity bean implementation. This way, when you decide to move to container-managed persistence at a later time, migration becomes much easier because you can just throw away the encapsulated data access object rather than try to pull out code that is potentially scattered throughout your entity bean.

The question arises as to why someone would ever want to use bean-managed persistence. The most common answer is exactly what we just described—namely to allow an easier way to transition from just writing data access code to using full-featured entity beans.

It should also be mentioned that entity beans are not intended to be the answer for every persistence requirement. If you just need simple access calls for data that is not expected to change very often, and you are not really worried about any concurrency issues, then continuing to just write your own data access objects is likely the best way to go. Figure 13-5 shows typical usage of the different approaches just described.

Transactions and Concurrency

All entity beans make use of container-managed transaction demarcation, which allows for the concurrency features to work properly. As such, any given entity bean instance is available to any number of clients at a time as long as the clients know how to locate it, and they have the proper security clearance.

As with session beans, transactional attributes are set on the methods a client can call to ensure the integrity of the entity bean and the data it persists. For this type of EJB, this includes all of the user-defined methods on both the Home and Remote interfaces. Valid attribute settings are exactly the same as those used for session beans.

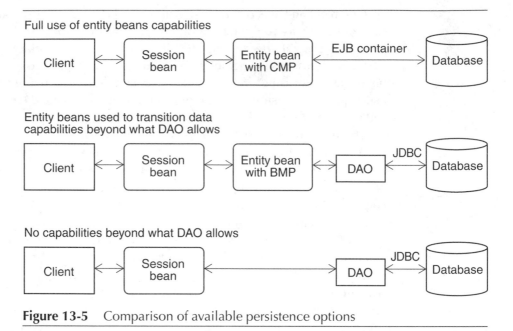

Full use of entity beans capabilities

Entity beans used to transition data
capabilities beyond what DAO allows

No capabilities beyond what DAO allows

Figure 13-5   Comparison of available persistence options

Abstract Persistence

J2EE 1.3 introduces an exciting new approach to entity bean persistence management. It applies only when using the container-managed persistence mechanism. The majority of the changes we are talking about revolve around the complete separation of the bean implementation from its persistent representation. The changes result in the introduction of two concepts we have not seen before: the *Abstract Persistence Schema* and the *Persistence Manager*.

Abstract Persistence Schema

One of the issues people had with data access code in general was that often the details of the database involved weren't fully known until very late in the development cycle. This stemmed from the fact that the database design and the EJB design were often done by two very separate groups. Or perhaps the design of the database was being updated for a new release, and the developers wanted to avoid completely retrofitting all of the existing EJBs they deployed in the past to work with it.

These are just a few of the compelling reasons to take the container-managed persistent (CMP) fields, also simply known as persistent fields, and completely abstract them out of the implementation for an EJB. By doing this, you effectively separate two major parts of your overall system that have a tendency to change somewhat independently from one another. This is a very useful separation.

Under the J2EE 1.2 persistence contract, you need to add normal Java fields to the implementation class for an entity bean, identify them as CMP fields in the deployment descriptor, and then provide **get** and **set** methods along with the necessary code for these methods. An example of this approach is shown in Figure 13-6.

With the new contract, you no longer add fields to the EJB directly, but instead indicate in the Abstract Persistence Schema the names of the fields that you would like the EJB container to create and manage for you. You also create **get** and **set** accessor methods, but mark them as abstract and therefore do not

```
Attributes declared in EntityBean class
:
public class AccountEJB implements EntityBean {
    /*
        Attributes declaration
    */
    public String AccountNum;
    public String AccountType;
    public BigDecimal Balance;
:
public String getAccountNum() throws RemoteException
  {
    return AccountNum;
  }
public String setAccountNum(int account)throws RemoteException
  {
    AccountNum = account;
  }
:
CMP field declaration in the Deployment Descriptor
:
<cmp-field>
      <description>bank account number</description>
      <field-name>AccountNum</field-name>
</cmp-field>
<cmp-field>
      <description>account type can be one of S, C, or
       I</description>
      <field-name>AccountType</field-name>
</cmp-field>
<cmp-field>
      <description>bank balance</description>
      <field-name>Balance</field-name>
</cmp-field>
:
```

Figure 13-6 J2EE 1.2 persistence management contract

```
Abstract get and set methods and no attribute declaration in EJB
public abstract class AccountEJB implements javax.ejb.EntityBean
{
:
    public abstract String getAccountNum();
    public abstract void setAccountNum(String newAccountNum);
    public abstract String getAccountType();
    public abstract void setAccountType(String newAccountType);
    public abstract BigDecimal getBalance();
    public abstract void setBalance (BigDecimal newBalance);
:
:
CMP Field Declaration in the deployment descriptor
:
<cmp-field>
    <field-name>AccountNum</field-name>
</cmp-field>
<cmp-field>
    <field-name>AccountType</field-name>
</cmp-field>
<cmp-field>
    <field-name>Balance</field-name>
</cmp-field>
:
```

Figure 13-7 J2EE 1.3 persistence management contract

need to provide any code. The Abstract Persistence Schema lives in the deployment descriptor for these EJBs. The information is then passed along to the Persistence Manager. An example of this approach is shown in Figure 13-7.

EJB Query Language (EJB QL)

The EJB QL is a very scaled down version of the typical SQL used for database access calls. It is intended to completely abstract the definition of finder and select methods from the underlying database. EJB QL is defined in J2EE 1.3 with entity beans to be used for certain required methods, like finders and select methods. EJB QL is used by the Persistence Manager and deployment tools to create the database access code for you under the covers during the deployment process. This means that you declare finder methods, and then specify EJB QL statements for them as part of the deployment process; however, you do not directly write the code for their implementation.

EJB QL statements are written using names corresponding to the Abstract Persistence Schema, CMP fields, and other related EJB names. The deployment tools then work to convert these statements into equivalent SQL queries, using actual database table and column names. From that point, the tools then generate the necessary code under the covers to execute these SQL statements at runtime.

In J2EE 1.2, EJB QL does not exist. In this case, SQL statements are provided to the deployment tools, which perform the final step where code to execute these statements is generated for you.

For the remainder of this chapter, we will use EJB QL. However, if you have J2EE 1.2, you can substitute EJB QL with SQL.

Persistence Manager

The Persistence Manager is a new tool in J2EE 1.3 and is typically shipped as part of the overall application server package. Its purpose is to process the Abstract Persistence Schema information for the entity beans and provide a mechanism to map the requested persistent fields to the underlying database.

Once the mapping is complete, the EJB container calls upon the Persistence Manager again at deployment time to actually create the necessary persistent fields, the accessor code for them, and the required database calls to keep things properly synchronized. These capabilities in and of themselves are a great bonus in helping to make entity beans easier to build and maintain, which leads us into the next area to take a look at—relationships.

Container-Managed Relationships

Container-managed relationships are also new in J2EE 1.3 and provide a function where the UML has applicability. The Abstract Persistence Schema discussed earlier has the additional capability to maintain information about relationships between container-managed entity beans using what are referred to as container-managed relationship (CMR) fields. Similar to CMP fields, these also use **get** and **set** accessor methods that you define as abstract, and you let the Persistence Manager create and manage the necessary code for them.

In a real J2EE project, it is common for sets of different types of entity beans to be related to one another and therefore require the use of these relationships. Continuing with our example of the entity bean representing a customer order, it is very possible that an additional entity bean might be used to represent the customer. This customer would therefore reference a collection of orders, which could be any number including zero.

In the UML, the visualization of this entity bean relationship can be drawn as shown in Figure 13-8.

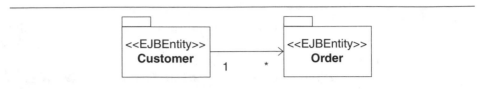

Figure 13-8   Example of a container-managed relationship

Multiplicity

In our example, we showed a situation where a customer referenced any number of orders. This was reflected in the UML by showing the relationship between the entity beans and a multiplicity of "*" on the order side. Note that a multiplicity of one is assumed if nothing specific is marked. In the preceding example, we have what is known as a one-to-many relationship. There are four possible multiplicity combinations:

- One-to-one
- One-to-many
- Many-to-one
- Many-to-many

The indication of "one" means that if an accessor method is provided, it passes back only a single instance of the entity bean it references. Likewise if "many" is used, it passes back a "collection" of instances of the referenced entity bean. In fact, the "collection" can be based on any of the following common types:

- **java.util.Collection**
- **java.util.Set**
- **java.util.List**
- **java.util.Map**

Note that the last two do not need to specifically be supported by an application server to be J2EE 1.3 compliant. So depending on your application server, you may or may not be able to use them.

The Persistence Manager takes care of creating the necessary code for you to handle the passing of references back and forth between entity beans. This greatly simplifies the task of developing complex systems with multiple entity beans.

Directionality

You might have noticed in the example in Figure 13-8 that the relationship was shown with an arrow from the customer to the order. This indicates that the relationship is *unidirectional*. The accessor methods for the customer EJB are not generated so that crossing over between EJBs is only allowed in one direction. For example, we might want the customer EJB to be able to access the related order EJB instances, but because of security reasons, we might not want confidential customer information to be directly accessible from an order instance itself.

You can also designate a container-managed relationship as being *bidirectional* by arrows in both directions. This means that accessor methods will be created for both processes. In this situation, the customer can access the collection of orders that have been made, and you can navigate from any given order over to the matching customer to access the information retained.

Duplicating Container-Managed Relationships in J2EE 1.2

In J2EE 1.2, container-managed relationships are possible to implement, and in fact often are. The only difference in J2EE 1.2 is that the accessor methods that provide the references to all of these entity bean instances have to be coded manually. There is no Persistence Manager to automatically handle this for you in J2EE 1.2.

Local Relationships

Note that the EJB relationships described in reference to the container-managed relationships imply the use of the local client approach, as was introduced at the end of Chapter 12. Simply put, if you want to take advantage of the work the Persistence Manager can do for you, the entity beans involved must all coexist in the same Java archive file, and they must all be running on the same Java Virtual Machine (JVM).

If you have cases where this is not true, relationships with the remote entities are still possible; however, the accessor code for these would need to be done manually, as is the case in J2EE 1.2.

Now let's look at the rest of the technology details of entity beans.

Entity Bean Technology

For the client, an entity bean is seen as a component that provides methods to easily retrieve business data in whatever format the client needs. The technology level of these J2EE components involves specific classes, interfaces, methods, and fields that must exist to support the client interfaces and life cycle of the entity bean.

Home Interface

Every entity bean needs to provide a Home interface. This is the interface used by the client to invoke the basic EJB life cycle methods. During runtime, the EJB container only creates a single copy of this interface per deployed entity bean. Through this interface, all of the instances of a particular EJB can be created, found, and destroyed.

The Home interface of an entity bean supports four different method types: create, finder, remove, and home methods. Note that the last type applies to J2EE 1.3 only.

Create Methods

Create methods are used to create an instance of the entity bean, and zero or more of these methods may exist. The return type must always be the Remote interface of the entity bean. Note that the EJB container can also create instances of the entity bean automatically in response to events that occur in the database, which is why it is possible to build a valid component with no create methods.

A **create<METHOD>** creates an instance of the entity bean, where **<METHOD>** can either be a name or empty, as long as **create** is the prefix. Any desired arguments can be used.

Finder Methods

Finder methods are used to locate an instance of an entity bean through the Home interface, and at least one of these methods, called **findByPrimaryKey(primaryKey)**, must always exist. The return type is either the Remote interface of the entity bean, which the required finder method must always return, or it can also be a collection of Remote interfaces from the multiple instances of the entity bean.

A **find<METHOD>** finds a single instance or collection of instances of the entity bean, where **<METHOD>** can either be a name or empty, as long as **find** is the prefix. Any desired arguments can be used. The actual code to run this finder method will not directly be created by the developer, but instead is automatically generated at deployment time through the interpretation of an appropriate EJB QL statement.

Remove Methods

Remove methods are used by clients to destroy their reference to the entity bean. Necessary remove methods are already defined in the base EJB interfaces for our entity beans and therefore do not need to be defined again. These methods, of course, have the name **remove**.

Home Methods

Home methods are used to specify business logic that does not apply to any specific entity bean instance. The concept of home methods was introduced in J2EE 1.3.

Any method name can be used for home methods, as long as it doesn't start with **create**, **find**, or **remove**. You can think of these methods as a type of static method to use within entity beans. They have a dual purpose: to support static data that all instances of the entity bean would need and to provide a way to help reduce the resources needed for business methods that are more static in nature because only one copy of a home method is ever available rather than one copy per instance of the entity bean.

Figure 13-9 shows an example of an entity bean Home interface.

Remote Interface

Every entity bean also needs to provide a Remote interface. This is the interface used by the client to invoke business methods that are specific to a particular entity bean instance. Most of your required business methods will be specified by this interface rather than through the more static type home methods discussed earlier. Just about any method names and arguments can be

```
package com.homedirect.ejb.account;
import java.rmi.RemoteException;
import javax.ejb.*;
import java.util.Collection;

public interface AccountHome extends javax.ejb.EJBHome
{
    public Account create(String accountid,
                String accounttype,
                float balance,
                int customerid,
                float limit,
                float userfee)
            throws java.rmi.RemoteException,
            javax.ejb.CreateException;
    public Account findByPrimaryKey(java.lang.String primaryKey)
            throws java.rmi.RemoteException,
            javax.ejb.FinderException;
    public Collection findAccounts(int customerid)
            throws java.rmi.RemoteException,
            javax.ejb.FinderException;
}
```

Figure 13-9   An entity bean Home interface

used, but you should avoid names that might imply an alternate meaning in the bean class.

For entity beans, business logic usually involves some sort of manipulation, checking, and validation of the persisted data, often formatting it to be more readily suitable to the needs of the client.

Figure 13-10 shows an entity bean Remote interface class.

Primary Key Class

In order to locate an entity bean in the underlying data store, each entity bean needs to be identified with a unique key known as the primary key. Each entity bean must have a primary key class identified to hold the methods required to process searches using the primary key. It is this primary key class that is used in the finder method **findByPrimaryKey()** to locate the entity bean.

The class may be a predefined Java class that already provides the necessary methods required to support primary keys, such as String or Integer, or it can be a user defined class, useful for cases where the primary key is a compound object not easily represented by a standard Java class. In any case, the methods this class must support are, at a minimum, **hashCode** and **equals**. A quick look at the source code used for these methods in classes like String or Integer will better show you what these methods need to accomplish. Note that the same primary key class can be shared across multiple entity beans if you so choose.

```
package com.homedirect.ejb.Account;

import java.rmi.RemoteException;
import javax.ejb.*;

public interface Account extends javax.ejb.EJBObject
{
public String getAccountid       () throws java.rmi.RemoteException;
  public void setAccountid       (String newAccountid) throws
                                 java.rmi.RemoteException;
  public String getAccounttype    () throws
                                 java.rmi.RemoteException;
  public void setAccounttype      (String newAccounttype)
                                 throws java.rmi.RemoteException;
 :
 :
}
```

Figure 13-10   An entity bean Remote interface

```
import java.io.Serializable;
:
public class AccountPK implements java.io.Serializable
{
  public int hashCode()
  {
      // implementation of hashcode function here
  }
  public boolean equals()
  {
      // perform the comparison to determine return value
  }
  public String toString()
  {
      // convert to string
  }
  public AccountPK     () { }
}
```

Figure 13-11   An example of a primary key class

The primary key class is a small but vital member of the entity bean. An example of a primary key class is shown in Figure 13-11.

Implementation Class

Additionally, there is the implementation class, also referred to as the entity bean class. It has the actual implementations for all methods declared in the Home interface and the Remote interface as well as the required entity bean life cycle methods.

The implementation class has some significant differences depending on the persistence type and J2EE version being used. For bean-managed persistence with all J2EE versions or for container-managed persistence using only J2EE 1.2, the implementation class must contain all of the following methods:

- **setEntityContext/unsetEntityContext:** These methods must exist and are called by the EJB container. The set allows the entity bean to store the context information in a local instance variable. The unset is called just before terminating the entity bean and allows for freeing any necessary resources.

- **ejbCreate<METHOD>:** For every **create** method called out in the Home interface, there must be a matching method in the bean class that differs only in that the prefix used on the method name is **ejbCreate** instead of **create**. Arguments must also match, but note that the return types are different. These methods typically perform simple initialization steps for the EJB.

■ **ejbPostCreate<METHOD>:** For every **ejbCreate** method used, there should be a matching **ejbPostCreate** method in the bean class. The EJB container calls this method after the normal **create** as a way to pass in arguments that otherwise would not be available until the **create** method has completed. Typically, this means that the entity bean needs to do more initialization, possibly requiring the Remote interface for the instance just created. Often these methods are simply empty.

■ **ejbRemove:** This method must exist with no arguments, and it gets called when one of the interface **remove** methods is invoked or when the EJB container initiates a remove action on its own. For entity beans, this method is equivalent to calling **ejbPassivate**.

■ **ejbHome<METHOD>:** For every home method called out in the Home interface, there must be a matching method in the bean class that differs only in that the prefix used on the method name is **ejbHome** instead of **home**. Arguments must also match. Note that this type of method does not exist in J2EE 1.2.

■ **ejbPassivate/ejbActivate:** These methods are called during instance passivation/activation actions. Often these methods will be left empty unless some special initialization/cleanup routine is needed for when the EJB is passivated or activated later on.

■ **ejbLoad/ejbStore:** These methods must be present and are called by the EJB container at various times to ensure that the persisted fields in the entity bean and the data in the database are kept synchronized. For container-managed persistence, these methods basically allow you to hook into the synchronization process to do something special whenever the load and store events occur. For bean-managed persistence, you write your database synchronization code within these methods. These particular methods are also very important to consider in regard to performance.

■ **Business methods:** All business methods defined in the Remote interface must have an exact match in the bean class in terms of method name and arguments. The actual implementation code for these business methods is done in the implementation class.

In addition to this list of methods, container-managed persistence using J2EE 1.3 introduces additional methods. The **ejbSelect<METHOD>** methods, known as *select* methods, are not exposed to the client through any interface, but instead live only within the implementation class. They are typically called from within other entity bean business methods and are always declared as abstract. Their implementations are achieved through the use of an EJB QL statement that gets interpreted at deployment time, which results in the necessary code being generated automatically for you.

There can be additional methods in the implementation class that exist simply as utilities to assist in supporting all of the other methods that are present, or there can be other classes present within the internal design of the entity bean that the implementation class can make use of as well.

Persistent Fields

The implementation class is also where the **EntityContext** field is kept as well as any persistent data fields. Persistent fields are usually placed in the implementation class along with the desired **get** and **set** accessor methods. Persistence is indicated for each desired field through a setting in the deployment descriptor.

For container-managed persistence using J2EE 1.3, you don't actually create the persistent fields, but as discussed earlier in this chapter, just create the abstract accessor methods for them and declare them in the CMP field area of the deployment descriptor. The rest is taken care of later through the use of the Persistence Manager. The same goes for CMR fields to handle container-managed relationships.

Figure 13-12 shows an example of an entity bean implementation class.

```
import java.rmi.RemoteException;
import javax.ejb.*;
:
:
public abstract class AccountEJB implements javax.ejb.EntityBean
{
  public javax.ejb.EntityContext EJB_Context;

   public AccountEJB()
   {
   }

   public AccountPK ejbCreate() throws javax.ejb.CreateException
   {
return null;
   }

   public void ejbPostCreate    () throws javax.ejb.CreateException
   {
   }

   public void ejbActivate    ()
   {
   }
```

Figure 13-12 A J2EE 1.3 entity bean implementation class (*continues*)

```
    public void ejbPassivate     ()
    {
    }

    public void ejbLoad      ()
    {
    }

    public void ejbStore     ()
    {
    }
    public void ejbRemove       () throws javax.ejb.RemoveException
      {
      }

public void setEntityContext      (javax.ejb.EntityContext ctx)
    {
    }



    public void unsetEntityContext     ()
    {
    }

    public abstract String getAccountid     ();
    public abstract void setAccountid     (String newAccountid);
    public abstract String getAccounttype     ();
    public abstract void setAccounttype     (String newAccounttype);
    public abstract float getBalance      ();
    public abstract void setBalance     (float newBalance);
    public abstract int getCustomerid      ();
    public abstract void setCustomerid     (int newCustomerid);
    public abstract float getLimit      ();
    public abstract void setLimit      (float newLimit);
  :
  :
    }
```

Figure 13-12 *(continued)*

Entity Bean Life Cycle

The life cycle of an entity bean uses essentially the same concepts as those discussed in Chapter 12 concerning the session bean life cycle, although the details differ somewhat. There are a couple of main differences to highlight.

The first is that the EJB container plays a role in initially creating a pool of instances for each entity bean you deploy. The size and behavior of the pool is controlled by various server settings. At this point, the Home interface for the EJB exists, so it is possible for home or finder methods to be called. Instances remain in this state until they are created or activated, either by the client or the EJB container.

The second point to note is that several of the state transitions an entity bean goes through can be the result of direct database actions including creation and removal of instances of the EJB. This is very important to keep in mind so that you don't get unexpected results as you build your enterprise application.

A UML state diagram is very descriptive in showing this life cycle. Figure 13-13 shows the entity bean life cycle as it applies to bean-managed persistence for all J2EE versions and container-managed persistence for J2EE 1.2 only.

Figure 13-14 shows the entity bean life cycle as it applies to container-managed persistence using J2EE 1.3. The addition of select methods is essentially the only difference.

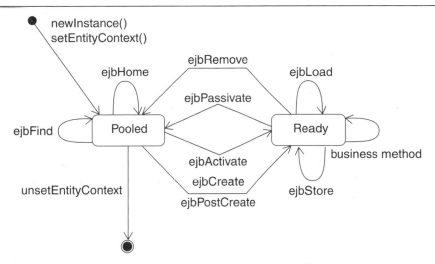

Figure 13-13 Entity bean life cycle for J2EE 1.2 and all bean-managed persistence

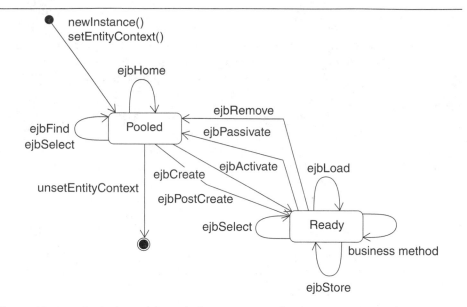

Figure 13-14 Entity bean life cycle for J2EE 1.3 with container-managed persistence

Entity Bean Common Scenarios

A standard scenario for using an entity bean is for the client to act as follows:

1. Call the **javax.rmi.PortableRemoteObject.narrow(…)** method to get a reference to the Home interface.

2. Any home or finder method can be called at this point. If you are trying to access existing data, the finder method will pass you back the Remote interface for the EJB instance you want. In this case, the desired instance would automatically be created for you by the application server, so the next step would be skipped.

3. If the instance you require is for new data you are planning to add to the database, using the Home interface reference, call the desired **create** method for the entity bean. Both the **ejbCreate** and **ejbPostCreate** methods will be executed. A reference to the Remote interface for the entity is returned.

4. Invoke any number of business methods using the Remote interface reference.

5. Call **remove** on either the Home interface or the Remote interface.

Figure 13-15 shows the code involved in the preceding scenario.

```
:
InitialContext initCtx = new InitialContext();
               Object objRef =
initCtx.lookup("java:comp/env/ejb/Profile");
ProfileHome profileHome = (ProfileHome)PortableRemoteObject.
narrow(objRef, ProfileHome.class);
Profile profileRemote = profileHome.findByPrimaryKey(username);
:
```

Figure 13-15   Entity bean usage scenario

Modeling Entity Bean Relationships

Entity beans may require other Java classes such as JavaBeans to fulfill their responsibilities and may interact with other J2EE technologies such as JavaServer Pages (JSP), servlets, and session beans to deliver enterprise application functionality. This section discusses details of modeling such relationships for entity beans.

Entity Bean and Other Java Classes

A common scenario involves an entity bean that has other Java objects as dependent data objects. A good example is an Account entity bean, which has one or more addresses associated with it (reflecting multiple account holders' addresses).

Because a dependent data object cannot independently exist from the entity bean, an appropriate way to model such a relationship is via the aggregation relationship between the entity bean implementation class and the dependent data object. An example is shown in Figure 13-16.

Another scenario requiring a relationship between an entity bean and other Java classes is the notion of a data access object discussed earlier. The idea is to facilitate an easier path to CMP by encapsulating the data access logic in a class by itself. This can be modeled as shown in Figure 13-17.

Entity Bean and JavaBeans

One of the challenges in using entity beans is that there is a significant overhead associated with each access to the entity bean due to its remote nature. Even if the bean is not located across the network, overhead is still involved as the call

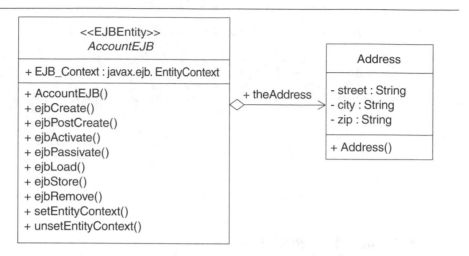

Figure 13-16   Entity bean and dependent data object

to access data from the entity bean must go through the container. As described in the previous chapter, J2EE 1.3 is expected to introduce the local client approach, which will eliminate these remote calls and greatly improve on the performance in this area.

Despite this improvement, there is still another fundamental mechanism that causes significant overhead for entity beans, which is the number of synchronization calls that are made to maintain the integrity of the data in the EJB instance with the underlying database. To illustrate this problem, imagine an entity bean persisting 20 different pieces of information. Whenever any one of the 20 gets or sets are called, the EJB container must ensure that the entity and database are in sync, so a necessary **ejbLoad** or **ejbStore** call is made. Many of these calls would be made for a typical amount of data requested from this entity bean.

One strategy for addressing this issue is to use the same approach as we did with session beans. That is, minimize the number of calls that need to be made to the entity bean for a particular action. This could be a good approach for some cases; however, if you have many points in your enterprise application where data from a particular EJB is needed, the performance improvement gained would not be as substantial.

The Value Object Approach

If your enterprise application is more complicated in nature, another more scalable strategy for addressing this issue is to use JavaBeans to encapsulate data and

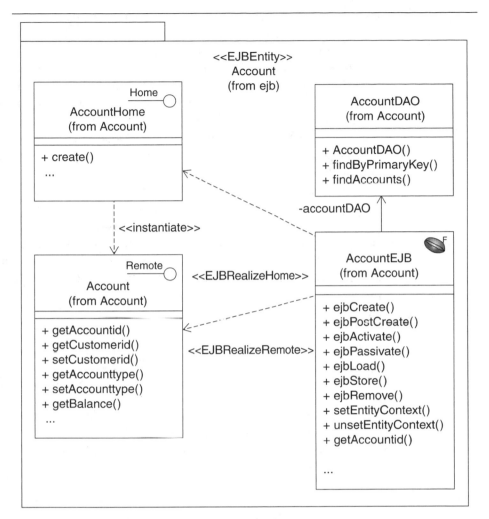

Figure 13-17   Entity beans and data access objects

employ a pass by value scheme using the JavaBeans as a *value object*. The Java-Bean is serialized and passed across the network where it can be repeatedly accessed locally. Because there is no data synchronization between the value object and the entity bean, a common strategy is to make the JavaBean immutable by only providing get operations on the data.

This value object approach has one major drawback. It essentially allows you to "short circuit" the normal data synchronization process that occurs automatically in the entity bean. This is because you are not really accessing the entity bean directly but another object that represents the data in that EJB instance at a particular point in time. You have to be careful that the value object does not inadvertently get out of sync with the real data in the database. In many cases though, this approach works well.

In our HomeDirect example, we use this value object approach; however, we take it one step further. Instead of introducing one JavaBean for every instance of an entity bean, we introduce one JavaBean per action initiated by the user. We do this because we want all data to be current at the specific point in time when a user initiates any particular action on the Web site. Anything kept around longer than an individual user action we treat as being potentially out of sync with the database.

This approach allows us to avoid issues concerning loss of synchronization, and it also tends to concentrate much of the presentation code processing in the JavaBean itself. Essentially, the JavaBean acts as the collection and processing agent for the data we are going to display. The JavaBean goes to each entity bean instance we need to access and collects the displayable data required for each row through a single business method. Once the JavaBean has collected and processed all of the EJB instance information it needs, it passes the final results back to a JSP page.

Keep in mind that this approach works well for this example, but might not for more complicated cases where the data the JavaBeans are holding actually must be accessed many times during a particular transaction or must be kept around for longer periods of time for some reason. The most important point to note in this situation is to fully understand your requirements so you can make the best design decisions and trade-offs for your particular enterprise application.

An example is shown in Figure 13-18.

Another slight variation on the value object approach is the *details object* pattern. In the details object pattern, the entire entity bean is marshaled into the

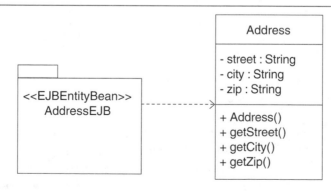

Figure 13-18 Entity bean with dependency on a JavaBean being used as a value object

Java object and also provides associated get operations. Set operations may also be provided to allow the user to "update the entity bean" locally, and then use the updated object to update the actual entity bean. You can even extend the details object to arrive at the entity bean class. However, this approach does entail some complications, similar to those discussed for the value object approach in the previous section.

Entity Bean, Servlets, and JSPs

For enterprise applications that do not have a lot of application logic, it may make sense to use a servlet to access an entity bean directly rather than use a session bean as an intermediary. In these types of scenarios, a servlet may have a relationship with an entity bean such that it creates the entity bean using the Home interface and later accesses or updates the data represented by the entity bean.

Such relationships are modeled as associations. An example is shown in Figure 13-19.

Although the same could be argued for JSPs (after all, they are compiled into servlets), it is still preferable to use JSPs for presentation logic and use an intermediary servlet to access entity beans as required. This maintains a cleaner partition between presentation and application logic. And unlike using a session bean as an intermediary between a servlet and an entity bean, this approach does not have the associated performance impact, as the servlets require less system resources.

An example is shown in Figure 13-20.

Entity Bean and Session Beans

Although there is no restriction in J2EE on accessing entity beans directly from a servlet or JSP, in most cases it makes more sense to access them via a session bean as session beans are responsible for managing the overall workflow in the

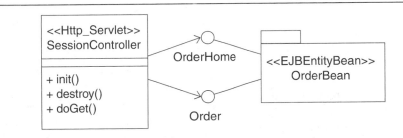

Figure 13-19 Entity beans and servlets

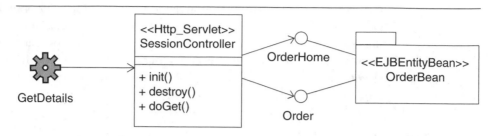

Figure 13-20 JSP accessing an entity bean via a servlet

application. Such session bean to entity bean relationships are easily depicted in the UML as dependencies or as unidirectional associations from the session bean to the entity bean. If the session bean does not retain information about the entity bean from one method call to the next, it can be modeled as a dependency. On the other hand, if it needs to know of the entity bean over an extended period of time, the relationship is modeled as an association.

An example is shown in Figure 13-21.

A common pattern is to use session beans as facades to entity beans.[1] The idea is to simplify the client interface by providing a singular point of entry in

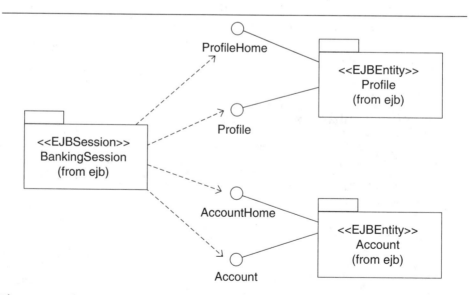

Figure 13-21 Session and entity bean relationship

1. Discussed in *Designing Enterprise Applications with the Java 2 Platform, Enterprise Edition* by Nicholas Kassem, Addison-Wesley, 2000.

the form of granular workflow-based interfaces via session beans and hide the details of various entity beans behind the session bean. Thus, a person placing an order on a Web site and an administrator monitoring the inventory may be working with the same underlying data, but they work with different session beans encapsulating their respective workflows.

Entity Bean-to-Entity Bean Relationships

Most of the entity bean-to-entity bean relationships were discussed in the context of the "Abstract Persistent Schema" section earlier in this chapter. The key fact to remember is to use entity beans for coarse-grained data and avoid using entity beans for maintaining fine-grained data.

Identifying Entity Beans in Enterprise Applications

Generally speaking, entity classes identified during the analysis phase should be used as starting points for determining the entity beans you will require for the system.

Referring back to the HomeDirect online banking case study, you might recall that we identified one or more entity classes as we went through specific use cases. For example, the entity classes involved in the Transfer funds use case included *Account* and *CustomerProfile,* among others. Both are good candidates for entity beans because each is fairly granular and stands by itself.

Of course, *Profile* also contains the user's name and customer identifier. Would it make sense then to create distinct entity beans for each *Profile?* Even though it is technically feasible, it is not advisable for two reasons. First, there is overhead associated with each EJB, so it would be preferable to maintain fewer EJBs in general. Second, entity beans typically represent a (logical) record in a database and splitting the *Profile* record between multiple EJBs would be counter-productive.

Figure 13-22 shows a partial revised class diagram for the HomeDirect case study involving all the technologies we have discussed so far.

Notice that the entity beans are not being accessed directly by the clients. The access is through a servlet in the case of login, or more commonly, through a session bean acting as a session controller. This is a common pattern. The technique is often referred to as wrapping the entity beans with a session bean. The idea is to reduce the number of network calls that are required and to achieve a cleaner separation of responsibilities. Note that some entity bean interactions are not shown in this diagram due to space constraints.

Another approach, which can also be used in conjunction with the preceding approach, is to place the entity bean information into a JavaBean and return that in response to a call. The key advantage, again, is the reduction in network

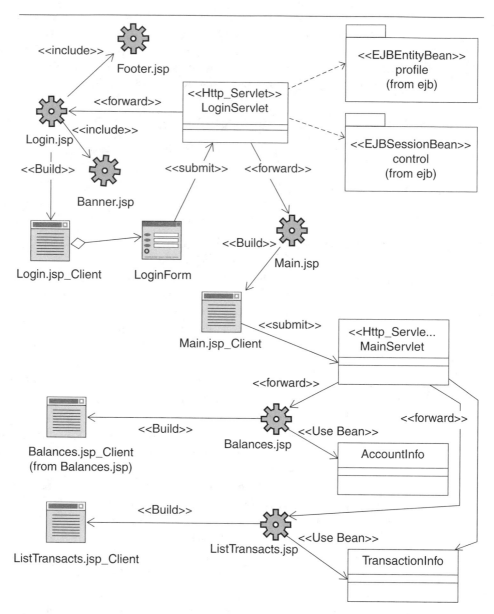

Figure 13-22   Partial HomeDirect class diagram using J2EE technologies

calls. The information can be accessed and even manipulated locally, and then the entity bean can be updated following a predetermined strategy.

Does it make sense to use entity beans to obtain an object-oriented view of every piece of data that is required by an application? The answer is no.

Remember that entity beans are expensive. In some situations, it may be appropriate to use a JavaBean instead and put the database access code directly in the JavaBean. This may be appropriate in situations where you are only reading the data and do not need to worry about transactions and updates to the information. The biggest disadvantage of this approach is that it violates the entity bean-based strategy envisioned by J2EE. Therefore, it may be appropriate to start with an EJB-based strategy and consider such approaches as implementation optimizations if necessary.

Layering

As discussed in Chapter 6, layering is concerned with the logical organization of packages and subsystems in order to achieve a functional partitioning of the system.

For the case study, we follow the RUP recommendations for organizing a J2EE project into layers. Specifically, the RUP proposes using a reuse-driven layering scheme. The following layers are used:

- *Application layer:* This layer focuses on application-specific functionality. The servlets associated with the application are placed within this layer. A "User Interface" (UI) sublayer within the application layer contains UI classes such as the JSP and HTML pages developed for the case study.

- *Business layer:* This layer contains two sublayers: "Business Entities" and "Business Services." The Business Entities layer contains the entity bean subsystems, and the Business Services layer contains the session bean subsystems. Had we used any dependent objects or JavaBeans to encapsulate database interactions (e.g., for use with a BMP entity bean or directly by a servlet), those classes would have been placed in a separate "Persistence" sublayer.

- *Middleware layer:* This layer contains third-party Application Programming Interfaces (APIs) and so on. It is not used in the case study.

This layering approach is shown graphically in Figure 13-23.

The distinction between layering versus packaging can sometimes be confusing. Layering is concerned with the logical structuring of the application, whereas packaging is concerned with the physical structure.

Consider the packaging structure that Java applications typically follow, for example, the package hierarchy *com.awp.homedirect* and so on. Although such packaging serves to partition a software application into well-defined packages, it does not provide a good representation of the logical organization of an application. For example, a physical packaging hierarchy cannot convey

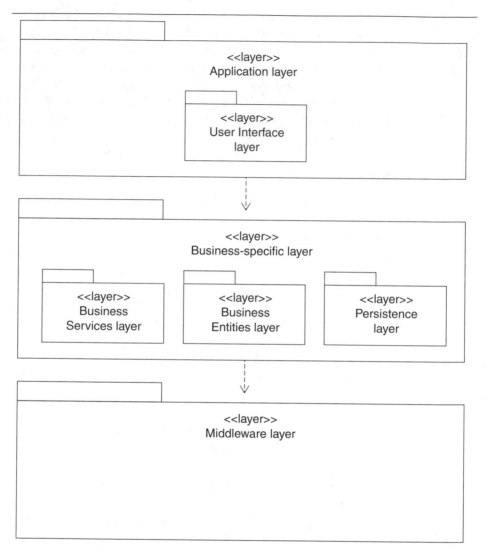

Figure 13-23 Layering

that an application might be structured such that you could easily extend the application by building on top of it or by replacing a "layer" of components.

This does not mean, however, that the physical packaging and layering are mutually exclusive. You can use packaging as a lower level mechanism to segregate or group specific details and map those onto the layers in your model.

For instance, in the HomeDirect application, the *com.awp.homedirect.web,* which contains all the servlets, is placed in the application layer. Similarly, the *docroot* package that contains the JSPs is in the application layer. The *com.awp.homedirect.ejb.control,* which contains the control session bean subsystem, is in the Business Services sublayer within the Business-specific layer. The remaining packages within *com.awl.homedirect.ejb* are mapped to the Business Entities sublayer and so on.

With such layering represented within the model, it would be easy to establish that if a new presentation format were desired or an application needed to be customized for a specific client, the activity could easily be accomplished by replacing the Application layer.

Summary

Although entity beans have not been adopted as widely as session beans, recent improvements should encourage their use. Modeling of entity beans is similar to the modeling of session beans and is accomplished using UML subsystems, classes, interfaces, methods, fields, and stereotypes, with relationships drawn between the different items.

An entity bean consists of a Home interface, a Remote interface, an implementation class, and a primary key class. The Home interface defines create, finder, and home methods. The Remote interface defines business methods. The primary key class must be included, but can also be shared between entity beans. The implementation class implements all of the life cycle, finder, select, and business methods.

Entity beans are all about persistence. J2EE 1.3 entity beans with container-managed persistence differ greatly from previous versions of entity bean types in terms of capability, behavior, and how persistent fields are specified.

Chapter 14

Message-Driven Beans

❖ **Process Check:**
We continue
with design as
we progress
through the
Rational Unified
Process (RUP)
analysis and
design disci-
pline. We also
discuss some
aspects of imple-
mentation in the
context of the
EJB technology.

The Enterprise JavaBeans (EJBs) we have talked about so far—session beans and entity beans—are both based on the synchronous method invocation paradigm. That is, if a session bean A wants to obtain some information from entity bean B, it calls a method on entity bean B (indirectly via the remote interface), and then the caller waits for the result to be computed and communicated back from the called bean.

In this chapter, we look at a very different paradigm recently added to the formal EJB specification for release in J2EE 1.3 in the form of message-driven beans *or more simply* message beans.

Introduction to Message-Driven Beans

The idea behind messaging is to send messages, essentially units of data, from one process to another. Messages can be about events that have taken place, requests for data, or replies to queries.

Message-driven beans are J2EE components that have been designed to be asynchronous message consumers. In other words, another J2EE entity, such as a session bean, can simply send a message on to the message-driven bean, and then go on about its business while the message-driven bean figures out how to process the message it has received.

The messaging paradigm offers various advantages over the conventional synchronous operation invocation paradigm.

For instance, it can be used as a relatively simple solution for communicating a large volume of events and/or data. In the J2EE, messaging and message-driven beans require the use of the Java Message Service (JMS).

The Java Message Service

The JMS is one of the J2EE Application Programming Interfaces (APIs). It provides an API to message-based systems, thereby allowing existing message-based systems to be used with the J2EE. Message-driven beans in J2EE 1.3 must use JMS for messaging purposes.

The JMS supports two kinds of messaging:

- *Point-to-Point:* In point-to-point messaging, one client acts as a sender of the message and another acts as the receiver. Incoming messages intended for a receiver are placed on a *queue* and processed by the receiver in the order they arrive. An e-mail system or traditional postal system is similar to a point-to-point paradigm.

- *Publish-subscribe:* In the publish-subscribe paradigm, multiple applications can send messages, and multiple applications can receive the messages. Messages are sent to a *topic* by one or more publishers and received by all those who have subscribed to the topic. A Web-based discussion forum is conceptually similar to a publish-subscribe paradigm.

Role of JMS and Message-Driven Beans in EJB

As stated earlier, message-driven beans leverage the JMS. Note that the EJB specification is not very clear concerning the possibility of using messaging services other than the JMS at this point. It is not ruled out, but it is not really explicitly supported. Message-driven beans are essentially built as JMS MessageListeners and are accessed by having the client locate the proper JMS destination, that is, a queue or a topic. This makes using them fairly simple.

Why Use Messaging and Message-Driven Beans?

There are several reasons why it is advantageous to use messaging and message-driven beans in an enterprise application setting:

- *Decoupling:* Different parts of an application can be developed such that they are not closely tied to each other. This allows for better reuse opportunities because the only common component is the destination.

- *Flexible integration:* Conversely, loosely coupled systems can be put together easily by using message-driven beans to "wrap" existing systems.

- *Efficiency:* Messaging can be used for separating those elements of the business logic that can be processed independently from the main timeline (e.g., logging specific event occurrences, sending e-mail informational messages). Doing so increases the overall efficiency because the same critical resource (e.g., a session bean) is spending less time waiting for nonessential operations to complete and can instead complete its task and handle new incoming requests.

Using JMS does not come without potential drawbacks. First, there is the additional overhead of messaging and associated message handling. Second, such messaging can lead to bottlenecks. Third, a message-based system has the potential to be a single point of failure. Appropriate strategies exist for addressing each of these drawbacks. So, all in all, a message-based system does offer significant benefits when used for the right reasons.

When to Use Message-Driven Beans

There are some scenarios where it makes sense to employ message-driven beans:

- You have a legacy application that needs to be integrated into the J2EE-based enterprise application. Rather than rewrite an entire application, you can use a message-driven bean to wrap the legacy application so that it acts as the intermediary to the legacy application.

- Your application requires low-level services that can be delivered offline. That is, although the service must be provided, the main workflow doesn't necessarily have to wait for its completion. An example of this is a logging service that records all orders being placed.

- Message-driven beans also provide a convenient mechanism to allow delivery of the same information to multiple parties. This is accomplished via the publisher-subscriber paradigm. Each message from a publisher is delivered to each subscriber. For example, if a publisher sends out a message and the topic has three subscribers, each of the subscribers receives the message without any work on the part of the publishers. The publisher/subscriber details can be changed easily without affecting the other parts of the system.

J2EE Version

As is the case with all EJB component types, message-driven beans are deployed with the help of an EJB container, which in turn is hosted by an application server. The particular capabilities and level of J2EE compliance of the server determines which version of the EJB specification you need to be working with.

Most of this chapter applies to J2EE 1.3 only because message-driven beans did not exist in previous releases of the J2EE platform.

The discussion of JMS is applicable to other versions as well.

Message-Driven Bean Views and the UML

Structurally, message-driven beans consist of a main Java class, often called the implementation class or the message-driven bean class. That's all there is to it. There are no interfaces nor other classes unless your design calls for some additional helper classes to be added to the EJB to assist in supporting your business logic.

Because there is really only one class to speak of, there are also no relationships between elements to consider. As you can see, this makes message-driven beans typically smaller and much easier to create and use than the other EJB types.

Client View

The primary interface between the client and the message-driven bean consists of the messages the client can send out to the message-driven bean. The client cannot refer directly to the message-driven bean.

As such, there is no client specific view of the message-driven bean analogous to the session bean and entity bean client views.

The client contacts a JMS destination that the EJB container provides for each deployed component. Other than that, there are no interfaces exposed to the client.

In terms of UML representation, the message-driven bean is simply represented as a UML class stereotyped as <<EJBMessage>> as shown in Figure 14-1. A message-driven bean could be represented in the same fashion as the session and entity beans; however, a message-driven bean does not have the same complexity and therefore a simple class approach is clearer and more consistent.

Note that in this case, we have shown the message-driven bean with the interfaces it realizes. Because a message-driven bean must always implements these interfaces, it would be appropriate to simply show the message-driven bean class itself. The presence of the stereotype implicitly identifies the interfaces being implemented by the message-driven bean.

UML Benefits for Message-Driven Beans

Message-driven beans rely on the destination and messages for incoming and outgoing communication. You can use UML modeling to clearly see and communicate how the message-driven bean fits into the overall system.

Specifically, you can

- Model the set of messages that can be sent or received by a given message-driven bean
- Model how destinations in your system are being utilized
- Show relationships between the message-driven bean classes and its users

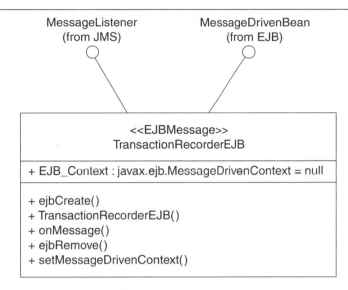

Figure 14-1   Client view representation of a message-driven bean in UML

Modeling Messages

All communication with message-driven beans is by means of asynchronous messages. Such messages must belong to *javax.jms.message* or one of its descendants.

Clearly, there is a need for the client to know which messages the message-driven bean expects. But there is no formalized mechanism in the message-driven bean itself to communicate this information to its users.

In the UML model of a message-driven bean, the appropriate message can easily be communicated via a dependency between the message types and the message-driven bean subsystem. The dependency can be used by the client to identify and communicate with the message-driven bean appropriately as the client would need to have the same dependencies on the client side to be able to successfully create and send the appropriate messages to the message-driven bean.

Figure 14-2 shows an example of this approach.

Modeling Destinations

A client does not see the message-driven bean itself. As such, it cannot address the messages to a specific message-driven bean. Rather, it simply locates and sends messages to a specific destination. A message-driven bean retrieves messages from the destination with which it is associated and processes it.

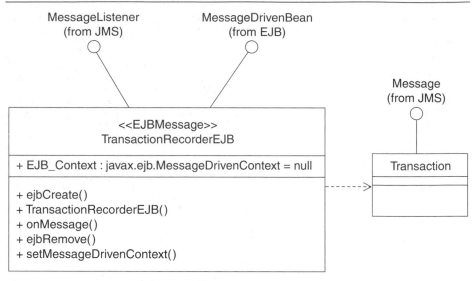

Figure 14-2 Modeling valid messages to a specific message-driven bean

JMS supports two types of message destinations:

- *Topic:* A topic enables what is sometimes referred to as the publisher-subscriber messaging paradigm. A topic can be published to by multiple clients and in turn multiple message-driven beans can subscribe to a topic to receive the incoming messages. A topic can be subscribed to in a durable or nondurable way. Durable subscription requires that messages sent to the topic be delivered even if the message-driven bean itself does not exist. Durable subscriptions are useful when you are building reliable and available systems.

- *Queue:* A queue differs from a topic in that although there can be multiple publishers to a queue, it can only have a single message-driven bean on the receiving end. Messages delivered by the senders are placed on the queue in the order received and processed by the message-driven bean as it retrieves them from the queue. In the simplest case, a queue can only have a single sender and receiver. This is sometimes also known as point-to-point messaging.

Interestingly, there is no direct programmatic relationship between the chosen destination for the message-driven bean and the message-driven bean itself.

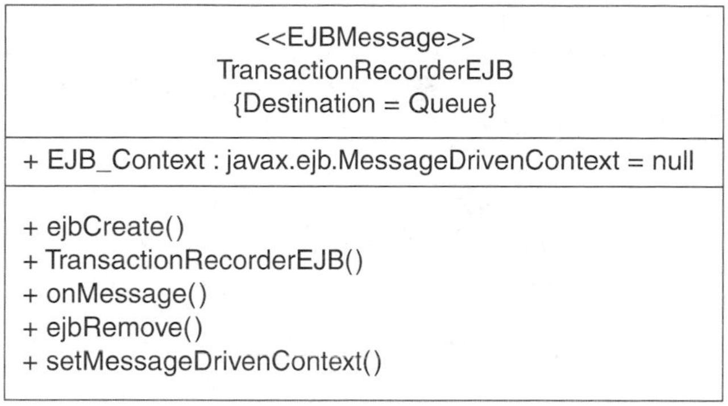

```
┌─────────────────────────────────────────────────────┐
│                   <<EJBMessage>>                      │
│               TransactionRecorderEJB                  │
│                {Destination = Queue}                  │
├─────────────────────────────────────────────────────┤
│ + EJB_Context : javax.ejb.MessageDrivenContext = null │
├─────────────────────────────────────────────────────┤
│ + ejbCreate( )                                        │
│ + TransactionRecorderEJB( )                           │
│ + onMessage( )                                        │
│ + ejbRemove( )                                        │
│ + setMessageDrivenContext( )                          │
└─────────────────────────────────────────────────────┘
```

Figure 14-3   Using a tagged value to model destination

The bean provider provides that information declaratively through the deployment descriptor. However, there is still value for the developer to identify this information at the UML model level in order to clearly identify the design intent and approach if it is material to the design. A tagged value of {Destination= Queue} or {Destination=Topic} can be used for this purpose. This is shown in Figure 14-3.

Message-Driven Bean Technology

For the client, a message-driven bean is a component that provides business logic to handle whatever JMS messages are sent to it. The technology level of these J2EE components involves specific classes, methods, and fields that must exist to support the EJB life cycle.

Transactions

Like session beans, message-driven beans can use either container-managed transaction demarcation or bean-managed transaction demarcation. The reasons for using either demarcation are the same as those described for session beans in Chapter 12.

As is the case for all other EJBs, transactional attributes are set on the methods a client can call. In the case of message-driven beans, the **onMessage** method is the only one that has these settings, and the client calls it only indirectly.

Implementation Class

The implementation class contains the implementations for all methods required by the EJB including life cycle methods. The implementation class must contain the following:

- **setMessageDrivenContext:** This method must exist and is called by the EJB container. It allows the EJB to store the context information in a local instance variable.

- **ejbCreate:** Only one such method must exist with exactly this name and no arguments, and the return type must be void. The EJB container uses this method to create new instances of the message-driven bean.

- **ejbRemove:** Only one such method must exist with exactly this name and no arguments, and the return type must be void. The EJB container uses this method to remove instances of the message-driven bean.

- **onMessage:** Only one such method must exist with exactly this name and a single argument that is the JMS message, and the return type must be void. The EJB container uses this method to process all JMS messages. The business logic for the EJB resides in this method, or at least is called from this method.

There can be additional methods in the implementation class that exist simply as utilities to assist in supporting the business logic in the **onMessage** method. There can also be other classes present within the internal design of the EJB that the implementation class can use. In addition, the required **MessageDrivenContext** field is part of the implementation class as well.

Figure 14-4 shows an implementation example of a message-driven bean.

Message-Driven Bean Life Cycle

The life cycle of a message-driven bean uses the same concepts used by other EJBs, and it is the simplest to describe. The EJB container initially creates a pool of instances for each message-driven bean you deploy. The size and behavior of the pool is controlled by various server settings. When a JMS message comes in, the EJB container simply dispatches the message to an available instance in the pool and calls the **onMessage** method. When that method completes, the instance goes back into the pool.

The state diagram in Figure 14-5 accurately shows this life cycle.

```
import javax.jms.Message;
import javax.jms.MessageListener;
import javax.jms.TextMessage;

public class LogBean implements javax.ejb.MessageDrivenBean,
javax.jms.MessageListener {
    private javax.ejb.MessageDrivenContext ctx;
    public LogBean() {      }
    public void setMessageDrivenContext(javax.ejb.MessageDriven
    Context context) {
      ctx = context;
  }
    public void ejbCreate() throws javax.ejb.EJBException,
    javax.ejb.CreateException {  }
    public void ejbRemove() throws javax.ejb.EJBException {   }

    public void onMessage(javax.jms.Message msg) {
      try {
         TextMessage tm = (TextMessage)msg;
         String text = tm.getText();
        // logging specific code here
      }
      catch (Exception ex) {
        // exception handling code here
      }
  }
}
```

Figure 14-4   Implementation code for a simple message-driven bean

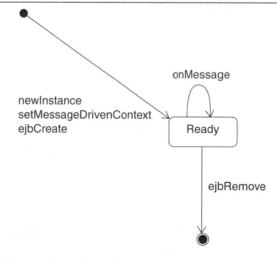

Figure 14-5   Message-driven bean life cycle

Message-Driven Bean Common Scenario

A standard scenario for using a message-driven bean is for the client to act as follows:

1. Client locates JMS destination for the message-driven bean
2. Client issues JMS messages to the destination

A UML sequence diagram showing a typical usage of a message-driven bean is provided in Figure 14-6.

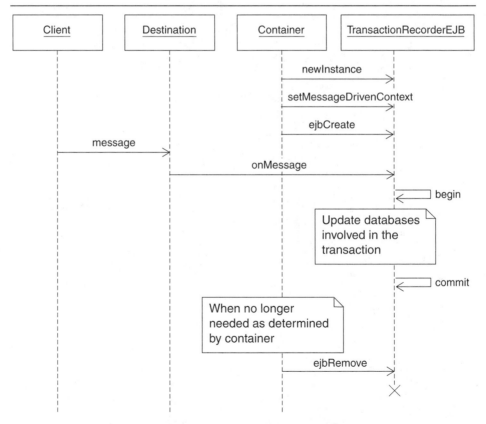

Figure 14-6 A sequence diagram showing the typical usage of a message-driven bean

Modeling Message-Driven Bean Relationships

Message-driven beans can utilize other Java classes to fulfill their responsibilities and may be utilized themselves by others. This section discusses modeling of such aspects.

Modeling Message-Driven Bean Relationships with Other Classes

Like any other Java class, a message-driven bean may utilize other Java classes to perform its responsibilities. Such relationships are modeled as usual.

Message-Driven Bean and Other J2EE Technologies

The relationship between a message-driven bean and each of the other J2EE technologies is similar. Each (servlet, session bean, entity bean, etc.) must use a destination to communicate with the message-driven bean. As such, there are no distinctive modeling aspects.

Identifying Message-Driven Beans in Enterprise Applications

Remote Procedure Call (RPC)-based communication, such as that employed by session beans, has the disadvantage that the sender must wait for a response. For instance, imagine that you invoke a business method on another session bean. You then need to wait for the method to return so you can undertake the next activity. What if the task you wanted to achieve was time-consuming and not particularly critical? Obviously, it would come down to a decision about how important the task really is and whether the performance impact is justifiable.

A message-based system, on the other hand, does not suffer from this drawback. So, in the same scenario, if the session bean were communicating with a message-driven bean, it could simply send the message along asynchronously to be processed by the message-driven bean in an independent fashion.

In the HomeDirect case study, we could use the message-driven bean to log any interesting operational information and report problems. HomeDirect components would just send the message on to the predetermined topic, and then go on about their business. When the message-driven bean received the message-based request, it would simply handle the message according to the message type. Message-driven beans can also be used to wrap legacy applications to make the integration effort easier.

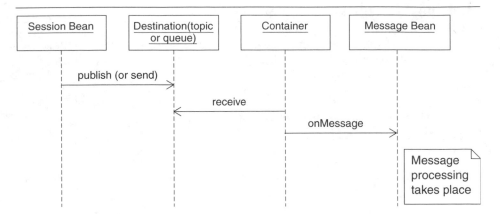

Figure 14-7   Example of an interaction between a session bean and a message-driven bean

An example of a session bean and message-driven bean interaction is shown in Figure 14-7. In this scenario, a session bean (after it looks up a Java Naming and Directory Interface [JNDI] destination) publishes a message to a destination. The message is retrieved by the container and leads to an **onMessage** method on the message-driven bean. At this time, the message-driven bean can process the message as indicated in the **onMessage** method.

The question of how to send a response back to the sending party often comes up. There is no formally defined mechanism in the current version of the EJB 2.0 specification. Typical strategies for dealing with this involve some variation on either setting up a temporary or permanent reply destination and providing information about the reply destination to the message-driven bean in the message itself.

Another thing to watch out for during the development of a message-driven bean is the message type. A message-driven bean should be prepared to handle any of the supported types of messages that are sent to it. For example, a message-driven bean should be able to receive and process a TextMessage while expecting an ObjectMessage. This is because any object that supports the message interface can be a valid message.

Summary

Message-driven beans are new in J2EE 1.3. They are designed to process JMS messages and are useful for situations where synchronicity is not required, nor desired. A good example is using message-driven beans for integrating loosely coupled systems.

UML class diagrams are used to model both client and internal views, even though there are no interfaces exposed to the client. Modeling is done using UML subsystems, classes, methods, fields, and stereotypes. Communication with message-driven beans takes place asynchronously via messages sent to a topic or a queue.

Message-driven beans use the transaction concept like other EJBs. As with other EJBs, the message-driven beans' implementation class implements the life cycle methods and business logic.

Chapter 15

Assembly and Deployment

- Component Modeling

- Component Modeling of J2EE Technologies

- Deployment Modeling

- Traceability Revisited

- Assembly and Deployment of Enterprise Java Applications

- Summary

Regardless of the specifics of your enterprise application and irrespective of the approach you use to analyze, design, and develop the software, there will come a point when you will need to identify how your software code will manifest itself in the physical world of files, binaries, executables, and libraries. You will further need to determine how the software code will be deployed for best results.

This is where component and deployment modeling comes in. You use component modeling to establish how the various pieces of your software are pieced together physically and deployment modeling to map out the overall layout of your distributed enterprise application.

Component and deployment modeling of Java 2 Platform, Enterprise Edition (J2EE) technologies and the enterprise application is the centerpiece of discussion for this chapter.

We conclude the chapter with a discussion of assembly and deployment in the context of enterprise Java applications.

Component Modeling

In our discussions with Java developers who use the Unified Modeling Language (UML), we often find that component modeling is usually not very prevalent. There are several reasons that warrant otherwise and suggest an increased focus on implementation modeling:

- *Complexity:* For a simple application, how the different elements of the model come together in the physical world to form the application is pretty trivial. But as applications grow larger, it becomes more and more important to model the physical implementation world to manage the overall complexity of your application. Component modeling can help in this regard by unambiguously showing the dependencies between the different model elements.
- *Reusability:* Reusability can take place at the design level when you reuse an existing class definition or interface in your application. But a more powerful force for usability is reusability of self-contained and packaged

components. Component diagrams provide the perfect vehicle for identifying such reuse opportunities.

Component Modeling of J2EE Technologies

A component diagram is primarily composed of UML components. In this context, however, the term *component* is slightly broader than the term commonly used in the software industry, as a UML component can be a source code component, a binary component, an executable component, or even a text file.

A component diagram provides a static view of the components and their relationships. Components on a component diagram may exist throughout development or may come into being after compilation, linking, and so on.

Stereotypes are used to distinguish between the different kinds of Java components on a component diagram:

- A Java class file (.class file extension) is represented by specializing the standard UML stereotype <<file>> and stereotyping a component with the stereotype <<JavaClassFile>>.

- A file containing a JavaServer Page (JSP; .jsp file extension) is represented via specializing the <<file>> stereotype and applying <<JSPFile>> to a component.

- A deployment descriptor is represented by specializing the standard UML stereotype <<file>> and stereotyping a component with one of the following stereotypes:
  - <<WebDescriptor>> for Web components composed of servlets and JSPs.
  - <<EJBDescriptor>> for Enterprise JavaBean (EJB) components.

- A Java Archive File (JAR) file is represented by stereotyping a UML package with the stereotype <<JavaArchiveFile>>. Different types of JAR files are distinguished by the use of one of the following:
  - JAR files (.jar file extension) containing EJBs are identified with stereotyping a package with the <<EJBArchiveFile>> stereotype.
  - Web archive files (.war file extension) containing JSPs, servlets, and HTML pages are represented via a package stereotyped as <<WebArchiveFile>>.
  - Enterprise archive files (.ear file extension) that contain entire enterprise Java applications are identified by stereotyping a package with <<EnterpriseArchiveFile>>.

Figure 15-1 shows an example of a simple component diagram.

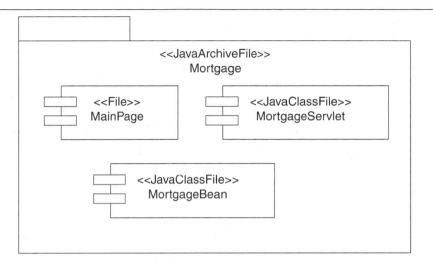

Figure 15-1 A simple component diagram

Representing Web Components

Web components can be composed of a servlet or JSP, static pages such as HTML pages, and a deployment descriptor. An example of a Web component on a component diagram is shown in Figure 15-2.

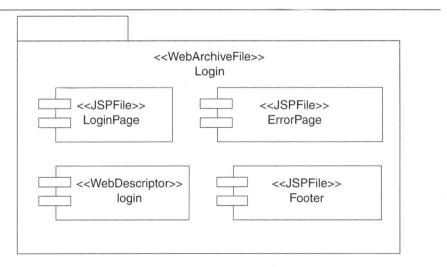

Figure 15-2 Web component on a component diagram

Representing EJBs

EJB components are packaged in archive files that contain the compiled class files for the EJB itself, any required supporting Java class files, and an EJB deployment descriptor.

Figure 15-3 shows a UML component diagram for an EJB component.

Note that several EJBs can exist within the same EJB archive file, and in fact, this is the most common way to group them. Grouping within the same file allows for local EJB-to-EJB relationships to be possible, so this is a very important point.

When grouping in this way, the descriptor fields for each EJB are usually merged into a single descriptor file, which is also the case for a Web descriptor in a Web archive file.

Figure 15-4 shows an example of multiple EJBs grouped in a single EJB archive. Note how both EJBs share a common primary key class in this example.

Component Modeling of Enterprise Applications

Enterprise Java applications represent all the different pieces that make up an enterprise application. Depending on the application, this may mean some Web components as well as EJB components.

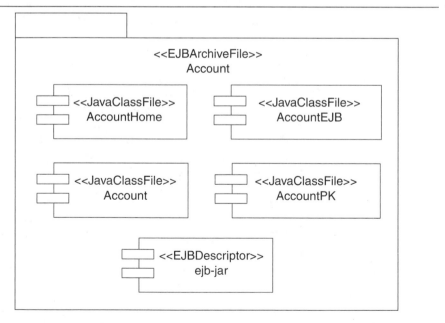

Figure 15-3   EJBs and component diagrams

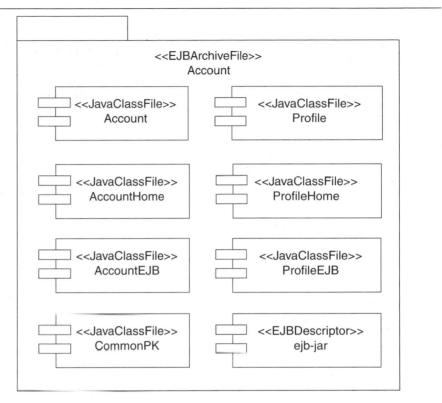

Figure 15-4   Multiple EJBs grouped in a single archive file

Figure 15-5 shows an example of an enterprise Java application via a component diagram.

It is also possible for an application to consist of just EJB components that are directly accessed via a thin client application. If the HomeDirect application had a client-based application interface, such a relationship could have been shown using the <<EJB ClientJar>> stereotype for a usage relationship as shown in Figure 15-6.

Deployment Modeling

Distribution is an essential aspect of enterprise applications. Deployment modeling is useful for modeling how the different pieces that make up the enterprise application are distributed across multiple processors and processes.

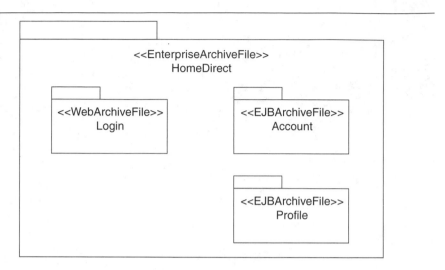

Figure 15-5 An enterprise component

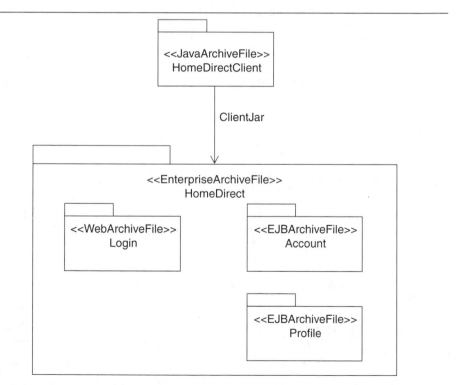

Figure 15-6 Showing client relationships for EJBs

Only those enterprise application elements that exist at runtime are modeled for deployment. In the case of J2EE, this includes the various archive files but excludes plain Java source files.

The central modeling concept in the deployment diagram is the *node*. In general, a node typically represents a processor or some similar hardware concept. Stereotypes can be used to distinguish different types of nodes. Nodes can have associations among them, which represent communication paths between nodes. Again, stereotyping is used to distinguish between different types of communication paths. Runtime component instances are mapped onto the nodes to show the runtime deployment.

In the J2EE world, you must also deal with different types of servers. This list includes Web servers, application servers, database servers, and so on. To model the enterprise application in a generic fashion, we use the following stereotypes to distinguish between the various types:

- <<WebServer>>

- <<ApplicationServer>>

- <<DatabaseServer>>

Figure 15-7 shows a deployment diagram for a simple enterprise application.

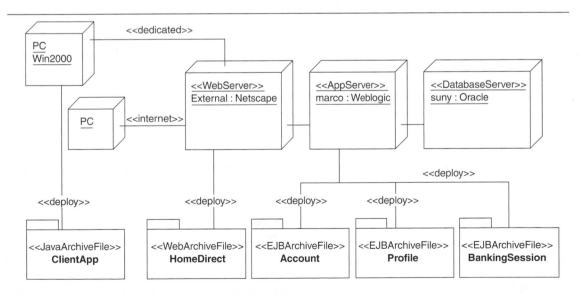

Figure 15-7   Modeling deployment of J2EE applications

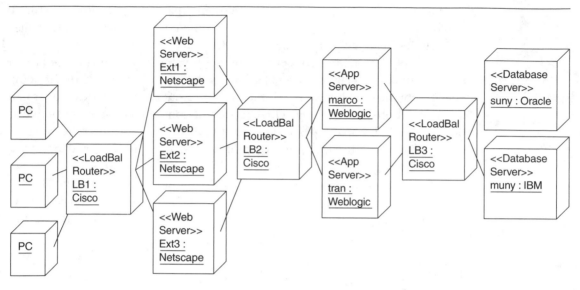

Figure 15-8 Redundancy modeling via deployment diagram

Additionally, a mission-critical enterprise application may call for redundant servers to ensure that services continue to be provided uninterrupted in case of failures. Deployment diagrams can be used to identify such configurations.

Figure 15-8 shows a deployment diagram with a load balancing setup.

Traceability Revisited

As discussed in earlier chapters, traceability is an important benefit of the Rational Unified Process (RUP) and the use case-driven development approach. Now that we have covered textual requirements all the way to the physical manifestation of the software, it is appropriate to revisit traceability and conclude with a concrete example to illustrate the concept of traceability across the entire UML model.

Figure 15-9 shows traceability graphically for the TransferServlet. It demonstrates clearly that we can easily justify the existence of the TransferServlet component based on the textual requirements by following the traceability chain from the requirements to the component. We can do so because the textual requirements directly lead to the use case in the use case model, which in turn results in the TransferFunds control object in the analysis model, and so on. We also benefit from knowing that should the requirements associated with the Transfer funds use case change, it will be relatively straightforward to identify the impacted pieces of software throughout the model.

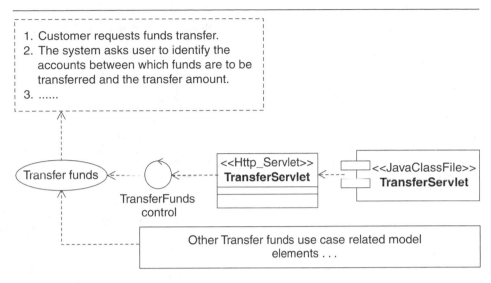

1. Customer requests funds transfer.
2. The system asks user to identify the accounts between which funds are to be transferred and the transfer amount.
3. ......

Transfer funds

TransferFunds control

<<Http_Servlet>>
TransferServlet

<<JavaClassFile>>
TransferServlet

Other Transfer funds use case related model elements . . .

Figure 15-9 Traceability across the model

Assembly and Deployment of Enterprise Java Applications

The J2EE specification places the responsibility of assembly and deployment on the *application assembler* and *deployer* roles, respectively. In doing so, it distinguishes between a person that develops an enterprise Java component such as an EJB and the persons who assemble and deploy that EJB. Although one person may take on all these tasks, it is equally acceptable for three different individuals to play these roles.

The *application assembler* role is responsible for locating and putting together individual components to form an enterprise application. Such assembly typically involves creating or updating an enterprise application deployment descriptor.

The *deployer* role focuses on configuring and installing an application assembled by the assembler onto an application server. This typically involves resolving external dependencies, configuring resources required by the application such as databases and mail services, configuring the application for transactions and security, and so on, and deploying the application to the app server.

Assembly can be carried out manually or with the help of assembly and deployment tools. Deployment involves using a deployment tool that generates container-specific classes to enable the container to provide the required runtime services to the enterprise application.

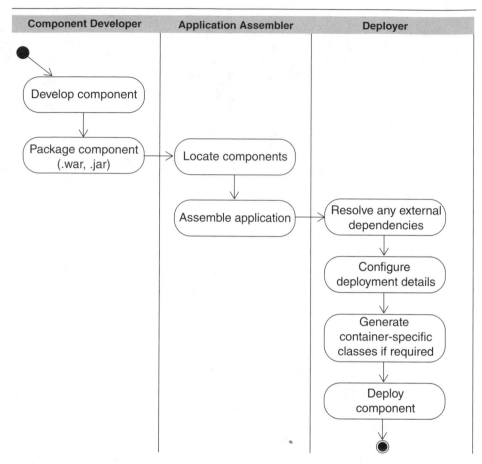

Figure 15-10   Division of responsibilities across J2EE roles

Figure 15-10 illustrates the division of responsibilities for the J2EE roles via an activity diagram.

Deployment Descriptors

J2EE components utilize eXtensible Markup Language (XML)-based deployment descriptors for communication between the component developer, the application assembler, and the deployer.

Each deployment descriptor is based on an XML Document Type Description (DTD), which specifies the grammar for that type of deployment descriptor.

A portion of the EJB XML DTD from the EJB 2.0 specification is reproduced in the following example. In this example, the first highlighted line indicates that an assembly-descriptor consists of zero or more security-roles, zero or more method-permissions, and zero or more container-transactions. In the second highlighted line, you see that each container-transaction can contain at most a single description, at least one method, a single trans-attribute, and so on:

```
<!ELEMENT abstract-schema-name (#PCDATA)>
<!ELEMENT assembly-descriptor (security-role*, method-permission*,
container-transaction*)>
<!ELEMENT cascade-delete EMPTY>
<!ELEMENT cmp-field (description?, field-name)>
<!ELEMENT cmp-version (#PCDATA)>
<!ELEMENT cmr-field (description?, cmr-field-name, cmr-field-
type?)>
<!ELEMENT cmr-field-name (#PCDATA)>
<!ELEMENT cmr-field-type (#PCDATA)>
<!ELEMENT container-transaction (description?, method+,
trans-attribute)>
<!ELEMENT dependent (description?, dependent-class, dependent-name,
cmp-field+, pk-field*)>
<!ELEMENT dependents (description?, dependent+)>
<!ELEMENT dependent-class (#PCDATA)>
<!ELEMENT dependent-name (#PCDATA)>
<!ELEMENT description (#PCDATA)>
<!ELEMENT display-name (#PCDATA)>
<!ELEMENT ejb-class (#PCDATA)>
<!ELEMENT ejb-client-jar (#PCDATA)>
<!ELEMENT ejb-entity-ref (description?, remote-ejb-name,
ejb-ref-name, home, remote, ejb-link?)>
...
```

J2EE has several distinct types of deployment descriptors:

- *Web deployment descriptor:* Used for servlets and JSPs. Web deployment descriptor XML files are named web.jar. A Web deployment descriptor may contain one or more servlets and JSPs.

- *EJB deployment descriptor:* Contains details of one or more EJBs. EJB deployment descriptor XML documents are named ejb-jar.xml.

- *Application deployment descriptor:* Contains details about a J2EE enterprise application. Application deployment descriptors are stored in application.xml files.

- *Vendor-specific deployment descriptor:* J2EE server vendors often require the use of one or more vendor-specific deployment descriptors to convey special parameters required by their server. These are in addition to the previously mentioned descriptors. For example, BEA Weblogic uses a weblogic-ejb-jar.xml deployment descriptor to allow the deployer to convey information required for caching, clustering, and so on.

An XML document uses a style very similar to HTML. Although HTML uses a fixed set of tags for conveying formatting details, XML tags associate meaning to data. XML tags can be nested to form complex structures.

A partial web.xml deployment descriptor is shown in the following example. In this example, XML tags are used to specify details of a servlet and a JSP contained in the Web application. For example, the tag <web-app> specifies that the remaining details are about a Web application that has a display name of *HomeDirect,* and so on.

```
<?xml version=1.0 encoding=Cp1252?>

<!DOCTYPE web-app PUBLIC' -//Sun Microsystems, Inc.//DTD Web Appli-
cation 2.2//EN' 'http://java.sun.com/j2ee/dtds/web-app_2.2.dtd'>

<web-app>
 <display-name>HomeDirect</display-name>
 <description>HomeDirect web application</description>
 <servlet>
   <servlet-name>ProfileServlet</servlet-name>
   <display-name>ProfileServlet</display-name>
   <description>no description</description>
   <servlet-class>com.homedirect.web.ProfileServlet</servlet-
class>
 </servlet>
 <servlet>
   <servlet-name>TransferJSP</servlet-name>
   <display-name>TransferJSP</display-name>
   <description>no description</description>
   <jsp-file>Transfer.jsp</jsp-file>
 </servlet>
 ...
```

Summary

As the applications being developed become larger, component modeling and deployment modeling become more important. Component modeling is useful for modeling how the various pieces are put together. Deployment modeling, on the other hand, is useful for modeling the distribution aspects of the application and how the runtime component instances that make up the enterprise application are deployed in the distributed system.

The J2EE specification partitions the responsibilities of development, assembly, and deployment into the developer, assembler, and deployer roles, respectively. Deployment descriptors are used as the chief means of communication between these roles.

Chapter 16
Case Study

- Case Study Background

- Problem Statement

- Rationale and Assumptions

- HomeDirect Requirements

- Inception Phase

- Elaboration Phase

- Remaining Phases

- Summary

Just reading theory will only get you so far. Inevitably, you must get your hands dirty in order to further your understanding.

This chapter provides a hands-on example for those interested in exploring the J2EE technology firsthand.

This is accomplished by:

- *Providing you with sufficient detail about a hypothetical but concrete problem*

- *Walking through several use cases from analysis to implementation*

- *Using simulated interaction with end users and others to approximate a more realistic iterative scenario*

- *Providing accompanying implementation to continue the case study*

- *Offering suggestions for changes to the implementation to enhance the functionality of the case study*

- *Providing guidelines on additional use cases to analyze, design, and implement in a reader-led iteration*

All this is done in the context of following a customized version of the Rational Unified Process (RUP) in order to reinforce the software development ideas discussed in this book.

All of the names of businesses, service marks, and so on used in this example are fictional. Any resemblance to real entities is purely coincidental.

The HomeDirect case study source code can be obtained from

http://www.awl.com/cseng/titles/0-201-73829-5/

Case Study Background

Despite the banking industry's image as a stoic and old-fashioned business, it has always been a heavy user of technology. Mainframe computers helped meet the heavy-duty data processing and record keeping needs. Automated Banking Tellers (ATMs) have now been in use for decades. So, it comes as no surprise that banks have seized upon the promise of the Web to provide enhanced yet cost-effective online banking services on a 24/7 basis to its customers.

Problem Statement

In order to better compete with its much larger competitors, ACMEBank of Sammamish, Washington has decided to offer a full range of online banking services, known collectively as *HomeDirect Bank,* to its customers.

HomeDirect will be available to all bank customers free of charge via the World Wide Web. Three key types of services will initially be offered as part of HomeDirect:

- *Inquiry services:* These include balance updates, viewing lists of transactions, and downloading past account history.
- *Bill Payment services:* Users will be able to pay bills electronically.
- *Transaction services:* These include facilities such as funds transfer, and for investment accounts, buying and selling of stocks,

A separate mechanism will be required for administrative functions related to HomeDirect. In addition to having full access to the online banking functions previously described, the administrative functions include the ability to create new accounts, close accounts, enable online banking for a given customer, manually adjust a given account balance, and cancel future bill payment transactions at the account holder's request.

HomeDirect online banking services must utilize the existing databases and other banking infrastructure at all times. Provision should also be made in the design for eventual integration with the existing loan processing system, LoansDirect, to enable customers to make requests for loans online. Enhanced bill payment services shall be offered for online customers that are using the BillsDirect service for tracking unpaid bills.

Rationale and Assumptions

The online banking example was used as the central project throughout this book. Although we considered various other possibilities, we felt this project to be most appropriate. Understanding the domain is half the battle, and the prevalence of online banking makes it much more likely that readers would already be familiar with what the case study is all about.

Obviously, it is beyond the scope of this book to implement a full and complete online banking system. As such, various simplifications and constraints have had to be necessarily imposed. The primary intent of this project is to illustrate the concepts related to the Java 2 Platform, Enterprise Edition (J2EE) and provide you with a hands-on learning resource.

Because this book is about applying the Unified Modeling Language (UML) and J2EE, we will use J2EE exclusively.

The following list contains some of the assumptions and constraints associated with our online banking example:

- Choice of technology is limited to the J2EE technologies (i.e., no ASPs or CGI scripts and so on, even though they may well be equally valid options in such a situation).

- A future payment cannot be for more than the current account balance (in real life, you may be allowed to do so due to pending deposits or overdraft protection setups).

- Only one customer can be associated with an account. Joint accounts are not allowed.

- In order to be a customer, a person must have at least one account.

HomeDirect Requirements

HomeDirect Bank shall utilize the existing databases and other infrastructure at all times. It shall be possible to easily migrate to a different platform vendor should the need arise.

The user interface shall be developed in such as way that customers can easily carry out inquiry or transaction services with minimal mouse clicks. Only valid user services shall be allowed at any given time. For example, if a user has no bills to pay, the service will indicate so and will not allow a pay bills transaction to be attempted.

Inquiry Services

Users shall be able to browse account-related information via the HomeDirect service.

HomeDirect users shall be required to login to the system prior to using it. A username and password shall be required. Once the username and password is verified for the customer, the user shall be able to use the full range of Home-Direct features.

Once a customer has successfully logged in, it shall be possible for the user to change the password and choose a new password. The user shall be asked to enter the previous password as a security measure. Once the old password is verified, the password shall be updated in the system.

The user shall be able to obtain the current balances summary from the database. The current balances shall be presented to the user with the account details.

The user accounts can include primary and secondary checking and savings accounts along with any number of bank-issued credit cards. Each account has its own limits and fees associated with it.

The user shall be able to obtain and view the list of recent transactions for all accounts. Each transaction in the list shall be displayed with the following information: transaction reference number, involved accounts or bills, explanation of fees if any, and the amount of the transaction.

Bill Payment Services

A user shall be able to use the ACMEBank HomeDirect service to pay bills electronically. An unpaid list of bills shall be provided to the user as obtained via the ACMEBank BillsDirect service.

The user shall be able to select any unpaid bill from the list for electronic payment from any registered account or credit card as long as sufficient balance, overdraft, or credit limit exists to cover both the amount of the bill and any associated fees.

Unpaid bills for existing users of the BillsDirect service are available via the bill database. New bills would be added to the bill database through existing banking processes outside of the HomeDirect system.

Alternately, a user shall be able to pay bills directly to registered vendors. Once a vendor has been added to the bill payees list for a given user, the user shall be able to make payments to the vendor as long as the vendor continues to be registered with the bank and is not removed by the user from the bill payee list.

To make a payment to a vendor in the bill payee list, the user shall be required to select the vendor from the bill payee list, indicate the exact amount of payment, and define a date for payment. When the user submits the bill payment request, the system shall verify the checking account balance to confirm that sufficient funds are available to pay the bill. If insufficient funds are available, the user shall be given appropriate notification, and the bill payment shall not be recorded.

If funds are available, the bill payment shall be queued to pending payments.

The user shall be able to remove a vendor from the bill payee list by selecting the vendor from the bill payee list and confirming the action. This shall result in the vendor being deleted from the associated account's bill payee list. Payments queued against pending payments shall not be affected by such removal.

Transaction Services

Although users shall not be able to carry out traditional transactions such as deposits and withdrawals via the HomeDirect service, they shall be able to undertake transfers between normal checking and savings accounts, credit cards, and unpaid bills as well as investment related actions.

A user shall be able to initiate fund transfers from one account to another account, for example, from savings to checking or checking to savings. The user shall provide two accounts and request fund transfers between accounts. Once the user has chosen the accounts and has indicated the amount of the transfer, the system shall verify that sufficient funds are available to perform the transfer. If successful, the transfer amount shall be debited from the current account and credited to the specified account. Otherwise, no transfer shall take place, and the user shall be notified appropriately.

If the user has investment accounts, the user shall be able to obtain a summary of account balances and list securities in the account as well as carry out buy and sell transactions against that account.

To initiate a buy transaction, the user shall select the investment account and provide a security symbol, quantity, and a limit price. The system shall provide approximate total charges and ask the user to select the account to which charges should be debited. The system shall then verify that the charge amount is available from the selected account. If the total charges exceed the balance, an appropriate message shall be displayed and no buy activity shall take place. Otherwise, the information shall be entered into the pending orders queue.

To initiate a sell transaction, the user shall select the investment account. A list of securities in the account shall be displayed. The user shall select a security to sell. The system shall display approximate total gain minus any required charges and tax withholding and prompt the account holder for the account to which the funds should be deposited. The funds shall then be credited to the chosen account (savings or checking).

Administrative Services

A separate application shall be provided for administration of the HomeDirect service. The administrator shall have full access to any functions available to the user. Additionally, the administrator shall be able to carry out account setup and maintenance tasks.

The bank employee shall be required to login prior to using the system. Such login shall require an employee ID, a password, and a valid authorization code.

The administrator shall also be able to enable and disable online access of ACMEBank customers. When online access is enabled for a customer, the customer shall be assigned a password. The password may be entered manually or if none is provided, may automatically be generated by the system. A confirmation e-mail shall be sent to the customer advising the customer of online access setup completion.

The administrator shall also be able to create new accounts for a selected user as well as close existing accounts for a selected user.

It shall be possible for the administrator to manually adjust a given account balance. This shall require the administrator to choose an account, indicate whether it is a debit adjustment or a credit adjustment, enter the amount of the adjustment, and provide a textual reason for the adjustment.

The administrator shall also be able to cancel future bill payment transactions at a customer's request. To do so, the administrator shall enter a transaction confirmation ID (provided to the customer at the time the transaction was set up). This shall be used by the system to retrieve details of the pending payment. Once payment information has been retrieved, the administrator shall be able to select the payment and cancel the payment on behalf of the user. If the payment is successfully cancelled, the associated account shall be credited with an amount equal to the cancelled payment.

Inception Phase

A single iteration was undertaken in the inception phase. The following items were developed as part of this iteration:

- A vision document providing an overview of the product, key stake holders and their needs, market positioning of the product, and the requirements
- A prioritized list of risk factors associated with the project
- A project plan identifying the phases and iterations to be undertaken
- An initial use case model consisting of important use cases and actors, and flows of events for the most critical use cases

In addition, the team undertook preparation of the environment for the project. This included installing required software, setting up configuration management, and so on.

Select items from the inception phase are presented in the following sections.

Initial Iteration

Risk Factors

Table 16-1 identifies the key risks for the initial iteration. (Note that the project risk list is reviewed and updated at the start of each iteration and adjustments made to the plan as necessary.)

Iteration Plan

The iteration plan was extracted from the project plan. To accommodate the risk factors listed in Table 16-1, it was decided to undertake three iterations during the elaboration phase. Table 16-2 presents an outline of the iteration plan.

Table 16-1   Initial risk factors

Risk Level (1–10, 10=highest)	*Risk Description*	*Mitigation Strategy*
9	Several new members on the team lack J2EE experience	Send team members to appropriate training courses as soon as possible
7	June delivery schedule too aggressive	Identify and use automation opportunities, for example, UML modeling and code generation tools, test tools
5	Upcoming release of EJB 2.0 specification	Develop on EJB 1.1 and investigate EJB 2.0 in parallel to understand the pros and cons of 1.1 versus 2.0
7	Administration related requirements not yet determined due to internal customer debate	Work with customer to stabilize requirements for the second elaboration iteration

Table 16-2   Preliminary iteration plan

Phase	*Iterations*	*Duration (in weeks)*
Inception	Initial Iteration	3
Elaboration	Elaboration Iteration#1 (basic use cases)	3
	Elaboration Iteration#2 (support for custom bill payment + administrative services)	3
	Elaboration Iteration#3 (investment services)	3
Construction	Construction Iteration#1	3
	Construction Iteration#2	3
Transition	Transition Iteration	2

HomeDirect Actors

The following list contains the complete list of actors in the HomeDirect case study:

- *Customer:* Uses HomeDirect to obtain information and perform banking transactions
- *Administrator:* Sets up users of the system. Obtains and updates information
- *Vendor:* Receives funds as a result of bill payments
- *Mail system:* Receives requests from HomeDirect to send confirmation e-mails
- *LoansDirect system:* Interacts with the HomeDirect system to provide loan services to customers
- *BillsDirect system:* Interacts with the HomeDirect system to provide automated bill tracking services to customers

HomeDirect Use Cases

The following list contains the use cases that were identified as important for the inception phase:

- Browse account balances
- List transactions
- Transfer funds
- Pay bills
- Login
- Logout
- Edit profile

Other use cases that were identified but marked for exploration and detailed flow of events that will be captured in a future iteration include

- Pay vendor bills
- Modify vendor list
- Display transactions
- Download transactions
- Buy security
- Sell security

- Manual account update
- Cancel bill payment

The flow of events for the important set of use cases is presented in the following sections. See the subsequent iterations for additional details on the other use cases.

Use Case: Browse Account Balances

Main flow of events: The use case starts when the customer successfully logs in and requests to browse his or her account balances. The system looks up information for the selected user and presents it to the customer on the display screen in a predetermined format. The use case ends when the customer logs out.

Alternate flow of events: The system is unable to obtain information for the specified user, or the user has no registered accounts. An error message is displayed to the user.

Use Case: List Transactions

Main flow of events: The use case starts when the customer successfully logs in and requests the list of transactions. The system obtains the list of transactions for the user. The list of transactions is displayed to the customer in the specified format. The use case ends when the customer logs out.

Alternate flow of events: The system is unable to obtain the list of transactions for the user. An error message is displayed to the customer.

Alternate flow of events: The system obtains a list of transactions containing zero elements. A blank list is displayed along with the message that no transactions were found in the account.

Use Case: Transfer Funds

Main flow of events: The customer logs in and requests a funds transfer. The system provides a list of existing accounts. The customer selects the account to transfer funds to and the account to transfer funds from, and then indicates the amount of funds to transfer. The system checks the account from which funds are to be transferred and confirms that sufficient funds are available. The amount is debited to the account from which funds are to be transferred and credited to the account previously selected by the customer. The transaction is recorded. The use case ends when the customer logs out.

Alternate flow of events: Sufficient funds are not available in the account from which funds are to be transferred. An error message is displayed to the customer. The customer is then presented with the opportunity to adjust the amount of the transfer or cancel the transfer transaction.

290 | Chapter 16 Case Study

Use Case: Pay Bills

Main flow of events: The customer successfully logs in and chooses to pay one of the unpaid bills that are identified via the BillsDirect service. The customer selects the bills and enters the required information. The system verifies that the customer's account has sufficient funds for the payment and asks the customer to confirm payment. The system debits the amount to the customer's account and records the bill payment. The system issues a confirmation number to the customer. The use case ends when the customer logs out.

Alternate flow of events: Sufficient funds are unavailable in the customer's account. An error message is displayed to the customer, and the bill payment transaction is cancelled.

Use Case: Login

Note that this is not a stand-alone use case, but is developed in this section to separate out common functionality to a large number of use cases in the HomeDirect case study. This use case is included in the preceding use cases.

Main flow of events: The customer is prompted to enter a customer name and password. The system verifies that the customer exists and verifies that the password entered for the user is valid. The system displays the main screen for the HomeDirect system so the customer can carry out online banking activities.

Alternate flow of events: The customer is not a customer of HomeDirect or the specified password is invalid. The customer is given an error message and offered the opportunity to log in again.

Use Case: Logout

Main flow of events: The customer selects logout to exit the system. The system ends the customer session.

Use Case: Edit Profile

Main flow of events: The customer chooses the change profile option. The system prompts the customer with his or her current profile details and allows the customer to enter any desired changes. All changes require entry of the customer's current password. Changes to the password additionally require entry of the new password twice for verification. The system verifies the changed information and updates the customer profile as appropriate. The use case ends.

Alternate flow of events: The old password entered by the customer is found to be invalid. The system displays an error message and asks the customer to reenter the old password.

Alternate flow of events: The first entry of the new password does not match the second entry of the new password. The system displays an error message to the customer and requests a correction by the customer.

Use Case Diagrams

Figure 16-1 and 16-2 detail the initial use cases for the case study.

Interaction Diagrams

The high-level flow of events for the important use cases are generally similar. A representative sample is shown in Figures 16-3, 16-4, and 16-5.

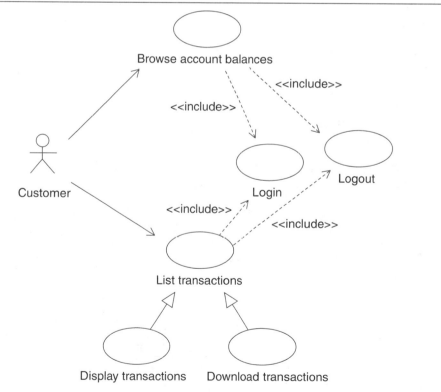

Figure 16-1   HomeDirect use cases—initial set

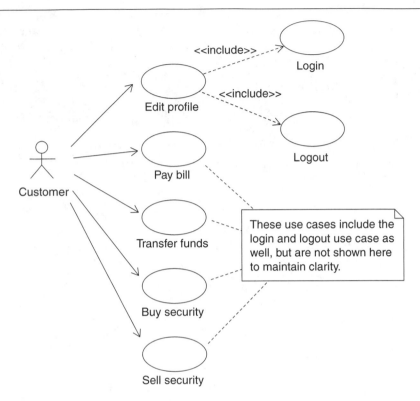

The note attached reads: These use cases include the login and logout use case as well, but are not shown here to maintain clarity.

Figure 16-2   Additional HomeDirect use cases

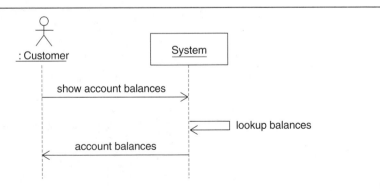

Figure 16-3   Browse account balances main flow of events

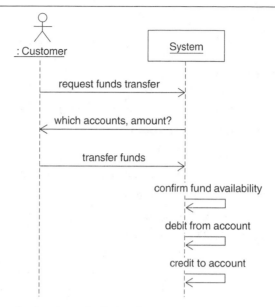

Figure 16-4 Transfer funds main flow of events

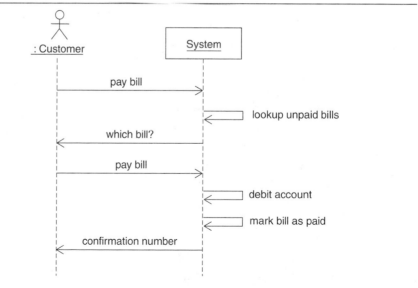

Figure 16-5 Pay bills main flow of events

Elaboration Phase

Three iterations were planned for the elaboration phase. The following items were updated or created as part of the first two iterations (the last iteration has not been started):

- Updated risks list (started during the inception phase)
- Initial architecture document
- Design model
- An executable prototype of critical functionality
- Initial implementation model
- A generally complete use case model (all use cases, all actors, and most flow of events completed)

Additionally, an analysis model was developed as part of this project. It was decided to maintain it for future reference and activities related to this project.

Elaboration Iteration#1

Updated Risk Factors
A new concern has been raised that the performance of Enterprise JavaBeans (EJB) may not meet expectations. This is a significant risk (risk level 8). To mitigate this risk, we decided to move to EJB 2.0 release early on to take advantage of enhancements in this area.

Requirements Update
Administrative services requirements are not yet sorted out due to scheduling issues (lack of availability) for key decision makers from the customer side.

After discussions with customer stakeholders about the scheduling risks, a decision was made to defer the investment services related use cases to a future release.

Updated Iteration Plan (Summary)
Table 16-3 provides an updated iteration plan.

Detailed Sequence Diagrams

Some representative sequence diagrams developed during this iteration are shown in Figures 16-6 to 16-9.

Table 16-3 Updated iteration plan

Phase	*Iterations*	*Duration (in weeks)*
Inception	Initial Iteration	Complete
Elaboration	Elaboration Iteration#1 (basic use cases)	3
	Elaboration Iteration#2 (EJB 2.0)	3
	Elaboration Iteration#3 (support for custom bill payment services and administrative services)	3
Construction	Construction Iteration	3
Transition	Transition Iteration	2

Class Diagrams

Figures 16-10, 16-11, and 16-12 show some of the class diagrams associated with use cases undertaken in this iteration.

Packaging Diagram

Figure 16-13 shows the initial packaging diagram for our example.

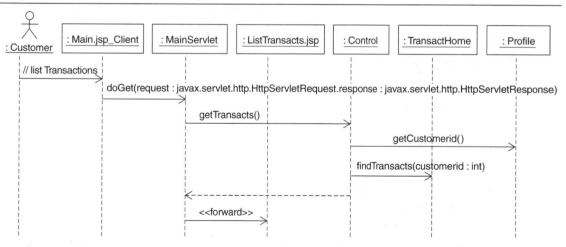

Figure 16-6 List transactions main scenario sequence diagram

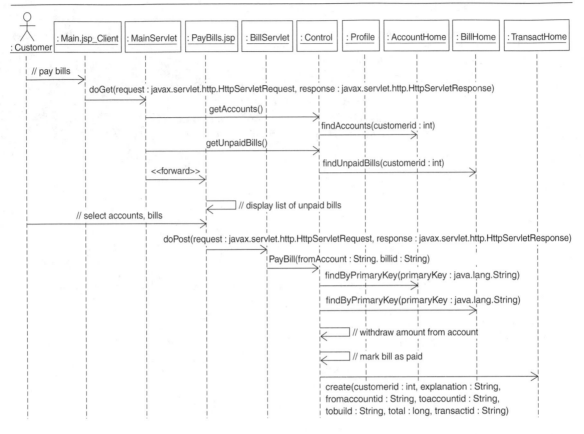

Figure 16-7 Pay bills main sequence diagram

Component Dependency Diagram

Figure 16-14 shows the component diagram for the account entity bean from the HomeDirect example.

Elaboration Iteration#2

This section summarizes the key points from the elaboration iteration#2.

Requirements Update

After reviewing the prototype, customers identified that the transaction confirmation procedures needed to be changed. Instead of displaying a confirmation

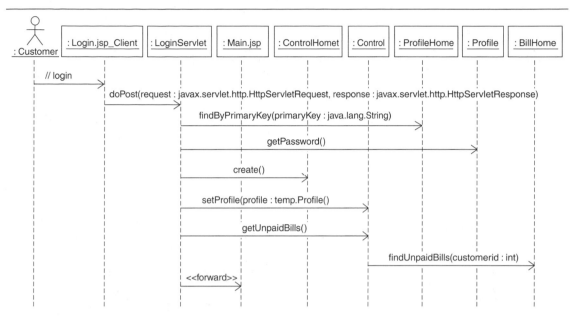

Figure 16-8 Login main sequence diagram

page, they would like the user to provide confirmation by entering a password along with other information. This change needs to be made.

Administrative services requirements were sorted out as well.

Implementation Details

The primary activity for this iteration was the migration of the work to the EJB 2.0 release. No new functionality was introduced in this iteration; however, some changes were made to the implementation in switching to the EJB 2.0 release.

A summary of implementation related changes required for the transition from EJB 1.1 to EJB 2.0 are as follows:

- All container-managed persistence (CMP) fields in the entity beans have been changed to work with 2.0 CMP. This involved removing the direct references to these fields from the EJB source and changing all accessors to be abstract and removing their code.

- Because of the modifications mentioned in the preceding implementation change, a few accessors that had nonstandard code bodies had to be

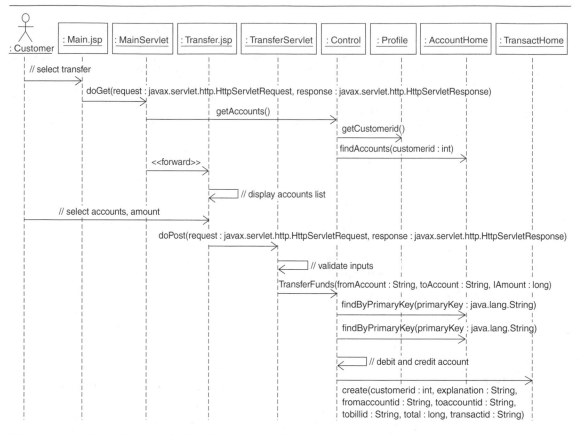

Figure 16-9 Detailed transfer funds sequence diagram

modified to use that code in a business method. Clients now call the business method first, which in turn calls the accessor as needed. (The AccountType accessors on the Account EJB are an example.)

- All components of the application needed to be reassembled from scratch because the deployment tools have changed significantly.

- Finder methods now use EJB QL to specify their queries rather than normal SQL.

- findByPrimaryKey methods are now hidden from the deployer and generated automatically by the tools, using specific naming conventions. To remain compatible with the deployment tools, all table names and column names needed to be modified to match these conventions.

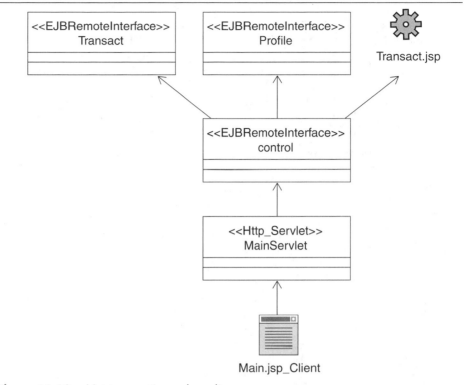

Figure 16-10   List transactions class diagram

Please see the README.html file accompanying the software for more information on the table and column name changes that needed to be made.

Elaboration Iteration#3

The elaboration iteration#3 is a reader led iteration. Instead of providing solutions, we identify problems that you can try to solve on your own. The problems build on the software provided, so you can continue on with the project outlined in this chapter.

Three sets of use cases have been provided in the form of detailed flow of events.

Requirements Update

The current list of transactions lists all transactions. The customer would like the ability to list only those transactions that are associated with a specific account as selected by the user.

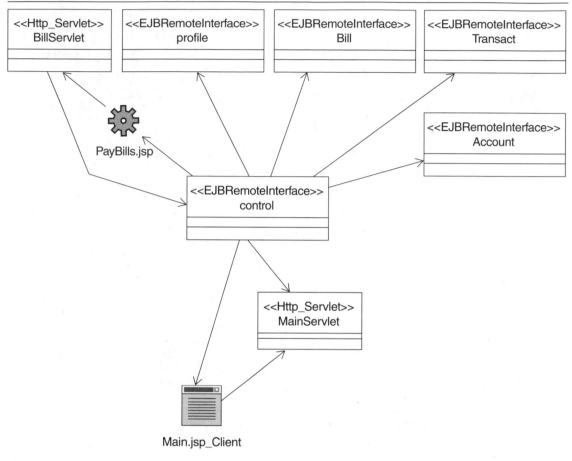

Figure 16-11   Pay bill class diagram

Suggestions for the Iteration

Suggestions and guidelines regarding activities to undertake during this iteration include

- Update the risks list and adjust iteration plans as required
- Incorporate the new use cases in the use case model as appropriate
- Develop initial sequence diagrams for each use case main flow of events
- Revisit architecture if warranted to ensure it can accommodate these requirements
- Develop View of Participating Classes (VOPC) diagrams for each use case

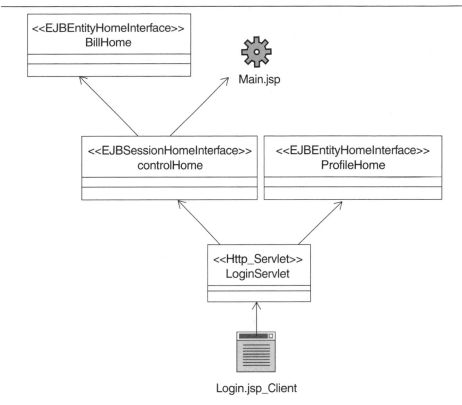

Figure 16-12 Login class diagram

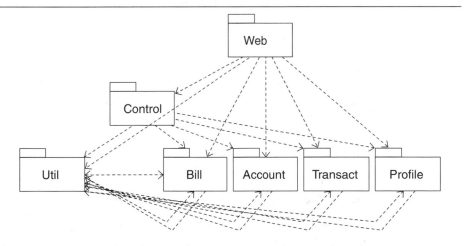

Figure 16-13 Initial packaging diagram

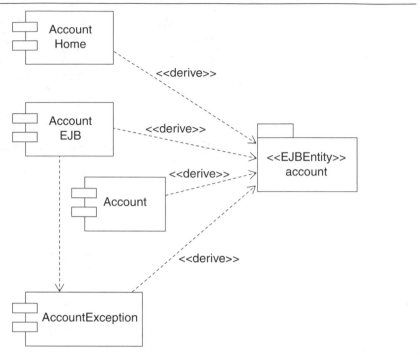

Figure 16-14   Component diagram for Account entity bean

- Update the implementation
- Update component and deployment diagrams to reflect the updated implementation model
- Modify the list transactions use case to match the requirements as outlined in the immediately preceding requirements update section of this iteration
- Enhance the user profile EJB to contain and report information such as e-mail information, user phone number, and address
- Set up asynchronous logging of every transaction to a backup file via a message-driven bean

Use Cases to Be Implemented in This Iteration

The following sections provide an overview of the use cases that will be implemented in this iteration.

Custom Vendor Bill Payment Services

The custom Vendor Bill Payment service consists of two main use cases. They are Pay Vendor Bills and Modify Vendor List. The main and alternate flow of events for these use cases are provided as follows.

Use Case: Pay Vendor Bills

Main flow of events: The customer successfully logs in and chooses to pay bills. The system presents the customer with a list of vendors previously set up by the customer and prompts the customer to choose a vendor, enter a total payment amount, and enter a payment date. The customer selects the vendor and enters the required information. The system verifies that the customer's checking account has sufficient funds for the payment and asks the customer to confirm payment. The system debits the amount to the customer's checking account and credits the amount to the vendor account. The system issues a confirmation number to the customer. The use case ends when the customer logs out.

 Alternate flow of events: The customer does not have a vendor list set up. The system displays an error message and directs the user to first add the desired vendors to the customer's vendor list.

 Alternate flow of events: Sufficient funds are unavailable in the customer's checking account. An error message is displayed to the customer, and the bill payment transaction is cancelled.

Use Case: Modify Vendor List

Main flow of events: The customer successfully logs in and requests that a change be made to the vendor list for future bill payments. The system presents the current list of vendors and buttons to add or delete a vendor. The customer chooses to add a vendor by selecting the Add button. The system prompts the user to enter a vendor name. The customer enters a vendor name. The system verifies the vendor name with the list of vendors registered with the bank. The system presents all matching vendor names to the customer, asks the customer to select one of the vendors, and provides vendor-related account information in the space provided. The customer selects the vendor and enters the number of the account being maintained with the vendor. The system verifies that the account number entered for the vendor matches the account number format provided by the vendor. The system displays an updated vendor list with the name of the vendor added to the list of vendors enabled for bill payment. The use case ends.

 Alternate flow of events: The customer chooses a vendor from the list of vendors already enabled for bill payment and specifies the delete operation. The system removes the name of the vendor from the list of vendors enabled for bill payment and displays an updated list of vendors.

Alternate flow of events: The vendor-specific account number entered by the customer as part of the add vendor function is invalid. The system displays an error message and prompts the customer to reenter the correct vendor-specific account number.

Administrative Services Use Cases

Administrative services are provided via a separate application. Use cases for the administrative application are detailed in the following sections.

Use Case: Manual Account Update

Main flow of events: The administrator logs in and selects to update an account manually. The system prompts the administrator for either the customer ID or the account number. The system locates the account based on the information provided and displays the types of transactions available. This includes credit and debit functions. The administrator chooses the transaction type and enters an amount and a text reason. The system carries out the transaction and debits or credits the account as selected. The use case ends.

Alternate flow of events: The customer ID or account number is invalid. The system displays an error message and prompts the administrator to reenter the information.

Alternate flow of events: The manual debit amount is more than the current balance. The system displays a reconfirmation dialog and informs the administrator of the imminent negative balance. Upon confirmation, the system performs the transaction even if the account produces a negative balance as a result of this action.

Use Case: Cancel Bill Payment

Main flow of events: The administrator logs in and selects the cancel bill payment option. The system prompts for a bill transaction confirmation number. The administrator enters the transaction confirmation number. The system retrieves the pending bill payment and prompts the administrator to confirm the cancellation. Upon administrator confirmation, the system deletes the record from the pending bills list and credits the customer account with an amount equal to the bill. The use case ends.

Alternate flow of events: The bill transaction number entered by the administrator is invalid. The system displays an error message and prompts the administrator to reenter the information.

The remaining use cases are optional as the customer has agreed to defer them to a future release.

Investment Services Use Cases

The initial investment services functionality revolves around two main use cases: buy security and sell security. Their main and alternate flow of events are described as follows.

Use Case: Buy Security

Main flow of events: The customer logs in, selects the investment account, and chooses to buy a security. The system prompts the customer to enter a security symbol, a quantity, a limit price, and other required information for the trade. The system verifies the accuracy of the symbol, calculates the approximate total charges for the security order, and displays a list of the customer's accounts from which payment will be deducted. The customer selects one of the accounts. The system verifies that sufficient funds are available, and then initiates the security purchase order on behalf of the customer. The system provides an order confirmation number to the customer. The use case ends.

Alternate flow of events: The security symbol entered by the customer is invalid. The system displays an error message and prompts the customer to reenter the symbol.

Alternate flow of events: Sufficient funds are not available in the chosen account. The system displays an error message and prompts the user to reenter the information or choose an alternate account for payment.

Use Case: Sell Security

Main flow of events: The customer logs in, selects the investment account, and chooses to sell a security. The system displays the list of securities currently held in the investment account and prompts the customer to choose the security, a quantity to be sold, and a price to be sold at. The system verifies that the required quantity of securities is available for the chosen security, calculates the approximate total charges for the security order, and displays a list of the customer's accounts to which the proceeds of the sale should be deposited. The customer selects one of the accounts. The system then initiates the security sale order on behalf of the customer. The system provides an order confirmation number to the customer. The use case ends.

Alternate flow of events: No securities are available in the customer's investment account. The system displays an error message to the customer.

Alternate flow of events: The chosen quantity for sale is more than the quantity available in the customer's investment account. An error message is displayed to the customer, and the customer is asked to reenter a smaller number for the quantity of security to be sold.

Remaining Phases

Due to time and space constraints, we do not cover the details of the remaining two phases identified by the RUP, namely the construction phase and the transition phase.

Some of the key items produced during the construction phase include

- A deployment plan
- An updated design model and an updated implementation model
- A test model
- The software system being implemented along with user documents and so on

The transition phase wraps up the effort with the following tasks:

- Delivery of the product to the end user
- Release notes for the product
- Any required training material

You are encouraged to continue with the case study by developing an interation plan for these phases and working through to the transition phase.

Additional suggested activities include porting the implementation to another application server (e.g., BEA Weblogic).

Summary

In this chapter, we undertook a hands-on case study and followed its progress through the different phases of the RUP. A sample requirements document was used as a starting point. Simulated changes to requirements and priorities along the way were used to show the impact on planned iterations. The chapter concluded with a reader-led iteration, which elaborated on the existing implementation by adding support for new requirements.

Glossary

A

ACID: *A*tomic, *C*onsistent, *I*solated, and *D*urable. Terminology used to identify principles that should be followed when designing transactions and session beans involving transactions.

activation: The reloading of a swapped out stateful session EJB that may be needed again.

activity diagram: A UML diagram that is an extension of a statechart diagram. Allows modeling of the systems behavior in terms of interaction or flow of control.

actor: Used in use case diagrams. An actor represents something or someone outside the system, for example, a user of the system.

aggregation: A stronger form of association. Used to show a logical containment relationship, that is, a whole formed of parts.

analysis: The process of understanding the requirements and transforming them into a system design.

analysis class: Classes created during analysis that are typically not implemented in software. Rather, they are refined later into design classes and subsystems.

architecture: The architecture of a software system deals with the structural aspects of the system as well as the system's usability, performance, resilience, reuse, and so on.

association: An association between two classes specifies that some sort of structural relationship exists between the classes.

B

bean: Refers generically to one of the two types of Java components: JavaBeans or Enterprise JavaBeans.

bean-managed persistence (BMP): When the details of the database access and manipulation are handled by the EJB itself.

boundary class: Analysis level classes that represent interaction with system and external entities, for example, other subsystems and so on.

C

class diagram: A UML diagram that shows the static relationships that exist among a group of classes and interfaces in a system.

collaboration diagram: A type of interaction diagram in the UML. The message exchange is captured in the context of the overall structural relationships among objects.

component: A UML component is used to model software entities in the physical world, for example, .java files, .class files, and so on.

component diagram: A diagram composed of components that show a static view of components and their relationships.

composition: Another form of association. Implies a stronger whole-part relationship between the participants such that parts cannot exist without the whole.

constraint: A UML mechanism for specifying restrictions and relationships that cannot be expressed otherwise.

container: A software entity that runs within the server and provides the execution environment for the J2EE components.

container-managed Persistence (CMP): One of the two persistence mechanisms supported by entity beans. In CMP, the container manages database access and synchronization details.

conversational state: Applies to session beans. Defined as the data describing the conversation represented by a specific client pairing with a session object. Stateful session beans maintain conversational state.

D

decomposition: Partitioning of a system into smaller, logical pieces to make it easier to manage the complexity.

dependency: When a class uses another class, it is said to have a dependency on that other class.

deployment: The act of installing an enterprise Java component onto an application server.

deployment descriptor: An XML document that is used to communicate information between the component developer, the application assembler, and the deployer.

deployment diagram: A UML diagram that shows the architecture of the system from the perspective of nodes and processors, and the relationships among them.

design: A phase during development that focuses on arriving at an implementation approach that will meet the requirements.

destination: Refers to a location to which messages can be sent. In JMS, a destination generically refers to either a topic or a queue.

Document Type Definition (DTD): Defines the XML document grammar for a specific language. In J2EE, XML DTDs are used for defining the deployment descriptors.

E

EAR file: An archive file that contains an enterprise application.

enterprise bean: Shorthand for an Enterprise JavaBean (EJB).

Enterprise JavaBean (EJB): A specification for a component model for building scalable, distributed server-based enterprise Java application components.

enterprise software: Refers collectively to all software involved in supporting the common elements of an enterprise.

entity bean: A type of EJB that encapsulates persistent data in a data store.

entity class: Analysis level classes that represent information of significance to the system.

extend relationship in use cases: A relationship used to model optional behavior for a use case.

F

forward: A programming technique used by JSPs and servlets to redirect requests to other servlets or JSPs.

framework: A framework provides a generalized architectural template that can be used to build applications within a specific domain.

H

Home interface: Session bean interface used by the client program to invoke the basic bean life cycle methods.

I

Include: A programming technique used by JSPs and servlets to include (the output from) other JSPs or servlets.

Include relationship in use cases: A relationship used in use case modeling where a common piece of functionality is captured in a separate use case, and the use case is then included in the other use case.

inheritance: A relationship between two classes where one class "inherits" from the other class. Also referred to as generalization.

interaction diagram: UML diagrams that are used for modeling the dynamic behavior of a system. Sequence diagrams and collaboration diagrams are types of interaction diagrams.

J

JAR file: A Java Archive file. Commonly used to package multiple Java classes into a single unit of distribution.

Java 2 Enterprise Edition (J2EE): A platform for developing complex, distributed enterprise-scale Java applications.

Java 2 Micro Edition (J2ME): Platform for the development of software for embedded devices such as phones, palm tops, and so on.

Java 2 Standard Edition (J2SE): Platform for developing Java applications. Also known as the JDK. Includes capabilities such as applets, JavaBeans, and so on.

JavaBean: Software components written in Java. Distinguished from Enterprise JavaBeans that are distributed server-side Java components.

Java Database Connectivity (JDBC): A generic API that provides vendor-independent interface to databases. Similar in spirit to Microsoft's ODBC API.

JavaMail: Provides an API to facilitate interaction with e-mail messaging systems in a vendor-independent fashion.

Java Messaging Service (JMS): Provides a uniform and generic interface to messaging oriented middleware.

Java Naming and Directory Interface (JNDI): Provides a generic and uniform way to access naming services.

JavaServer Pages (JSP): A type of J2EE Web component that combines elements of Java with HTML to provide dynamic content creation capabilities.

JSR-26: Java Specification Request # 26. An industry-led formalized effort under the Java Community Process (JCP) to develop a UML profile for EJB modeling.

L

layering: A pattern for decomposition that is used to organize the system into layers to restrict and constrain the usage of the subsystems, modules, and so on in the system.

M

message: Units of data used in message-based systems. Messages can communicate events, requests for data, replies to requests, and so on.

message-driven bean: A type of EJB that provides a convenient paradigm for creating asynchronous consumers of Java Message Service (JMS) messages.

model: An abstraction of a system that conveys what the system is.

Model1: A presentation-centric architectural approach used in developing systems involving JSPs and servlets.

Model2: An MVC-based architectural approach for building systems involving JSPs and servlets.

Model-View-Controller (MVC): An architectural pattern for minimizing coupling among objects in a system by aligning them with a specific set of responsibilities in the area of the persistent data and associated rules (Model), presentation (View), and the application logic (Controller).

N

node: Represents a processor or some device on the deployment diagram.

n-tier: Refers to the number of tiers software is organized into.

P

package: A grouping mechanism in Java as well as the UML.

pattern: A reusable design that has been captured and abstracted out through experience.

Q

queue: A type of destination used for delivery of messages in a messaging system.

R

Rational Unified Process (RUP): A software development process that provides best practices and detailed guidelines on developing software.

Remote interface: The interface used by a client program to invoke the business methods on a session bean.

Remote Method Invocation (RMI): Enables access to components in a distributed environment by allowing Java objects to invoke methods on remote Java objects.

request object: An object passed to servlets or JSPs as a parameter at the time of invocation. The object can be used to obtain details provided by the user, for example, form data and so on.

response object: An object passed to servlets or JSPs as a parameter. Servlets and JSPs use it to provide a response back to the invoking party.

S

scriptlet: Snippets of Java code embedded within a JSP.

sequence diagram: A type of interaction diagram where objects and the interaction between them is shown along object lifelines.

servlet: A server-side component that handles incoming requests and generates a response dynamically.

session bean: A type of EJB best used for transient activities. Session beans often encapsulate the majority of business logic within an enterprise Java application. Can be stateful or stateless.

SQL: Structured Query Language. Used to query, extract, and write data to databases.

statechart diagram: A UML diagram that is used to define state machines. Excellent for capturing dynamic behavior of a system.

stateful session bean: A session bean that is capable of retaining its conversational state with the client.

stateless session bean: A session bean that does not retain its conversational state from one method call to another.

stereotype: A mechanism in the UML that allows you to create a new, incrementally different model element by changing the semantics of an existing UML model element.

T

Tag Libraries: A collection of custom tags that can be called from within a JSP.

tagged value: A UML extension mechanism that can be used to define and associate a new property for a model element.

tier: An architectural concept that is primarily concerned with the distribution of software over multiple processes.

topic: One of two kinds of destinations for delivery of messages. A topic follows the publisher-subscribe paradigm.

transaction: A group of activities that are carried out as if they were a single unit of work.

U

Unified Modeling Language (UML): A graphical language for the modeling and development of software systems.

use case: A UML concept used in use case modeling. A use case encapsulates a sequence of steps performed by the system on behalf of an actor.

use case diagram: Part of the UML. Use case diagrams capture the precise requirements for the system from a user's perspective.

use case realization: A use case realization captures how a specific use case is implemented within the system.

V

visual modeling: The act of modeling the software graphically. This is typically done via graphical models constructed in the UML.

W

WAR file: A Web archive file. Contains a J2EE Web component.

Web component: A J2EE component that consists of servlets or JSPs (along with any required HTML pages, etc.).

Web server: A software application that provides the execution environment for servlets and JSPs.

X

XML: Refers to the eXtensible Markup Language. Used in J2EE deployment descriptors for presentation and so on.

References

Books

Arrington, C.T. *Enterprise Java with UML*. OMG Press, New York: John Wiley and Sons, 2001.

Asbury, Stephen and Scott Weiner. *Developing Java Enterprise Applications*. New York: John Wiley and Sons, 1999.

Bass, Len, Paul Clements, and Rick Kazman. *Software Architecture in Practice*. Reading, MA: Addison-Wesley, 1997.

Booch, Grady. *Object-Oriented Analysis and Design with Applications*. Reading, MA: Addison-Wesley, 1994.

Booch, Grady, James Rumbaugh, and Ivar Jacobson. *The Unified Modeling Language User Guide*. Reading, MA: Addison-Wesley, 1999.

Conallen, Jim. *Building Web Applications with UML*. Reading, MA: Addison-Wesley, 1999.

Hofmeister, Christine, Robert Nord, and Dilip Soni. *Applied Software Architecture*. Boston, MA: Addison-Wesley, 2000.

Jacobson, Ivar, Magnus Christerson, Patrik Jonsson, and Gunnar Overgaard. *Object-Oriented Software Engineering*. Reading, MA: Addison-Wesley, 1992.

Kassem, N. and Enterprise Team. *Designing Enterprise Applications with the Java 2 Platform, Enterprise Edition*. Boston, MA: Addison-Wesley, 2000.

Kruchten, P. *The Rational Unified Process*. Reading, MA: Addison-Wesley, 1999.

Monson-Haefel, Richard. *Enterprise JavaBeans*. Sebastopol, California: O'Reilly and Associates, 1999.

Perrone, Paul and Venkata Chaganti. *Building Java Enterprise Systems with J2EE*. Indianapolis, IN: Sams Publishing, 2000.

Rumbaugh, James, Ivar Jacobson, and Grady Booch. *The Unified Modeling Language Reference Manual*. Reading, MA: Addison-Wesley, 1999.

Selic, Bran, Garth Gullekson, and Paul Ward. *Real-Time Object-Oriented Modeling*. New York: John Wiley and Sons, 1994.

Articles and Online Sources

Ahmed, K. "Building reusable architectures using Rose frameworks," Rational Software Corporation White Paper, 2000.

Ambler, S. "Enhancing the Unified Process, Software Process for Large Scale, Mission-Critical Systems," White Paper, November 2000, www.ronon-intl.com.

Bauer, C. "Components make the banking world go 'round," IBM Developer-Works, October 2000.

Bergin, J. "Building Graphical User Interfaces with the MVC Pattern," www.wol.pace.edu/~bergin/mvc/mvcgui.html.

Bollinger, G. and B. Natarajan. "Building an E-Commerce Shopping Cart," Java Pro, June 2000.

Brown, Kyle. "What's it going to take to get you to go with EJB components?" IBM DeveloperWorks, May 2000.

Brubeck, S. "Application Programming in Smalltalk-80: How to use Model-View-Controller (MVC)," www.st-www.cs.uiuc.edu/users/smarch/st-docs/mvc.html.

Carlson, B., S. Gerard, and J. Carey. "Constructing Applications from Components: A Tutorial," IBM WebSphere Business Components, presented at the JavaOne Conference, 2000.

Carnegie Melon Software Engineering Institute. "How do you define software architecture," www.sei.cmu.edu.

"Developing Large-Scale Systems with the Rational Unified Process," Rational Software Corporation White Paper, 1999.

"d-tec Distributed Technologies GmbH. 3- and n-Tier Architectures," www.corba.ch/e/3tier.html.

Duffey, K. "On Model1, Model1.5 and Model2," www.brainopolis.com/jsp/mvc/KDuffey_MVC.html.

Edelstein, Herb. "Multitier Architecture in Data Warehouses," www.powersoft.com/inc/symbag/quarter4_96/arch/multitier.folder/multitier.html.

Evans, G. "A Simplified Approach to RUP," January 2001. www.therationaledge.com.

"Finding the Middle Ground," www.networkcomputing.com.

Fisher, P. "Enabling Component model integration," Application Development Trends, November 2000.

"General information about Extreme Programming," www.Xprogramming.com.

Kobak, P. "Servlet Session Display," Java Developer Journal, February 2000.

Kruchten, P. "The 4+1 View of Architecture," IEEE Software, 12(6), November 1995.

Lacy, M. "Presentation Logic and EJBs: Using Session Beans to Help Bridge the Java-HTML Gap," Java Developers Journal, May 2000.

Lavandowska, L. "JSP Architectures: An explanation and comparison of the methodologies commonly known as 'Model I' and 'Model II'," www.brainopolis.com/jsp/book/jspBook_Architectures.html.

Lilly, S. "How to Avoid Use-Case Pitfalls," www.sdtimes.com/articles/2000/0001/0001d/0001d.htm.

Oberg, R. et al. "Applying Requirements Management With Use Cases," Rational Software White Paper, TP505, 2000.

Petschulat, S. "JSP or Servlets—Which Architecture is Right for You?" Java Report, March 2001.

Price, R. "The Art and Architecture of Client Server Systems," www.tp.ac.sg/content/irbd/Journal/tj5/Art.htm.

Rosenberg, D. and Scott, K. "XP: Cutting through the hype," ObjectView, Issue 3, www.ratio.co.uk.

Sharon, Y. "Extreme Programming: A lightweight OO Development Process," ObjectView, Issue 3, www.ratio.co.uk.

Sheil, H. "Frameworks save the day: Use an extensible, vendor-independent framework to accomplish the top tasks in server-side development," JavaWorld, October 2000.

Sheshadri, G. "Understanding JavaServer Pages Model 2 architecture," www.javaworld.com/javaworld/jw-12-1999/jw-12-ssj-jspmvc.html.

Spence, I. and L. Probasco. "Traceability Studies for Managing Requirements with Use Cases," Rational Software White Paper, 1998.

Stack, C. "Establishing a Strategy for the Reuse of Enterprise JavaBeans Architecture-Based Components," presented at the JavaOne Conference, 2000.

Tataryn, C. "Introduction to MVC and the Jakarta Struts Framework," www. computer-programmer.org/articles/struts/ppframe.htm (online presentation)

The OPEN process Web site, www.open.org.au/.

Tost, A. "Using JavaBeans as accessors to Enterprise JavaBeans," IBM Developer-Works, October 1999, www.ibm.com.

UML Resources section on www.rational.com.

Volter, M. "Building Component Based Systems," MATHEMA AG, 2000.

Williams, J. "Raising Components, Application Development Trends," September 2000.

Index

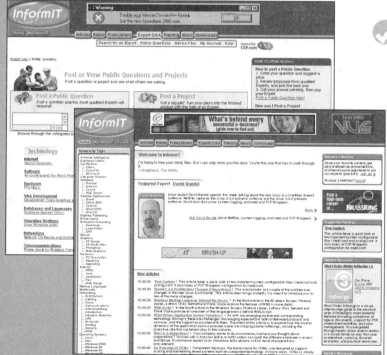

Register
Your Book
at www.aw.com/cseng/register

You may be eligible to receive:

- Advance notice of forthcoming editions of the book
- Related book recommendations
- Chapter excerpts and supplements of forthcoming titles
- Information about special contests and promotions throughout the year
- Notices and reminders about author appearances, tradeshows, and online chats with special guests

Contact us

If you are interested in writing a book or reviewing manuscripts prior to publication, please write to us at:

Editorial Department
Addison-Wesley Professional
75 Arlington Street, Suite 300
Boston, MA 02116 USA
Email: AWPro@aw.com

Addison-Wesley

Visit us on the Web: http://www.aw.com/cseng